LIGHT & TRUTH

A LATTER-DAY SAINT GUIDE
TO WORLD RELIGIONS

LIGHT & TRUTH

A LATTER-DAY SAINT GUIDE
TO WORLD RELIGIONS

ROGER R. KELLER

RELIGIOUS STUDIES CENTER
BRIGHAM YOUNG UNIVERSITY

DESERET
BOOK

In memory of
Spencer J. Palmer,
friend and mentor,

and dedicated to
the Reverend Dean Jackson and his wife, Marlys,
who have always reached out to people of all faiths.

Published by the Religious Studies Center, Brigham Young University, Provo, Utah, in cooperation with Deseret Book Company, Salt Lake City. http://rsc.byu.edu

Cover and interior design by Art Morrill.

US $28.99
ISBN 978-0-8425-2817-7

Library of Congress Cataloging-in-Publication Data

Keller, Roger R., 1942–
Light and truth : a Latter-day Saint guide to world religions / Roger R. Keller.
    pages cm
ISBN 978-0-8425-2817-7 (hardcover : alk. paper)
1. Christianity and other religions. 2. Religions. 3. Church of Jesus Christ of Latter-day Saints—Relations. 4. Mormon Church—Relations. I. Title.
BR127.K45 2012
261.2—dc23

CONTENTS

CHAPTER 1

WHY BOTHER WITH OTHER FAITHS?

Latter-day Saints may have different answers to common questions from those of other faiths, but each offers insights into the grave and challenging issues of what it means to be a human being struggling to be in harmony with the ultimate power in the universe.

In 1984 and 1985, while still a Presbyterian minister in Mesa, Arizona, I served on a committee to evaluate a movie entitled *The God Makers*. It purported to be the true story of the Mormon faith, and hundreds of people left the showing believing they finally knew what their Latter-day Saint neighbors believed. It was clear to anyone who had even a little knowledge about The Church of Jesus Christ of Latter-day Saints that it was a series of twisted half-truths perpetrated by persons who called themselves "Ex-Mormons for Jesus." Latter-day Saints were justifiably upset. The Arizona chapter of the National Conference of Christians and Jews (now the National Conference for Community and Justice or NCCJ), a group of persons dedicated to fairness and accuracy in religious dialogue, decided to examine the film. They asked me to be a member of the examining committee, since I had called it "religious pornography" in a letter to the editor of the *Mesa Tribune* after having seen it. No Latter-day Saints served on the committee, to ensure that the effort of the committee would not be self-serving.

In the interest of accuracy, it should be said that I had been a member of The Church of Jesus Christ of Latter-day Saints for three or four months in 1964 while serving in the military, but due to a lack of fellowshipping, no calling, and a failure to understand the Apostasy, I had returned to my prior tradition, Presbyterianism.

The committee examined the film, interviewed those who either made or distributed the film, and then talked with various Latter-day Saints, among them Truman Madsen, then holder of the Richard L. Evans Chair of Christian Understanding at Brigham Young University. In the end, the Arizona chapter of the NCCJ issued a statement, in the context of a larger statement on appropriate standards for inter-faith dialogue, saying that the film did not appropriately represent the faith of their Latter-day Saint neighbors. The investigation and state-ment were models of how the religious community should care for one another to ensure religious freedom for all. Untruths and partial truths about anybody else's faith are both wrong and inappropriate.

This statement now leads me to the title of this chapter, "Why Bother with Other Faiths?" Do we as Latter-day Saint Christians really need to know anything about other faiths? Do we not know all we need to know? In asking these questions, we should remember that Latter-day Saints were deeply offended by *The God Makers* with justification. But sometimes in our ignorance of the true beliefs of our neighbors, we create our own skewed version of other faiths in our priesthood quo-rums, our Sunday Schools, and our Relief Societies. As converts to the Latter-day Saint faith, my wife and I have seen our previous faith expe-riences denigrated and demeaned. It was to such ignorance about their beliefs that Latter-day Saints objected when they saw *The God Makers*. Thus, if we are to be a world church, we need to understand and appre-ciate all the good that God has given to persons beyond the Latter-day Saint pale and to represent it accurately. President George Albert Smith said as he spoke to persons who were not Latter-day Saints:

> We have not come to take away from you the truth and virtue you pos-
> sess. We have come not to find fault with you nor to criticize you. We
> have not come here to berate you because of things you have not done;
> but we have come here as your brethren . . . and to say to you: "Keep all
> the good that you have, and let us bring to you more good, in order that

you may be happier and in order that you may be prepared to enter into the presence of our Heavenly Father."[1]

Likewise, President Howard W. Hunter told Latter-day Saints:

In the gospel view, no man is alien. No one is to be denied. There is no underlying excuse for smugness, arrogance, or pride. Openly scorning the pettiness and intolerance of rival religious groups, the Prophet Joseph Smith said in an editorial:

"While one portion of the human race is judging and condemning the other without mercy, the Great Parent of the universe looks upon the whole of the human family with a fatherly care and paternal regard; He views them as His offspring, and

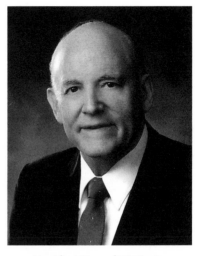

President Howard W. Hunter
© Intellectual Reserve, Inc.

without any of those contracted feelings that influence the children of men, causes 'His sun to rise on the evil and on the good, and sendeth rain on the just and on the unjust.' He holds the reins of judgment in His hands; He is a wise Lawgiver, and will judge all men, not according to the narrow, contracted notions of men, but, 'according to the deeds done in the body whether they be good or evil,' or whether these deeds were done in England, America, Spain, Turkey, or India."[2]

In the spirit of President George Albert Smith, President Howard W. Hunter, and the Prophet Joseph Smith, this book will attempt to show the good that God has placed among his children and upon which the Restoration may build to bring more good. It will be done in the spirit of conversation and dialogue, seeking to appreciate all the good that each religion brings. At the same time, this book will seek to show what makes each religious tradition unique, for it is our unique qualities that make us who we are.

— Five Thousand Years of Questions —

I remember being in a meeting in which a prominent evangelical was going to speak. A fellow Latter-day Saint sat down next to me and asked, "What is he doing here? We are supposed to teach, not be taught." My question to him was, "Do you know all the questions?" For five millennia, human beings have been asking about the meaning of life: Where have we come from? Why are we here? Where are we going? The big questions are not new with Latter-day Saints. Humans have been asking them since the time of Adam. They have also wondered why some persons are born wealthy and others poor, why some are born perfect physically and others have birth defects, why some have religious inclinations while others do not, why some are born into a privileged part of the world and others are not. And the questions go on and on.

Unfortunately, the study of philosophy and world religions is not required at many universities. If it were, more students might at least understand the issues about which people have wondered for so long. At Brigham Young University, they would also come to realize that the Latter-day Saints have answers, thanks to prophets and apostles, to these questions that need to be considered in any setting where the great questions of life are being discussed. Latter-day Saint answers need to be taken seriously in the realm of philosophical and theological exchange. All too often, Latter-day Saints feel at a disadvantage because they do not have a professional clergy. While that may be true, they have no shortage of thinkers among them who have imbibed the teachings of prophets and apostles who themselves have drunk from the well of divine revelation where these questions are answered. Thus Latter-day Saints can all participate in meaningful discussions with their neighbors of whatever faith about the essentials of life. As we study the religions of the world, we will learn their questions and their answers and see what Latter-day Saints have to bring to the discussion.

— Prophets, Apostles, and Scripture —

President Spencer W. Kimball stated, "The great religious leaders of the world such as Muhammad, Confucius, and the Reformers, as well as philosophers including Socrates, Plato, and others, received a portion of God's light. Moral truths were given to them by God to enlighten whole nations and to bring a higher level of understanding to individuals."[3] Notice that persons like Muhammad, Confucius, Luther, Calvin, Wesley, and even philosophers like Plato and Aristotle did not teach simply the best of their own thought. They taught what God had given them to teach, undoubtedly mixed with their own views. And although this passage could suggest that they simply drew from the Light of Christ, real content comes through manifestations of the Holy Ghost, which are available to all members of the human family.[4]

Another very interesting statement was made in 1921 by Elder Orson F. Whitney, an Apostle:

Elder Orson F. Whitney

© *Intellectual Reserve, Inc.*

[God] is using not only his covenant people, but other peoples as well, to consummate a work, stupendous, magnificent, and altogether too arduous for this little handful of Saints to accomplish by and of themselves. . . .

All down the ages men bearing the authority of the Holy Priesthood—patriarchs, prophets, apostles and others, have officiated in the name of the Lord, doing the things that he required of them; and outside the pale of their activities other good and great men, not bearing the Priesthood, but possessing profundity of thought, great wisdom, and a desire to uplift their fellows, have been sent by the Almighty into many nations, to give them, not the fulness of the Gospel, but that portion of truth that they were able to receive and wisely use.[5]

Note that Elder Whitney says that the Latter-day Saints cannot accomplish what God has called them to do by themselves. They need the help of others beyond the priesthood in its various offices. To accomplish his work, the Lord has actually sent other great figures, not holding the priesthood, to give to people what they need to hear in their particular time and circumstances. This is an amazing statement, and how true it is.

Suppose that the only truly moral, spiritual persons in the world were fourteen million Latter-day Saints. What would this world be like? It would be a terrible place to live. Thank heaven for all our brothers and sisters who have moral and spiritual values given to them by God and who make it possible for all of us to live above the level of a hunted animal. Thank heaven for my Hindu, Muslim, Buddhist, Christian, Jewish, Sikh, and Bahá'í neighbors, as well as all the other religious persons I haven't yet mentioned. By the spiritual values they hold, they make the world habitable. We do not have to live in terror, for there are others like us who seek to do God's will.

To extend these thoughts, we need to turn to the Book of Mormon. There are two passages which deal with the themes we have been considering. Every Latter-day Saint is thoroughly familiar with them and could probably quote them from memory. However, I wonder if we have ever read them with the world's religions in mind. The first passage, 2 Nephi 28:30, says:

> For behold, thus saith the Lord God: I will give unto the children of men line upon line, precept upon precept, here a little and there a little; and blessed are those who hearken unto my precepts, and lend an ear unto my counsel, for they shall learn wisdom; for unto him that receiveth I will give more; and from them that shall say, We have enough, from them shall be taken away even that which they have.

We know that we learn line upon line and precept upon precept. We know that is exactly the way Joseph Smith learned. But have we thought that it is the way the whole human family, the family of God, learns? God never gives any of us, including Latter-day Saints, the whole truth. Sometimes my students say that they as Latter-day Saints know all truth, but in reality, they know so little of what there is to know. What they mean is that they know the fullness of the gospel. They know how to get back to their Heavenly Father, but "all truth" will actually be sought into the eternities. Thus all persons are on their own pilgrimages back to their Heavenly Father. All of us who were reserved for and born in these latter days are working on an aspect of our spirituality that our Heavenly Father knew we needed to hone. Perhaps I am a Latter-day Saint because I need to learn how to serve. Perhaps a Hindu is learning how to unite himself or herself with God. Perhaps a Buddhist is learning how to let go of the things of the world. Perhaps a Muslim is learning how to live an ethical life before God. Perhaps a Jew is learning how to obey the law of God. And many more scenarios could be developed.

Each one of us is exactly where our Father knows we need to be to grow. There are no accidents in a universe governed by our Heavenly Father. We all learn line upon line, precept upon precept, and we will be held accountable if we do not receive the "more" that God has to give us as we walk the upward path. When we stop somewhere on the path and want no more, we do not remain stationary; we actually slide backward. We even lose what we have.

The second passage from the Book of Mormon is 2 Nephi 29:11–12, which says:

> For I command all men, both in the east and in the west, and in the north, and in the south, and in the islands of the sea, that they shall write the words which I speak unto them; for out of the books which shall be written I will judge the world, every man according to their works, according to that which is written.
>
> For behold, I shall speak unto the Jews and they shall write it; and I shall also speak unto the Nephites and they shall write it; and I shall also speak unto the other tribes of the house of Israel, which I have led away, and they shall write it; and I shall also speak unto all nations of the earth and they shall write it.

Here we have the Lord's declaration that he will speak to all the peoples of the earth, no matter where they are. We could hardly find a broader statement about the universality of God's care for all his children. What the Lord speaks to the human family will be written down and kept in books, and it is against the content of these books that the peoples of the world and their works will be judged.

What books? The text tells us. The first book is the one which the Jews shall write, the Bible, for both the Old and the New Testaments arise from authors of the Jewish faith, except perhaps Luke. The second book is also clear. It will arise from the Nephites, and that is the Book of Mormon. The next books arise from the tribes of Israel that the Lord has led away, so those are writings from the ten lost tribes of Israel. In reality, they will probably be very much like the Book of Mormon, bearing witness of Christ in expectation and then as the Risen Lord. When we finally get those, we might need a large backpack or a wagon to get them all to church!

The last phrase is the most interesting from a world religions perspective, for it tells us that God will speak to all nations of the world and "they shall write it." These books have to be the Qur'an of the Muslims, the Bhagavad Gita of the Hindus, the Analects of Confucius, the Tripitaka of the Buddhists, the Guru Granth Sahib of the Sikhs, and the many other religious writings found among the great religions of the world. This means that God has also given these books to his children, and thus they are holy scripture for them. They are as sacred to them as any holy writ that we have for us. In them, God addresses members of his family. He ignores none of his children. He gives them all guidance against which they will be judged, for God is a just God. Thus, the Muslim is judged against the Qur'an, the Christian against the Bible, the Buddhist against the Tripitaka, the Hindu against the Bhagavad Gita, and the Latter-day Saint Christian against the four canonical volumes which God has given them. God holds no one accountable for what he has not given them, but each of us is responsible to live by what God has personally given to us.

Given the above, one can imagine a scene in which Heavenly Father called before him a choice spirit and commissioned him to bring more light and truth to South Asia knowing that he would never hear the gospel. Would he do that? Of course, the only request being that someone later perform the saving ordinances for him in a temple. His name on earth was Siddhartha Gautama—the Buddha. Likewise, another choice spirit was asked if he would do something similar for those in Southwest Asia. Again came the positive response with its request for someone to eventually perform his temple work. His earth name was Muhammad.

Now imagine today as Buddhists and Muslims pass through the veil. Each is greeted by the Buddha or Muhammad with the words,

"Welcome. Now let me tell you the rest of the story!" Is this not what Doctrine and Covenants 138 is about—missionary work to the dead who have never heard the fullness of the gospel in this life and who need its saving ordinances so that they may have all that their Heavenly Father wishes for them? Perhaps it is appropriate to paraphrase some of the prophets of the Book of Mormon by saying, "Oh, how great the breadth and depth of our Heavenly Father's plan."

— SETTING TRAJECTORIES —

In harmony with what has just been said, let me suggest that each of us sets a trajectory in mortal life. The greatest step that members of the human family will ever take in their spiritual journey is to enter mortality, for only here can we encounter the sharp edges of life that will smooth us into a disciple that the Lord Jesus can use. Thus those of every faith that seek *truth* will set a trajectory with a steep incline upward, much like an F-16 taking off. Some enter mortality, however, with a somewhat laissez-faire attitude. They do nothing particularly bad, but neither do they do anything particularly good. Their trajectory is flat, similar to a tractor plowing a field. Finally, there are those who use mortality to diminish and destroy themselves. They set a trajectory straight down, similar to a parachutist whose backup chute will not open. If unaltered in mortality, these are the trajectories that we will take out of this life with us to the next.

For those who set the trajectory upward, they will find Truth with a capital *T*. In the Gospel of John, Pilate asked Jesus, "What is truth?" (John 18:38). Earlier, Jesus had stated, "I am the way, the truth, and the life" (John 14:6). Thus, truth is not a series of philosophical propositions but rather a person, the person of Jesus Christ. Those of all faiths who pursue truth will encounter it in all its fullness in the Lord Jesus Christ and, having pursued it, will accept Jesus as their Lord without reservation. They will also accept the authority of the priesthood through which God always works, and they will accept without hesitation the saving ordinances of the gospel done for them by proxy. These persons will be of all religious traditions, for they received what God originally gave them and then accepted more when it was offered. They will be admitted to the celestial kingdom to the joy of all the saints of heaven.

Those, however, who set a level course will also gain what they desire. Again, these are persons from all faith traditions, including, sadly, many Latter-day Saints. It is certainly possible that their trajectory can be changed on the other side of the veil, but if they persist in their present self-satisfied stance, they will gain the terrestrial kingdom. Those who are plummeting to their own dooms may also be turned, but it will not be easy to change their self-destructive ways. If no change occurs, they will receive the glory of the telestial kingdom. Again, all faith traditions will be represented, including Latter-day Saints. However, there is a note of hope, even for those who seem bent on self-destruction. Truman Madsen, in his book about the temple, notes that President Wilford Woodruff said that there would be few who would not accept the ordinances of the temple when they are done for them. Similarly, he notes that John Taylor said that only about 10 percent of persons would refuse the ordinances. He quotes President Taylor as saying, "How many who are kept in prison are not ready to come out?"[6]

— APOSTASY AND RESTORATION

Another way of seeing the connection between the world's religions and Latter-day Saints is to examine the concept of apostasy. Latter-day Saints claim that an apostasy took place in the second half of the first century CE. But what does that mean? We know that in the meridian of time, Jesus came to atone for our sins. He called and set apart twelve Apostles and a group of seventy others to carry forward his work during his ministry and afterward. However, both of these groups were lost. Most importantly, the Quorum of the Twelve Apostles vanished through persecution and even martyrdom in many instances. Latter-day Saints claim that to perpetuate the apostolic authority, it is not sufficient for an Apostle to have ordained at one time an early Church father. When the Apostles were taken from the earth, so was the authority to perform the saving ordinances of the gospel. Thus with the loss of the Twelve also came the loss of authority—the heart of the Apostasy. This did not mean, however, that all truth was lost.

Latter-day Saints often say to me that they are glad that I have found the gospel. My response is that I knew the gospel long before I was a Latter-day Saint—what I found is the fullness of the gospel.

How could I have known the gospel? I knew it because faithful Roman Catholics, Eastern Orthodox, and Protestants passed along the biblical witness of Jesus across the centuries, thereby bringing billions to Christ, myself included.

The heart of the Restoration is that the same authority that was lost in about 100 CE was restored to Joseph Smith by Peter, James, and John in the summer of 1829. By 1835, the Quorum of Twelve was reestablished, although there were always twelve men around Joseph. However, I have to believe that prior to 1835 the full authority of the Restoration lay with the original Twelve in the heavens. In God's economy, what happened over that roughly 1,800-year period between the loss of authority and its restoration? Did not Jesus know that it would be lost? Of course he did, for if Paul knew it in 2 Thessalonians, then so did Jesus. Why, then, did he go to the trouble of establishing the Twelve and Seventy in the first century? To give us a template of what the church would look like when it was time for the church to be on the earth in its fullness. With the Restoration, we see the return of the original order of things with the Twelve and the Seventy leading the church on earth.

But we also see that Catholicism, Orthodoxy, and Protestantism were part of the Lord's plan. They were Eliases, or forerunners, to the Restoration, for without their ministry across the centuries, no one would have been prepared or looking for something more than what they had. Sidney Rigdon and Oliver Cowdery, for example, were looking for a restoration of the New Testament Church, based on their reading of the Bible. Their only question was whether the Lord had restored it through Joseph Smith.

What then of the other religions of the world? How do they fit into this picture? Much in the same way that traditional Christianity fits. They are Eliases to the Restoration, preparing their followers for the "more" that the Lord is waiting to give them as they are ready. In the meantime, he is molding their spirits through their own traditions.

— MISSIONARIES AND GOOD NEIGHBORS

From a Latter-day Saint perspective, however, these other religious traditions, including traditional Christianity, are incomplete. They have much good, but we desire to offer them more good. This is why we preach to all faith traditions. We believe that we have a precious pearl that will enhance their lives and their spirituality. We build on a foundation already laid. We should never denigrate that which God has put into place, for to do so is to despise what the Lord has planted. If we must denounce someone else's faith to make our own look good, that would mean we have very little to offer. If we have truth, truth will validate itself as the Holy Ghost bears witness of that truth.

The missionary effort of The Church of Jesus Christ of Latter-day Saints covers most of the countries of the earth, and in this mobile society, most of the nations of the earth with their religions are represented in the United States. If we know something about the religions we will encounter in our missionary efforts both here and abroad, we will be better missionaries. While the Spirit can guide in all things, we need to be able to find common ground with those that we teach, as did Ammon with Lamoni, so that we build from a common foundation. Knowledge of other faiths also gives an appreciation of and respect for what God has already given them. We can rejoice in the truths that they already know, thanking God for guiding these particular children to the point where we may offer them the "more of Mormonism."

Similarly, the earth is shrinking. If we are to be good citizens of this world village, we need to know and appreciate our brothers and sisters of all nations, colors, and religions. God would not have us at odds with one another, and religion is very close to the hearts of most people. To know the hearts of our brothers and sisters, we must know their religions.

— FORMAT

In the past when I have written on the world's religions, I have always tried to let the various traditions have their own say without interruption. At the end of a chapter on Hinduism, for example, I would put a section of Latter-day Saint reflections on the philosophical and theological issues that had been raised by the presentation of the Hindu faith. For a textbook, I still believe this is an appropriate approach, but in this book, I am going to take a different path. I believe that there can be constructive dialogue between faiths in which both parties respect and appreciate one another. My experience with the study of the world's religions is that I learn much about my own religion through my dialogue with other faiths. I see things in my own faith that I might never have seen had I not looked at it through the lens of another faith. The study of other faiths has only deepened and strengthened my own beliefs and commitments.

I had a teaching assistant who said it well. He was a Sikh from New Delhi who had come to Brigham Young University for his undergraduate work. He attended his ward and participated in the social events that went with ward life. He had his share of missionaries who wanted to convert him to the Latter-day Saint faith, but he resisted them because he did not find his faith to be deficient. With deep respect for Latter-day Saints, he said that being at Brigham Young University among so many faithful Latter-day Saints had deepened his own understanding of and commitment to his Sikh faith. So it is for me. The more I study other faiths, the more committed I become to my own. I become a better Latter-day Saint through my interactions with my brothers and sisters, who are the sons and daughters of a common Heavenly Father.

Thus in this book I will interlace the traditions of the various faiths we treat with the thoughts of Latter-day Saints on the issues that a given faith raises. This is not an attempt to show that Latter-day Saints are better than their neighbors. Rather, it is to show that we all wrestle with the common issues of human life and that we all have sensible answers to common questions. We need to remember that no one believes anything that is unreasonable. We all believe things that give meaning, purpose, and direction to our lives. We may have different answers to common questions, but each offers insights into the grave and challenging issues of what it means to be a human being struggling to be in harmony with the ultimate power in the universe. It is in this spirit of respect and appreciation that we as Latter-day Saints will examine our religiously diverse neighbors who hold deep faiths just as we do.[7]

--- NOTES ---

1. George Albert Smith, *Sharing the Gospel with Others: Excerpts from the Sermons of President Smith*, comp. Preston Nibley (Salt Lake City: Deseret News, 1948), 12–13.

2. Howard W. Hunter, "The Gospel—A Global Faith," *Ensign*, November 1991, 18. The quote from Joseph Smith is found in *History of the Church of Jesus Christ of Latter-day Saints*, ed. B. H. Roberts, 2nd ed. rev. (Salt Lake City: Deseret Book, 1970), 4:494–96.

3. Spencer W. Kimball, *Statement of the First Presidency Regarding God's Love for All Mankind*, February 15, 1978; quoted in Carlos E. Asay, "God's Love for Mankind," in Spencer J. Palmer, ed., *Mormons and Muslims: Spiritual Foundations and Modern Manifestations*, rev. ed. (Provo, UT: Religious Studies Center, Brigham Young University, 2002), 54.

4. Dallin H. Oaks, "Always Have His Spirit," *Ensign*, November 1996, 59. Elder Oaks explains that the manifestations of the Holy Ghost are available to everyone, with the purpose of acquainting "sincere seekers with the truth about the Lord and his gospel." Though this statement could be interpreted to mean only the doctrine of the church, this chapter suggests throughout that God gives direct guidance to any of his children who are open to it (manifestations of the Holy Ghost). When followed, those manifestations will eventually lead them to Christ and the priesthood, which is the point made by Elder Oaks.

5. Orson F. Whitney, in Conference Report, April 1921, 32–33, quoted in Hunter, "A Global Faith," 18.

6. Truman G. Madsen, *The Temple: Where Heaven Meets Earth* (Salt Lake City: Deseret Book, 2008), 31.

7. In the Western world, era designations are typically expressed in one of two ways: (1) AD (anno Domini, "in the year of the Lord" or "in the year of our Lord") and BC ("before Christ"), or (2) CE ("of the Common Era") and BCE ("before the Common Era"). By convention, the "Common Era" begins when Jesus was born, so it is correlated with AD, but BCE and CE are not centered on Christ. Because this is a book about world religions, BCE and CE are used throughout.

SOUTH ASIA

Temple in Belur, India. Central to Hindu worship is seeing the god housed within his or her temple. All images courtesy of author unless otherwise noted.

CHAPTER 2

HINDUISM

Hinduism is a highly varied faith, but it is beautiful in its diversity. People seek God, and for those who live their faith well, they live very much as do Latter-day Saints with similar standards and values.

Hinduism is a vibrant, multifaceted faith with roots deep in India's soil. Most of its nine hundred million adherents[1] are in India, but many Hindus have left India for educational or vocational reasons, creating thriving communities all over the world. The Hindu umbrella is large, incorporating polytheists, monotheists, and atheists. It is generally a nonmissionary faith, with the belief that all persons follow the way they made for themselves in prior lives and that the way they follow is uniquely theirs. Not only is it hard for Hindus to understand the missionary zeal of Christianity and Islam, but they also resent the implication that their indigenous religion is inferior or inadequate when compared with other faiths. Hinduism has many sensible answers to human questions and meets many human needs, so this chapter will attempt to show Hinduism in its beauty and diversity while in conversation with Latter-day Saint thought.

— ORIGINS

A HINDU POSITION

Hinduism holds itself to be one of the oldest faiths, if not the oldest faith, on the face of the earth. From a Hindu perspective, the precepts that make up Hinduism can be traced back to ancient wise men living far back in the mists of time who heard the vibrations of the universe, received them, and passed them along orally to others who continued the transmission. These oral traditions were passed along among a people known as the Aryans, whose origins are not clear. Eventually their oral traditions were written down, and today these make up the most sacred portion of the Hindu scriptures. They are texts that are believed to have no human authors but rather emanated from either the depths of the universe or the all-encompassing deity, dependent upon one's Hindu perspective.[2]

A HISTORICAL VIEW OF THE RELIGION

From the standpoint of the history of religions, Hinduism is viewed by scholars as an amalgamation of the Aryan religion and the religion of a people known as the Dravidians from the Indus Valley Culture. The Dravidians were the original inhabitants of the Indus Valley, which lies in current-day Pakistan. We know very little about them, since the written script they used is found in few places and has therefore not been translated. Thus our knowledge of the Dravidians is based on archaeology. Archaeology suggests that they were agriculturalists and that they had a highly developed civilization as evidenced by the population centers of Harappa and Mohenjo Daro. Both centers had public water and sewage systems, public baths, and other refinements. Small figurines of bulls and nude women suggest that the religion of the Dravidians was a fertility cult. In addition, we know that they were a black-skinned people but not African, based on their descendants, known as Tamils, who still live in India, especially in the south.

By contrast, the Aryans were a Caucasian nomadic, herding people, perhaps coming from the steppes of Russia, although scholarly opinion is not at one on this issue. Around 1500 BCE, they began to migrate in search of pasture for their flocks and herds. Some moved into the Indus Valley; others traveled into Persia, the Greek

Peloponnesus, Europe, and Scandinavia. In other words, the Aryans are the ancestors of those whose roots lie in Europe. Among scholars, there seems to be a growing consensus that there was a gradual Aryan migration, with the Dravidians already beginning to move out by the time the Aryans arrived due to a changing climate that was making it harder to raise crops. The land was becoming more suited to a pastoral life than to an agrarian one. Be that as it may, a great deal is known about the Aryans because we have their writings, known as the Vedas. We learn from the Vedas that the Aryans worshiped nature gods, had an elaborate sacrificial system, and had a priestly structure to carry out their sacrifices. The scholarly argument contends that Hinduism arose from the interaction of these two cultures, which lived side by side for a millennium.

Scripture

Shruti. The Hindu scriptures are divided into two categories: the Shruti and the Smriti. Shruti means "that which is heard," and these contain those texts which were heard by the ancient wise men eons ago. The wise men were not the authors of these texts; rather, they received them more in the manner of a court reporter who writes down what has been said. These texts are in Sanskrit and are the

Bull Nandi, Birla temple. Small figurines of bulls suggest that the religion of the Dravidians was a fertility cult.

province of scholars and priests; most are used in support of sacrificial rituals.

The foundational Hindu texts, the Vedas, include the Rig Veda ("wisdom consisting of verses"), which is recited by "caller priests" who invite the gods to the sacrifices; the Sama Veda ("knowledge of melodies"), which is sung by "singer priests" in support of the sacrificial rituals; the Yajur Veda ("knowledge of sacrificial sayings"), which is chanted by the "sacrificial priests" during the sacrifices; and finally the Atharva Veda ("knowledge of magic sayings"), which is primarily concerned with diverting disasters.

In addition to the Vedas, the Shruti contain philosophical commentaries on the sacrificial process; internal meditative rituals to be performed in the forest;[3] and philosophical treatises which begin to deal with reincarnation, the identity between the world soul and the human soul, and the ascetic life of the forest monk.

Smriti. The Smriti, meaning "that which is remembered," have human authors who write what they know, often in story form, and incorporate in their stories the principles that are contained in the Shruti. However, the Smriti are much more "user friendly." Many of them are attractive stories that keep the interest of the lay reader, and they are read and told in the average home. Thus, most Hindus are far more familiar with parts of the Smriti than they are with parts of the Shruti. The Smriti contain stories and legends about gods and their activities that are somewhat similar to Aesop's Fables, which are told to educate as well as entertain. They also contain the Mahabharata, a huge epic poem which exceeds in length *The Iliad* and *The Odyssey* combined. The poem narrates the wars and interactions between two ancient Indian families—the Pandavas and the Kauravas—and very probably has its roots deep in the soil of ancient India. One chapter within the Mahabharata is the Bhagavad Gita, the most sacred book of the Hare Krishna sect of Hinduism. The power in the Bhagavad Gita is Krishna's teaching about the role of devotion to him in salvation, and this teaching is loved by all Hindus. The Ramayana is a wonderful story of the love between the god Rama and his wife, Sita, and the battle between good and evil. Because of these themes, the Ramayana is a popular story among all Hindus, but it also cuts across cultural lines. The author has seen it performed in the Sultan's palace in Yogjakarta, Indonesia, a country that is 95 percent Muslim. He has also seen it performed in Bangkok, Thailand, a country that is virtually all Buddhist, and of course it has been performed in India and the United States. In all cases, it is thoroughly enjoyed. Finally, the Laws of Manu addresses the laws that guide the various castes, as well as the proper roles for women and the various rites of passage in Hindu life. It is clearly written from the male, priestly perspective.

— THE HINDU WORLDVIEW

ARYAN DEITIES

Some of the gods that were part of the Aryan religion still play a significant role in present-day Hinduism. For example, Indra is the king of the gods and a storm god. He is the ruler of the middle sky and the god of the monsoon storms, which bring life to India annually. He was very much the patron god of the Aryans, and those who attacked the Aryans attacked Indra, who would fight on behalf of his people.

Agni is the god of fire. Essentially, he is the messenger boy who carries the sacrifices from earth to heaven. Soma is the god of immortality, and by drinking soma, a hallucinogenic drink, one may take on the characteristics of the god. Thus warriors often drank soma before entering into battle. It may seem strange that there is the close tie between something material (i.e., the drink soma) and the god Soma. However, if Latter-day Saints will think about what actually happens in taking the sacrament, they will realize that there is a close connection between the elements of bread and water, which worshipers take into themselves, and Jesus Christ, with whom the worshipers identify through the material elements of bread and water and the Spirit. Because of that identification, worshipers leave the sacrament table as clean and pure as they were the moment they emerged from the baptismal pool. They have taken upon themselves the name of Christ (or Christ himself) and have thereby received his perfection.

One final god derived from the Aryans is Brahmanaspati, who is the god who knows how to influence the other gods, or is the power in prayer which moves the gods. People who know how to control Brahmanaspati have tremendous power—the power that the Brahmins, the priests, are believed to hold. For this reason, the priests stand atop the social structure known as the caste system. While there may be many persons with power in the temporal realm that can kill and destroy, only the priests have the power to influence the gods. They have cosmic power through Brahmanaspati. A parallel to Brahmanaspati in Latter-day Saint thought could be priesthood power. Through it, we can draw on the very power that God himself uses. However, rather than influencing God, as do the Brahmins, priesthood is used to bring God's power and influence to earth and to people.

CASTE AND SOCIAL RESPONSIBILITY

Probably one of the most recognized but least understood aspects of Indian life is the caste system, or the system of social segregation. It is probable that the hierarchical social structure defined by priests did not exist among the Aryans, for nomadic societies tend to be divided on the basis of responsibility, creating a horizontal structure. However, when the Aryans finally settled in the Indus Valley, what previously was a vocational grouping became vertical and hereditary, and thus one's caste was defined by the caste of one's parents. Marriage and social relationships were and still are to be within castes, thereby stratifying the society. A text that defined traditional caste responsibilities comes from the *Institutes of Vishnu 2—1.17* and reads:

> Brahmins, Kshatriyas, Vaishyas, and Shudras are the four castes. The first three of these are called twice-born. They must perform with mantras the whole number of ceremonies, which begin with impregnation and end with the ceremony of burning the dead body. Their duties are as follows. A Brahmin teaches the *Veda*. A Kshatriya has constant practice in arms. A Vaishya tends cattle. A Shudra serves the twice-born. All the twice-born are to sacrifice and study the *Veda*.[4]

From the above, it is clear that Brahmins perform the priestly tasks and are at the top of the system, because they know how to influence events at the cosmic level. A Brahmin presides at the sacrifices and performs them on behalf of others. In return, they give him alms which support him and his family. Kshatriyas were the warriors and the nobles who had tremendous temporal power and could make life good or bad for people, but they did not have the special knowledge of the Brahmins. Their basic job was to protect the community. Vaishyas were the people who really made society work. They were the farmers, merchants, accountants, money lenders, etc. Finally, the Shudras were the servant class and were involved in various trades or crafts.

Twice-born. We should notice the reference to the "twice-born" in the passage above. The male members of the first three castes may be twice-born, meaning that they could be initiated into the full range of responsibilities within Hindu society, particularly that of studying the sacred texts and performing the prescribed ceremonies of religious life. At various canonical ages, the three twice-born castes can receive a sacred thread which is worn over the left shoulder for life. The ceremony marks the entrance of the young man into adulthood. There are certain appropriate times for the ceremony, depending on caste, as well as certain things which are received, again depending on caste. Twice-born they may be, but equal they are not.

The fourth caste, the Shudras, are not twice-born, because they are not believed to have sufficient spirituality to perform the rituals and sacrifices, much less study the sacred texts. Given this, however, all castes have certain common responsibilities according to the *Institutes of Vishnu 2—1.17*:

> Duties common to all castes are patience, truthfulness, restraint, purity, liberality, self-control, not to kill, obedience toward one's gurus, visiting places of pilgrimage, sympathy, straightforwardness, freedom from covetousness, reverence toward gods and Brahmins, and freedom from anger.[5]

Few religious persons could fault these values.

In addition to the classical four castes, there is also another group that is outside the caste system, but for all intents and purposes, it is a caste in itself. These people are known as the Untouchables or Outcasts. These were probably people of Dravidian descent, while the four castes were probably of the Aryan race. The Untouchables were and are those who hold the lowest and most impure jobs in society, such as tanners and persons who work with sewage, clean the streets, or burn dead bodies. Because Gandhi did not believe that people should be categorized by parentage, he called the Untouchables *Harijans*, which means "children of God." In other words, people are what they make themselves by their actions, not by their birth.

There are Brahmins who behave as Untouchables, and there are Untouchables who behave as Brahmins. People should be accepted in society based on their behavior, in Gandhi's view. Today, the Indian Constitution prohibits discrimination based on caste for jobs and political offices. There are even parliamentary seats reserved for members of the "scheduled castes" (Untouchables) so that all persons are represented. There are also groups within Hinduism that do not believe in the caste system, one of which is the Hare Krishnas.

The traditional four-caste system has been modified over time. Today, in each historical caste, as well as among the Harijans, there are many subcastes known as *jatis*. Usually, these are based on occupations, and it is around these that most Hindu life is oriented, for they function like the historic castes. One is born into them, has social relations within them, and marries within them. Thus jatis are open or closed to one another, as were the historic castes, and India is still very conscious of caste or jati standing.

In closing the discussion of caste, it should be said that the caste system is not about economics but rather about spiritual standing. Shudras or Untouchables may be very rich, but they are spiritually light-years behind a dirt-poor Brahmin. The higher castes have some advantages educationally and financially, but neither of these is the ultimate goal of Hinduism. Rather, spirituality is the goal, and all else must ultimately be left behind to attain this. Consequently, the measure of a person is not his or her wealth but his or her spirituality. Thus people are socially where they belong. Since they must live out the way they created for themselves, the caste and jati system creates a highly stable society.

This is quite different from the Latter-day Saint view, in which individuality and personal agency are stressed. Human beings control their own destinies. There is social mobility through hard work, education, and seizing opportunities. People are not locked into social positions by birth but may grow and advance through their best efforts. Among Latter-day Saints, class stratification is denied because God is not a respecter of persons. All are equal before him. All are his children, and he loves none more or less than others. However, he does give commands, and based on obedience to those commands, he rewards or condemns. Goodness, however, does not necessarily ensure material wealth or well-being.

Hence, caste in any form is anathema to Latter-day Saints. In the end, everything belongs to God, who gives all and who calls all to the service of their brothers and sisters. No church member is better than any other. All have been called to their own roles, but not because one is inherently better than another. We may show our differences in the way we respond to God, but for all of us, leadership is finally service, not status.

— HINDU PHILOSOPHY

MONISM

The traditional Brahmin worldview begins with a concept known as monism, the belief that all things are one. There is only one reality, and all things are simply extensions of that one which is called Brahman. Perhaps the best definition of Brahman is simply "Brahman is." Thus it is an illusion to believe that persons or other things have an identity separate and distinct from this world soul. As long as persons hold to the illusion of individual identity apart from Brahman, they will continue to return to the rounds of rebirth. Only when they come to an experiential knowledge of their oneness with Brahman will they finally be released.

The best example of the monistic worldview is that it would be an absolute illusion for a wave on the surface of the ocean to believe that it was something separate and distinct from the ocean. The human soul is the wave which appears momentarily and then vanishes. This would be pure monism.

However, most Hindus believe they have individuality and thus hold a modified monism. Their view would be more that of an ocean wave slamming into a cliff, and while the droplets of water, the souls, are in the air, they are truly separate from the ocean. But ultimately, they fall back into the ocean and all individuality is lost in the sea. In the end, all things are Brahman.

The concept of monism is foreign to the Latter-day Saint way of looking at the universe. The LDS perspective begins with the eternal nature of things. Matter, energy, intelligences, and God are all eternal and uncreated, but they are held to be distinct and separate.

Matter, energy, and intelligences are not God, and thus he can organize them into universes, galaxies, star systems, animals, plants, fish, and fowl. The highest of God's acts is the clothing of intelligences with spirit forms that bring men and women into the spirit world and ultimately, as with all life, to an earth. Thus there is individuality to all things, though we share the thought with Hinduism that all is uncreated. Salvation is to find union with the Father through Christ, like Christ's union with the Father, in which there is oneness in love, purpose, and will. In this union, however, humans do not lose their individuality in God; what they lose is their ego. We cannot take into God's presence a will different from his. Satan tried that and was expelled. Neither are humans just an extension or piece of God. Instead they bear a divine spiritual nature derived from God. Consequently, the union Latter-day Saints experience is a spiritual union, not a material union.

KARMA

How does monism fit with other concepts within Hinduism? Very well, for the system is quite tight. A principal concept is that of karma. Karma is what results from past actions, and it comes to fruition at various times and ways in various lives. In physics, every action has an equal and opposite reaction. So it is with karma, which explains many of the differences we observe in life. Why are some born wealthy and others poor? Because of karma. Why are some born perfect in body while others have birth defects? Because of karma. Why do some die early and others live to a ripe old age? Because of karma, and we did it all to ourselves. We are reaping what we have sown perhaps many lifetimes ago. We can have no objections to our situation in life because we created it for ourselves; and now we must live it out, although we can exercise our agency in how we live it. How we live it is defined by our caste laws and laws related to our sex or other stations in life.

Latter-day Saints have the idea of the law of the harvest, the point being that we reap what we sow. If we reject the offer of the Atonement, we are left responsible for our own acts. If we accept the Atonement, we will be blessed according to how faithfully we cling to Christ, how we live out the Christian life, and whether we accept the saving ordinances of the gospel offered through the priesthood. Thus the Atonement can pay the price for our sins. The result of sin is not inexorable, as are the results of karma, thanks to Jesus Christ.

What about the relation between the premortal life, this life, and the consequences of our deeds in the former? By our very presence in this second estate, we know that we were faithful to the Father and to Jehovah when Satan led his revolt. Beyond that, we know very little about the exact correlation between the two estates, although we know that the great and valiant were reserved for the latter days. Often we assume these valiant persons to be only the Latter-day Saints, but there are many other persons of deep faith being born in these last times who improve the moral and spiritual content of human life, as we have already noted. They seem to have a role for which they too were foreordained. Given this, perhaps we as Latter-day Saints should concern ourselves more with the mercy and inclusiveness of God than with his justice and exclusivity. Perhaps, as President Hunter and Elder Orson F. Whitney suggested, God's reach is much broader and more inclusive through his servants of many faiths than we might have supposed.

REINCARNATION

Hindus believe in multiple lifetimes (i.e., the doctrine of reincarnation). It is clear to them that in one lifetime people cannot attain perfection sufficient for release from the rounds of rebirth, so there must be multiple lifetimes through which humans grow spiritually. While punishment for bad deeds certainly happens during the cycle of reincarnation, the underlying idea is one of growth toward spiritual things. Thus the Brahmins, the most spiritual of all groups, stand at the top of the caste system. Dependent upon their karma, persons may be reincarnated as any number of life-forms. The spectrum of life is as below.

Gods

Humans

Animals

Vegetation

Demons

Only as a human being may one find release from the wheel, for it is only as a human that one has agency or choice. Even the realm of the gods is only a place of rest and relaxation, but in the end, the gods must enter human life to find release. So it is with the lower life-forms. They are what they are because of karma, and they must remain as they are until the karma that placed them there is burned off. Karma is like a candle. When the candle finally burns down, all the fuel is exhausted. When the karma that placed one in a particular situation is burned up, new karma will come to fruition, and a new lifetime or life-form will occur with new opportunities for growth, if one is reincarnated in the human realm.

Latter-day Saints generally dismiss without much thought the doctrine of reincarnation. That, however, is too easy a response to the issue. The real question is, what is the problem with which the doctrine deals? The answer is that it deals with the reality that no one is able to be perfect in one lifetime. We all recognize that fact, no matter what our faith is.

Latter-day Saints also recognize the problem, although they give a different answer to it than does Hinduism. The Latter-day Saint answer lies in two principal doctrines: (1) the Atonement worked by Jesus Christ and (2) the doctrine of eternal progression. In the first instance, we do not have to become perfect, for Christ through his Atonement offers us his perfection. Each time we take the sacrament, we are made momentarily perfect in Christ. Ultimately, our goal is to live so near the Holy Ghost that we can be like Nephi in the book of Helaman, who was granted the right to ask for whatever he wanted, since he would never ask amiss. Most of us never attain that level of spirituality, but even Nephi leaned on Christ's Atonement.

The second doctrine, that of eternal progression, simply means that we began our spiritual growth in the premortal life, continue that growth exponentially in mortality, and will continue to grow in our knowledge of God in the postmortal existence. Therefore, we may grow toward perfection in ourselves, a process that other Christians call sanctification. In this manner, Latter-day Saints deal with the issue of their imperfection. We must recognize that both approaches, the Hindu and the Latter-day Saint, make sense, given their underlying views of the world and of God.

TRANSMIGRATION AND RELEASE

Coupled with reincarnation is the concept of transmigration, which many authors equate with reincarnation. However, as we will see with Buddhism, they are not equivalent. Transmigration means that something—my soul—moves from one life to another, and thus I am reborn. The soul is my essence until it falls back into the ocean, and until then, it moves from life to life.

In the end, however, the goal is to get out of these rounds of rebirth through *release*. To gain release, persons must break the illusion of their separateness from Brahman and come to a knowledge of their oneness with Brahman. But this is not "head knowledge." The head only gets us into trouble, for our thoughts are not reality. Only Brahman is real. Historically, according to the Brahmin priests, when persons have lived lives of such merit that their karma is reduced to the degree that they have the propensity for release, they can enter the Brahmin path of study and meditation which ultimately leads to the enlightenment experience. This is a profound experience of oneness with all things, or oneness with Brahman. It is not an intellectual knowledge but rather an experiential knowledge. When persons become enlightened and experience their oneness with Brahman, it is equivalent in Latter-day Saint terms to having our "calling and election made sure." Persons know at death that they will be released from the rounds of rebirth. But release means what? It is the drop of water falling back into the ocean. This is nirvana, the loss of individuality and selfhood.

NIRVANA

But why would one want to reach a state of nonexistence? To answer this, we must walk in the shoes of persons who live in a different world than do we, which is not the comfortable world of the West. In the United States, only a relatively few people have wanted for the essentials of life. Most have far more in goods and privileges than they can ever use. However, most of the world does not live this way, nor have our brothers and sisters across the millennia had such luxury. Most have lived on the edge of death. They were lucky to have any kind of meal every couple of days; they watched their children die; they were subject to the brutality of the more privileged; they were enslaved. If persons believed that lifetime after lifetime they would return to such situations, release might look good.

Latter-day Saints too experience the vicissitudes of life. Rather than seeing them as something to be escaped, they are viewed as growth opportunities. If we are not challenged, we cannot grow. With that said, we must still stand silent before some of the incredible suffering that people have to endure in our world. Much of it is due to the inhumanity of people to people, the hoarding of resources, and the desire for power. Some would suggest that it is due to choices we made in the premortal life, but I find that hard to accept. In considering the relationship between premortality and mortal life, Elder B. H. Roberts probably set the right tone:

> Between these two extremes of good and bad, obedient and rebellious [in the premortal life] were, I doubt not, all degrees of faithfulness and nobility of conduct; and I *hazard the opinion* that the amount and kind of development in that pre-existent state influences the character in this life, and brings within reach of men privileges and blessings commensurate with their faithfulness in the spirit world. Yet I would not be understood as holding the *opinion* that those born to wealth and ease, whose lives appear to be an unbroken round of pleasure and happiness, must therefore have been spirits in their first estate that were very highly developed in refinement, and very valiant for God and his Christ. . . . I hold that the condition in life which is calculated to give the widest experience to man, is the one most to be desired, and he who obtains it is the most favored of God. . . . I believe it consistent with right reason to say that some of the lowliest walks in life, the paths which lead into the deepest valleys of sorrow and up to the most rugged steeps of adversity, are the ones which if a man travel in, will best accomplish the object of his existence in this world. . . . Those who have to contend with difficulties, brave dangers, endure disappointments, struggle with sorrows, eat the bread of adversity and drink the water of affliction, develop a moral and spiritual strength, together with a purity of life and character, unknown to the heirs of ease, and wealth and pleasure. . . . In proof of this I direct you to the lives of the saints and the prophets; but above all to the life of the Son of God himself.[6]

Recognizing that the above is only Roberts's opinion, the views certainly fit with all that we know from the restored gospel. It seems that life is not meant to be easy. It is designed to stretch and mold us, and it is definitely not to be escaped. We can be sure that evil is derived not from God but from those of us who use our agency for ill in mortal life. Unfortunately, far too many of us use it to elevate ourselves rather than our brothers and sisters.

Four Permissible Goals of Life

A Hindu may pursue four goals in life. The first two of these are self-directed. In other words, they focus on the person, while the last two are directed away from the self.

Pleasure. The first permissible goal is pleasure, but not just any pleasure. Pleasure must be pursued within the context of caste law and social propriety. While pleasure is a permissible goal, it is not the highest goal, and hopefully either in this life or in some future life people will ask if there is not a higher way. And there is.

Power or wealth. The second permissible goal is not, however, a higher way because it focuses once again on the self. The second goal is power or wealth. Again, it cannot be pursued in ways that are at variance with caste and social convention. Persons may have to be a bit thick-skinned to climb the corporate or political ladder or to gain wealth. Once again, sooner or later should come the question of whether or not there is a higher way, which, of course, there is.

Duty. The third goal begins the higher way, and it is the goal of duty. As students, for example, people owe duty to their teachers. As householders, they owe duty to their spouses, their children, aged parents, the community, an employer, the PTA, the soccer league, and any number of other organizations. Persons cease to focus on their own wants and needs and become more concerned about those of their neighbors, family, and friends.

Release. For all its good, duty is still not the highest goal of a Hindu because the ultimate goal is to break the rounds of rebirth and gain release. But this sounds rather self-directed. "I want to gain release from the rounds of rebirth." If we think about it, however, what does release mean? It means the drop of water falls back into the ocean or the wave vanishes from the surface of the ocean and all individuality is lost. In other words, release is the ultimate of nonself, because the self is lost in the ocean of Brahman.

FOUR STAGES OF LIFE

Student. Just as there are four permissible goals in life, there are also four stages of life—namely, student, householder, hermit, and holy man. The stage of student is what determines whether persons are twice-born or not. Persons who are twice-born can participate in all aspects of Hindu life, including the study of sacred texts. Shudras are not spiritually mature enough to study these texts and therefore cannot be twice-born and cannot be students. Today, few actually study the religious texts as young men. Some may, but most in India study in public or private schools and thereby have moved away from the religious nature of the student stage.

Householder. The stage of householder is just what one would imagine (i.e., persons marry, have children, earn a living, care for the home, and owe responsibility to the community). The twice-born householder is expected to perform all the rituals related to various passages in life from conception to death. This is the last stage that most Hindus ever enter. The responsibilities and joys of family life are so all-consuming that there is no room for anything else. Both this stage and the stage of student are oriented toward the permissible goal of duty, since both draw people beyond themselves, although for the householder there are aspects of pleasure in marriage and family, as well as the seeking of wealth as men try to support their families.

Hermit. If persons want to pursue yet a higher goal, that of release, they must withdraw from the home and enter the stage of hermit, in which they seek to become detached from all things, be they persons, places, or things. Historically this stage has always meant that persons withdraw from society, often joining a guru in a place of spiritual retreat. There they leave their past behind, going beyond family, caste, or vocation. They are no longer who they were, since all of that was transient and impermanent.

Holy man. There is no sharp demarcation between the stages of hermit and holy man. To enter into the latter stage simply means that one has left all attachments behind and is fully focused on attaining release. They have no past, for it is gone. They have only the future hope and goal of attaining release, and many Hindus believe that when a holy man dies, he automatically gains release from the rounds of rebirth. These last two stages are not normally entered by women, although some will enter the third stage within the household, turning daily duties over to daughters-in-law while they focus on the spiritual. Almost no women enter the final stage, although there are some (few and far between) renowned female ascetics.

Latter-day Saints also have their stages of life. At eight years of age, children are baptized and are believed to become accountable for their choices. At twelve, young men are ordained to the priesthood, and young women enter the Young Women organization. At fourteen, both genders start seminary. Shortly after eighteen years of age, young men are expected to be ordained to the Melchizedek Priesthood and at nineteen to go on a mission. Girls move into the Relief Society at eighteen. At twenty-one, women may also go on a mission, if they have not yet been married. For both young men and women, normally the next stage of life is marriage and having a family while also getting an education and preparing for their future careers. This would be the householder stage. At the time of retirement, there is a stage of conse-cration for married couples who can once again give their lives to the church as missionaries. There is no retirement in the church.

THREE WAYS OFF THE WHEEL

The ultimate goal, as we have seen, is to gain release from the rounds of rebirth. This may be accomplished by following one of three paths—works, knowledge, or devotion.

The way of works. The way of works is the way that all must follow. Fundamentally, it means living out individual lives within the context of caste laws, which indicate what is right and wrong for those per-sons. One follows his or her "way" in hopes of gaining a better rebirth in a future life. No one of any caste can escape the need to follow the route laid out by caste laws, so all castes walk this path. However, if persons are Brahmin males, another path is open to them which can lead directly to release.

The way of knowledge. The way of the Brahmin male is the way of knowledge. This is the path through which experiential knowledge of oneness with Brahman may be attained. Brahmin males held that only they had progressed sufficiently spiritually to be able to walk this path, since they had reduced karma to the degree that they were on the verge of release. The way of knowledge usually meant withdrawal into the stages of hermit and holy man, learning from a guru, and ultimately sitting in meditation that led to the experience of enlightenment, thus assuring release from the rounds of rebirth at death. As noted earlier, most Hindus assume that holy men achieve release upon death. We should probably also say here that if women want to gain release from the rounds of rebirth, it was assumed historically that eventually they had to become Brahmin males.

The way of devotion. The way of devotion was always part of the Hindu life, but it was not always viewed as a way to gain release from the rounds of rebirth. According to Brahmin males, that could be accomplished only through the way of knowledge. However, with the rise of Jainism and Buddhism, both of which offered paths to release that cut across sex and caste lines, the Brahmins validated the way of devotion to deities, which offered the same benefits as did Buddhism and Jainism but within a fully Hindu context.

We need to remember that the traditional goal of Hinduism was to gain release from the rounds of rebirth by gaining an experiential oneness with Brahman. However, concepts like Brahman, the wave on the

Ganesha, the remover of obstacles, is one of the gods worshipped in the Hindu pantheon.

ocean, droplets of water, and illusion are hard to comprehend because we try to understand the infinite with a finite mind. So Brahman accommodates itself to our level of comprehension by manifesting itself in personal forms as creator, preserver, and destroyer. In these aspects, Brahman the infinite is known as the gods Brahma (creator), Vishnu (preserver), and Shiva (destroyer). It is through these three that the power of the devotional path of Hinduism arises.

Because these gods are aspects of Brahman or of the infinite, none of them are captured on the rounds of rebirth, and they can therefore free devotees from the realm of rebirth. Brahma is rarely worshiped by himself, and there are only two temples in all of India dedicated solely to him. He is the creator god, has essentially done his job, and is thus off on a long break. However, the two most popular male deities to whom devotion is directed are Shiva and Vishnu.

Shiva is the god of destruction and meditation. He destroys evil and ignorance particularly. Many who follow the meditative way model themselves after Shiva and devote themselves to him. A follower of Shiva can normally be identified by the horizontal stripes of white on his or her forehead.

Vishnu is the preserver deity. He preserves the earth and its people and has come in nine incarnations to preserve the world or its order. Some of those incarnations have been animals. One was a man-lion. Others were in human form, such as Rama or Krishna. Vishnu may be worshiped directly or indirectly through his incarnations.

The male deities also have female counterparts who give them power. No god has power without a female partner, and these partners may be worshiped. Through them, people can gain release because of their devotion. In addition to these male figures and their consorts, there is also Devi, the great goddess personified in Durga and Kali, both of whom strike fear into those who oppose them. Many Hindus worship them.

For those who follow the devotional way, and virtually all Hindus do so, they conceive of the god whom they worship as the god who manifests himself or herself in all the other deities. Henotheism is the name given to this practice of worshiping one god who is manifest in many other deities. The power of the devotional way is captured in the words of Krishna in the Bhagavad Gita. He says, "Be certain none can perish, trusting me. O Pritha's son, whoso will turn to me, though they be born from the very womb of sin, woman or man; sprung of the Vaisya caste or lowly disregarded Sudra—all plant foot upon the highest path."[7]

In other words, one does not need to be a Brahmin male to gain release from the rounds of rebirth. It can be done by becoming one through devotion with any one of the above deities who are manifestations of Brahman. Thus, as noted above, virtually all Hindus today are devotional Hindus. They worship a deity who can give them release. Even so, all must still follow the path of works, since all must live their caste laws. Some may follow the path of knowledge, living a more ascetic, meditative life and perhaps worshiping Shiva. In the end, the way of devotion is open to all.

— WORSHIP IN HINDUISM

To say that Hindu worship is varied is an understatement. There are probably almost as many ways of worshiping as there are worshipers, but there are some common elements that may be pointed out. The heart of Aryan worship was the sacrificial rituals that were designed to placate or please the various gods. Sacrificial rituals are still done today, generally with vegetable materials, as ways of expressing renunciation and penance.[8] Images also play a major role in Hindu worship. Some Westerners mistakenly believe the images themselves are worshiped, but they are not. They symbolize that which is divine, and they direct the worshipers' attention in that direction. Since Brahman is viewed as being in all things, anything can be used to focus or crystallize people's attention on God. Even a stone may represent deity, if that is the intention of the person setting up the stone. The ultimate impersonal, invisible god Brahman may be manifest in many ways through the personalized Brahman and thus may be worshiped under many forms and names. As we have seen, Brahman can be seen as Brahma, Shiva, Vishnu, Rama, Krishna, Devi, or any other number of gods or goddesses. Since the male gods must have their female counterparts to have power, their wives may also be worshiped. For example, persons may worship Lakshmi, the wife of Vishnu, or Parvati or Durga, wives of Shiva. Most Hindus have a personal god whom they worship, and there may also be a god that is worshiped by their family to whom they submit. Simultaneously, there will probably be a local god who is worshiped. In the end, however, these are all manifestations of Brahman.

"Tools" of worship are *mantras* (chants), *yantras* (geometric pictures), and *darshan* (seeing the god). Chants are reality in sound. The vibrations from the chant when recited benefit both the reciter and the hearer. They focus the mind through sound and exclude distractions as the worshiper focuses his or her mind on the reality that the sound represents, usually a god. However, the most powerful chant is simply the syllable *om* or *aum*. When pronounced properly, it captures the very essence of the universe.

Geometric pictures function in the same way that chants do, but rather than focusing the mind through sound, they focus the mind through a visual geometric representation and are often made of colored powders on the floor. The aim is to be able to visualize these and stop the flow of extraneous thoughts.

Seeing the god is also central to Hindu worship. Thus one goes to the temple to see the god housed there. The god in turn sees the worshiper and blesses his or her life.

Ritual worship is called *puja*, although there are many names for worship forms. Common elements that may be observed in ritual worship are the reciting of chants inviting a particular deity to be present, the chanting of hymns of praise, and the waving of lamps, which is

The Ganges River is considered sacred and is personified as a goddess.

called *arati*. At the end of the waving of the lamps, worshipers will move their hands over the lamps and draw the warmth and the light to themselves, thereby being purified. At the end of worship, the priest may sprinkle the worshipers with holy water from the Ganges River.

The most spectacular worship experience is known as the Kumbha Mela, a mass gathering that occurs four times during a twelve-year cycle. There are four sites where the Kumbha Melas are held. Up to ten million people gather at a Kumbha Mela, and the central ritual is all the pilgrims bathing together in the river at a predetermined time.

— WOMEN IN HINDUISM

According to Sharada Sugirtharajah, society in the period of the Veda was based on the family and was patriarchal and life affirming. Initiation was open to men and women, and both could receive a spiritual education. In the realm of religious activities, men and women were equal.[9] However, with the rise of both Brahmin religious specialization and the ascetic ideal, the gap between men and women widened in society.

Historically, Hinduism has been ambivalent about women, seeing them on the one hand as goddesses and on the other as temptresses. Generally, they were viewed as dependent beings for their entire lives. As girls, they were dependent on their fathers. As wives, they were dependent on their husbands, and as widows, dependent on their sons. In essence, they were not autonomous persons. When married, a woman moved into the home of her husband and became subject to his mother and other women in the household, which was often very difficult. If a husband died, the widow could not remarry, no matter how young she was. It was only in 1856 that a law was passed permitting widows to remarry, although not many do so now, since it would run against custom and culture. While widowhood may be inauspicious, there is a breaking down of the public prejudice against it. For example, Indira Gandhi, a widow, was prime minister of India. However, the true feminine ideal is that of a mother, especially if she produces a son; this is because having a son will allow the family name to be continued and will thus ensure salvation of the family.

Latter-day Saints also have a patriarchal order, but it is an order shared by a man and a woman. They should be equal partners. In that partnership, both have roles that they are to fulfill—the husband is the provider and priesthood head of the home, and the wife is the primary nurturer of the family. Both roles are essential to the growing of an eternal family unit. If a man or woman loses a spouse to death, each is permitted, if not actually encouraged, to remarry. In Latter-day Saint thought, human beings were not meant to live alone.

— CONCLUSION

Hinduism is a highly varied faith, but it is beautiful in its diversity. People seek God, and for those who live their faith well, they live very much as do Latter-day Saints with similar standards and values. These values, because they are common and good, must have their roots in a common God who is the Father of us all. Thus he leads the Hindu toward him, just as surely as he leads the Latter-day Saint toward him, but the paths are different in external form, especially where Jesus Christ and priesthood authority are concerned.

— NOTES

1. "Major Religions of the World Ranked by Number of Adherents," Adherents.com, last modified August 9, 2007, http://www.adherents .com/Religions_By_Adherents.html.
2. Swami Bhaskarananda, *The Essentials of Hinduism: A Comprehensive Overview of the World's Oldest Religion*, 2nd ed. (Seattle: Viveka, 2002), 1–5.
3. Constance A. Jones and James D. Ryan, *Encyclopedia of Hinduism* (New York: Facts on File, 2007), 42.
4. Robert E. Van Voorst, *Anthology of World Scriptures*, 6th ed. (Mason, OH: Cengage Learning, 2008), 41.
5. Van Voorst, *Anthology*, 42.
6. B. H. Roberts, *The Gospel: An Exposition of Its First Principles and Man's Relationship to Deity*, 10th ed. (Salt Lake City: Deseret Book, 1965), 277–79; emphasis added.
7. David S. Noss and John B. Noss, *A History of the World's Religions*, 9th ed. (New York: Macmillan College, 1994), 133.
8. Anuradha Roma Choudhury, "Hinduism," in *Worship*, ed. Jean Holm with John Bowker (New York: Pinter, 1994), 64.
9. Sharada Sugirtharajah, "Hinduism," in *Women in Religion*, ed. Jean Holm with John Bowker (New York: Pinter, 1994), 59–60.

Jain temple in Sarnath, India. The principal ritual for all Jains is veneration of the Ford Finders, which involves going to the temple. Courtesy of Ken Wieland.

CHAPTER 3

JAINISM

In a world fraught with violence, materialism, and sensuality, it is important that someone remind us that these things are not eternal and that they separate us from that which is ultimate.

J ainism is a religion with which most people in the West are not familiar. It is small, with only about 4.2 million adherents,[1] most of whom reside in India, but it claims roots in antiquity which rival those of Hinduism. Its principal tenets focus on nonviolence, nonattachment, and relative pluralism. The principle of nonviolence deeply influenced Mahatma Gandhi in his nonviolent opposition to oppression. By extension, it also influenced Martin Luther King Jr.'s approach to the issue of segregation and his nonviolent marches through the southern United States. Underlying Jainism is a strong moral foundation and a unique view of the universe and how human beings fit into it.

— ORIGINS

FOUNDER

While Hinduism traces its roots back through the Aryan civilization to the wise men who stand at the beginning of history, the Jains trace their origins back through the Indus Valley civilization, often equated with the Dravidians mentioned in the previous chapter. Throughout this long history, there were twenty-four Ford Finders, spiritual leaders who discovered the Jain way and taught it to their contemporaries. Essentially, they found the way when it had been lost. Each time the way became lost, a new Ford Finder arose to show the way once again, similar to how a scout would show a wagon train the ford across a river. The closest thing in Latter-day Saint thought to a Ford Finder would be the founding prophet of a dispensation. The first of these Ford Finders was Rikhava, whom one author assumes lived at least five thousand years ago.[2] The same author believes that the Indus Valley civilization showed no signs of having been warlike, that there were no deities depicted on seals, and that persons are shown meditating in the same way that Jains today meditate. In other words, he believes that archaeology is showing that the Indus Valley civilization, rather than being a proto-Hindu cult, was the forerunner of modern Jainism. Following Rikhava were twenty-three other Ford Finders, all men except the nineteenth, Malli Natha, whom the White Clad Jains believe to have been a woman. The Sky Clad Jains, however, hold Malli Natha to have been a man.

The most recent Ford Finder is known as Mahavira (meaning "great hero"). Mahavira was born in 599 BCE and died in 527 BCE. His father was a raja and thus a noble, but Mahavira was not the eldest son, so he had options that he would not have otherwise had. According to tradition, Mahavira was raised in great luxury. He married the princess Yasoda and had a daughter, but he found himself discontented with the life of a prince. Outside the town where he lived was a group of monks, and Mahavira felt drawn to them. However, out of respect for his parents, he felt he could not leave the palace to seek a religious life. Upon the death of his parents when he was about age thirty, Mahavira felt free to pursue the spiritual dimensions of life. Thus he left his wife and daughter. Mahavira took off his royal regalia and, keeping only one robe, pulled his hair out in five handfuls and vowed, "I shall for twelve years neglect my body and abandon the care of it. I shall with a right disposition bear, undergo, and suffer all calamities arising from divine powers, men or animals."[3] He then joined the ascetics.

Why would a man leave his wife and daughter for the withdrawn life? Having examined Hinduism, we know the answer to that

Mahavira, the twenty-fourth and final Ford Finder.
Courtesy of Dayodaya.

question. Mahavira was following the four stages of life and was simply moving from the stage of householder to that of hermit. While this step is usually taken when a spouse has died and children are grown, it was not beyond possibility to make the step while the wife still lived with the expectation that she should and would support her husband in his search for release. In the case of Mahavira's family, we can be sure that they were well cared for, being of royal birth, but we have no insight into the emotional trauma that his decision might have caused.

It did not take long for Mahavira to decide that the monks were not very serious about the ascetic life. After about six months, he left them, threw off the one remaining robe that he had, and began to wander nude through central India. His asceticism consisted of eating very little, seeking not to take life, and practicing extreme ascetic activities. For example, in the cold season, he would sit in the shade; in the hot season, he would sit in the sun, all in an attempt to bring his body under the control of his spirit. In addition, he practiced extreme nonviolence, meaning that he was conscious of life in almost all things and tried to injure nothing. Normally, he wandered, so that he would not become attached to people, places, or things. During the rainy season, however, he would stay in one place, in order not to injure the multiplicity of life that would come out on the paths. He was often badly treated by various householders who would encourage their dogs to bite him or who would disturb him in his religious meditation, even picking him up, throwing him into the air, and letting him fall to the ground. Mahavira persevered through all of this.

Finally, after thirteen years of extreme asceticism, Mahavira came to enlightenment. In Jainism, this means that he became omniscient and knew all things about people and the universe.

This event was a bombshell in the Hindu religious landscape because according to Brahmin males, the only persons who had the spiritual maturity to gain enlightenment were Brahmin males, but now a Kshatriya (noble) had proven that not to be so. A whole new way to release had been opened by Mahavira's enlightenment, a way not dependent upon Brahmins, castes, Vedic sacrifices, or scriptures. It was a way that cut across caste and sex lines. Everyone, male or female, could gain enlightenment, no matter what his or her station in life was. This self-help way certainly was not easy, but it was a way! The models for the way were the Ford Finders.

SCRIPTURES

The only thing certain about scriptures in Jainism is that the two major sects, the Sky Clads and the White Clads, do not agree on what is canonical. The Sky Clads accept only two texts as canonical, and the White Clads accept forty-five. Each sect believes that their scriptural canon contains the essence of Mahavira's teachings, but the Sky Clads hold that his exact words have been lost. The White Clads believe that the texts they use are close to, if not actually, the words of Mahavira.

— SECTS —

We have already used the names of the two major sects within Jainism—the Sky Clads and White Clads. As may be guessed, the former have monks who wear only the sky (i.e., they wander nude), and the latter have monks and nuns who wear white robes. The two groups and some of their beliefs are contrasted in the chart below.

— SKY CLADS —	— WHITE CLADS —
1. Ascetics must be nude.	1. Nudity is not essential.
2. Women cannot gain liberation.	2. Both men and women can gain liberation.
3. Mahavira was not married.	3. Mahavira was married.
4. Ford Finder images are unclad.	4. Ford Finder images are clad and adorned.
5. Monks eat once a day.	5. Monks and nuns may eat more than once a day.
6. Monks have only two possessions.	6. Monks and nuns may have up to fourteen possessions.
7. Monks may carry scriptures.	7. Monks and nuns may carry scriptures.

This sketch suggests that the monks of the Sky Clads live more severely ascetic lives and are doctrinally more conservative than the White Clads. Given the above, a few comments are in order. First, the Sky Clads have only male ascetics who wander nude, and there are probably only about one hundred of these. They feel that women do not have either the physical strength or the spiritual development to gain release. Another doctrine that underlines the conservatism of the Sky Clads is their denial of Mahavira's marriage. Theirs is an ascetic tradition, and things of the "flesh" are forbidden for ascetics. Surely, from their point of view, the founder of such a tradition could not have participated in marriage relations and thus could never have been married. The truth, however, is that Mahavira was almost certainly married. One can easily see, though, how the Sky Clad monks, who themselves didn't marry, would want to deny it.

A White Clad Jain priest.

Another practice that underscores the more ascetic Sky Clad practice is eating once a day. In addition, they may eat only one dish from one home, and this must be eaten with the hands. In contrast, White Clads can go from house to house, use utensils, and eat more than once per day. Similarly, Sky Clads are allowed only two possessions (i.e., a whisk broom made from peacock feathers for sweeping away insects or other life from the path or a seat, and a wooden water pot). White Clads may have up to fourteen possessions, including their loincloth and shoulder cloth. A further sign of the more conservative Sky Clads is the nudity of the Ford Finders in their temples. These statues are unadorned in any way. On the other hand, the statues of the Ford Finders in White Clad temples wear a loincloth and may be highly decorated, even with jewels.

In addition to these two sects, there are also two subsects which have arisen from the White Clads. Both of these are non-image-worshiping groups, meaning they do not have statues of the Ford Finders in their temples. Both cover their mouths with white masks to prevent harm to insects and the air.

— JAIN PHILOSOPHY

There are three fundamental principles that support Jain life and thought: nonviolence, nonattachment, and relative pluralism. We will see the role each plays in the Jain worldview.[4]

NONVIOLENCE

Jains love to categorize things, so what follows is a kind of taxonomy of life. Although their view of life may differ somewhat from ours, we should always remember that what may be different for Westerners makes logical sense to Jains. Having said this, there are two kinds of souls: a liberated soul, released from the rounds of rebirth, and a soul still on the rounds of rebirth. The soul still on the rounds may be composed of anywhere from one to five senses. For example, one-sense life would be plants. Two-senses would be worms, birds, and fish. Three-senses include lice. Four-senses encompass bees, and five-sense life includes humans, animals, heavenly beings, and hell beings. The important thing to remember is that from the Jain perspective, all have the possibility of gaining liberation from the rounds of rebirth, and thus each soul or life is potentially as valuable as any other. Even a demon has the potential to become a released soul. Therefore, all life should be preserved as much as possible.

It is recognized, however, that it is impossible to remove all violence from life. Some is inevitable, so Jains classify the types of violence. There are two major categories, intentional and unintentional, and people's intent in an action is what really matters. In the intentional category are animal sacrifice, meat eating, hunting and fishing, robbery, and exploitation. Notice that the last two do not do physical harm but violate personal space and rights.

Unintentional violence is obviously that which is committed accidentally or is an unavoidable outgrowth of one's daily life and duty. There are three kinds of unavoidable violence: domestic, professional, and defensive. The daily chores may endanger life whether one is washing clothes, preparing food, walking to work, or traveling to a meeting. Multisense life may end up in the wash tub, fly into the gas ring, crawl underfoot, or impact a car's grille. None of these events was intentional, and the person who did life harm is not held responsible for that violence.

Professional violence is carried out by doctors or farmers. Doctors take life to preserve higher life as they give inoculations, for example. Farmers take life as they plow and plant crops, but both doctors and farmers do what they do to help other life, and while farming may not be a vocation of first choice, it is still what most of India does to survive. When involved in medicine or farming, doctors and farmers should regret all violence that is necessary and minimize it as much as possible.

Finally, defensive violence is that which occurs when persons protect their family, village, or nation. When violence is necessary in these circumstances, it should be minimized and regretted. However, it is possible within the framework of Jainism to be a soldier or policeman, which would involve defensive violence. Neither of these, however, would be vocations of first choice for most Jains.

At first blush, nonviolence does not seem to be quite as strong among Latter-day Saints as among Jains. Latter-day Saints are not pacifists. During the Second World War, they were counseled to support their nations and be obedient to their leaders, even if this meant that Saint might face Saint on the battlefield. They till the soil, even though this takes the life of some beings. There are no vocations that are outside a Latter-day Saint's ability to do for the reason of nonviolence. Certain vocations would be shunned for moral reasons, but vocations such as butchers, fishermen, and others are honorable and acceptable.

However, the Prophet Joseph Smith gives us a glimpse of a future in which we may need to think more like Jains than we do today. We read the following from the Prophet:

In pitching my tent we found three massasaugas or prairie rattlesnakes, which the brethren were about to kill, but I said, "Let them alone—don't hurt them! How will the serpent ever lose his venom, while the servants of God possess the same disposition, and continue to make war upon it?

Men must become harmless, before the brute creation; and when men lose their vicious dispositions and cease to destroy the animal race, the lion and the lamb can dwell together, and the sucking child can play with the serpent in safety." The brethren took the serpents carefully on sticks and carried them across the creek. I exhorted the brethren not to kill a serpent, bird, or an animal of any kind during our journey unless it became necessary in order to preserve ourselves from hunger.[5]

It would seem that nonviolence will be at the heart of the Millennium and that perhaps it needs to begin to grace our lives in the church today. Perhaps those of us who hunt should ask why we take the lives of defenseless creatures. Do we like to watch death overtake a beautiful deer or an elk or a lovely pheasant? Do we really need the food they provide, or do we like the sport of killing? Joseph in the above quote indicated that it was legitimate to kill to stave off hunger, but how many of us hunt for this reason? This thought is further extended in D&C 49:21, which, although it permits the eating of animals, adds the caveat "And wo be unto man that sheddeth blood or that wasteth flesh and hath no need." It seems that the challenge of both Jainism and Joseph Smith should cause us to examine our motives and discover where the pleasure in hunting lies for each of us. Are we diminishing our humanity when we take life for sport? Perhaps there is more to nonviolence in the church than we realized.

An obvious corollary of nonviolence is vegetarianism, and Jains take this very seriously. All meat products are forbidden, and even some vegetable life that is believed to stimulate the senses is forbidden. What about Latter-day Saints? In answer, there are few Latter-day Saints who are vegetarian, but D&C 89, the section called "the Word of Wisdom," might require us to think about this a bit more. Notice first its message is "adapted to the capacity of the weak and the weakest of all saints, who are or can be called saints" (D&C 89:3). It meets us at a point where we can handle its requirements, but it may not be what the Lord will ultimately ask of us.

Verses 5–7 deal with alcohol, or as the text puts it, strong drink. These are forbidden except as body washes. Verse 8 bans tobacco except for use in healing, and verse 9 bans hot drinks, which have historically been understood as tea and coffee. Verses 11–12 approve the use by humans of all kinds of herbs in their season. Verses 12–15 then talk about the use of flesh and various kinds of grains.

> Yea, flesh also of beasts and of the fowls of the air, I, the Lord, have ordained for the use of man with thanksgiving; nevertheless they are to be used sparingly; and it is pleasing unto me that they should not be used, only in times of winter, or of cold, or famine. All grain is ordained for the use of man and of beasts, to be the staff of life, not only for man but for the beasts of the field, and the fowls of heaven, and all wild animals that run or creep on the earth; and these hath God made for the use of man only in times of famine and excess of hunger. (D&C 89:12–15)

This passage begins by affirming the use of animal flesh, thus being congruent with D&C 49. However, there are constraints and parameters within which flesh is to be used. First, it is to be used "sparingly," but even more, it is to be used only in winter or cold or famine. Essentially, animals and birds are to be used in times when it is not possible to raise vegetation (e.g., when the ground is covered with snow, when it is too cold, or when there is insufficient rain). Otherwise, all grain is for the use of both people and beast, including the wild animals. The passage ends with the admonition once more that the animals ("these") are to be used in times of famine and excess hunger. They are to be used in emergencies.

Now, let us turn to the Isaiah passages about the Millennium. Isaiah describes the millennial reign in these words.

> The wolf also shall dwell with the lamb, and the leopard shall lie down with the kid; and the calf and the young lion and the fatling together; and a little child shall lead them. And the cow and the bear shall feed; their young ones shall lie down together: and the lion shall eat straw like the ox. And the sucking child shall play on the hole of the asp, and the weaned child shall put his hand on the cockatrice' den. They shall not hurt nor destroy in all my holy mountain: for the earth shall be full of the knowledge of the Lord, as the waters cover the sea. (Isaiah 11:6–9)

Clearly, if this is to be a reality, animal life cannot be taken. Joseph indicated what had to happen before the millennial reign of the Lord, and that included peace between humans and animals. While this idea is a bit speculative, the millennial diet may well be vegetarian. While there is no mandate that Latter-day Saints be vegetarian, it would appear that the Jains may be pointing to a reality in the future for all of us.

NONATTACHMENT

Jains are to become unattached to persons, places, things, or attitudes. We have already seen in Hinduism how this becomes the goal of the person who moves into the hermit stage of life, but Jains, especially in the ascetic life, take this as far as they can. Attachment causes bondage to the material world, which is bad and is to be left behind. Not only are material possessions to be left behind, but so are attitudes such as likes and dislikes and emotions. In terms of physical possessions, nonattachment is a vow of no possessions for ascetics and of limited possessions for laypersons. People should move beyond those things which tie them to the material world.

As we have seen, Jains are ultimately not to be attached to people, places, and things. In the end, the only material things the Lord promises Latter-day Saints is "sufficient for their needs." No matter how righteous we may be, we may still be poor. Large incomes and large homes are not guaranteed by adherence to the gospel and in reality may be more of a curse than a blessing. Jesus said it was easier for a camel to go through the eye of a needle than it was for a rich man to get into heaven (Matthew 19:24). The reason? Because we cannot serve two masters (Luke 16:13). We will be drawn either to the things of the world or to the things of the Spirit. We cannot live with one foot mentally in each world. We have to make a choice.

The things we spend virtually all our lives to attain will be left behind us. The law of consecration should teach us this. In this vein, Billy Graham once said that he had never seen a hearse going to the cemetery with a U-Haul trailer behind it. So it is with us. The only things that we can take out of this world at the time of death are our knowledge of and relationships with the Father, the Son, and the Holy Ghost and our family relationships. And yet, we live our lives as if all the material things in the world really mattered in the long run. Perhaps we should learn from the Jains that the labels on our jeans and the places we buy our shirts are irrelevant. We should learn this in the temples of the Lord, where we are given the eternal view of our lives. Too many of us have forgotten that our passports say "Celestial Kingdom" and not "Earth" on the front. We cannot be like Esau, who traded his birthright for a mess of pottage. The Lord does not accept the "Earth" passport at the gates to the celestial kingdom.

RELATIVE PLURALISM

Relative pluralism refers to the fact that Jains believe only omniscient persons see reality as it truly is. Other persons see reality only partially, and thus an object or event may receive many descriptions from various observers or witnesses. Every police officer knows that if there are five witnesses to an accident, there were five accidents. Each view is right and each view is wrong, because no one perceives reality as it truly is. Jains often illustrate this with the story of the blind men and an elephant. Each man feels the elephant and attempts to describe it. One holding the tail says it is like a vine. Another with his arms around a leg says it is like a tree. A third feeling the side says it is like a wall. Another feeling the trunk says it is like a great snake. In a sense, all are right while being wrong. They each encounter a part of reality.

The awareness that there may be many ways to perceive the same thing should lead people to be open to other viewpoints, recognize they may not have all truth, and thus have greater respect for others' perspectives. It is generally true that an idea can be made better when others with slightly different perspectives on the issue get together and discuss the idea, amplifying it with respect for others' ideas.

As stated, relative pluralism means that we all perceive things differently and that only omniscient beings see things as they really are. To a large degree, Latter-day Saints can agree with this. It is evident in a court of law that witnesses perceive the same event in different ways. We can also agree that different people see spiritual reality differently than do others and that two perceptions may bear truth. Thus, there should be humility in the religious person who recognizes that the Spirit may speak to different people of different cultures in different ways. The Spirit does not, however, contradict itself, so the various spiritual experiences must complement one another, which consideration may require us to go beyond superficial reactions to others.

However, in the end, Latter-day Saints cannot be relativists. There are rights and wrongs as they are revealed by God. We firmly believe that there is "more to Mormonism," which takes us beyond other religions to the saving ordinances of the gospel which can be obtained only under the hands of the authoritative priesthood found in The Church of Jesus Christ of Latter-day Saints.

ASSUMPTIONS

Jainism has an optimism about the human being. No gods are needed to help persons free themselves from the effects of the world. The view that humans are dual beings is shared by many faiths which recognize the spiritual and material sides of humanity, but for the Jain, the material world must be escaped. The body is not good but rather is a prison from which the spirit or soul must free itself. This is hard for imperfect human beings, but latent within humans is perfection. The dust must be brushed off the soul to allow the infinite attributes that are hidden within persons to appear. Nothing new is added to the person, only the negatives are shed, and human beings have the power to do this, according to Jains.

WORLDVIEW

The universe is believed to be formed roughly in the shape of a human being. The realm in which humans live would be at the waistline. The upper body and head would be the heavenly realms, and the lower portion would be the hells. As with Hinduism, there are various life-forms into which souls may enter. They may be deities in the heavenly realms, none of which can be of assistance to human beings, so Jainism is nontheistic (i.e., gods are not involved in human lives). Souls may enter human bodies, and this is to be desired because only as human beings with agency can souls find release. Souls may also return as animals, insects, plants, bacteria, and so on. Finally, they may be reincarnated as hell-beings or demons.

The same concepts of reincarnation and transmigration are present in Jainism that are in Hinduism. However, there is no concept of monism. Instead, Jainism believes that there are billions of independent, uncreated, eternal souls that inhabit the universe. These all have the same potential (i.e., to become gods when released from the rounds of rebirth). Thus, it is clear why the concept of nonviolence is so important to Jains, for if every life-form has the same potential, it is mandatory to treat each with as much respect as possible.

Perhaps one of the most interesting points of contact between Latter-day Saints and Jains lies in the Jain concept of the soul. The soul is an independent, individual, eternal, self-existing entity which dwells in all life. This is essentially the definition of the "intelligence" which the Father clothes with spirit form and which is then born into the premortal realm. Just as there is no end to intelligence, there is no end to the soul. The similarity between these two ideas is striking.

The concept of karma in Jainism differs from that in Hinduism. While karma is a kind of "cosmic computer" in Hinduism and is nonmaterial, in Jainism it is actually a substance and is known as karma-matter. Thus, when I do bad deeds (violating the principles of Jainism described above), my soul accrues karma-matter, is weighed down and darkened, and sinks in the universe and on the spectrum of life. On the other hand, when I do good deeds in congruence with the above principles, my soul becomes lighter and brighter and rises in the universe. Eventually, a person purifies his or her soul to the point that all the dust has been removed from the soul, and he or she can see things as they really are. This is the experience of enlighten-ment—universal knowledge.

At the top of the universe is a heavenly realm. This is where the released souls which have attained godhood dwell. This is the realm of the Ford Finders and all others who are conquerors (*Jina*, from which the word Jain comes), who have infinite faith, knowledge, energy, and bliss. They have gone beyond the rounds of rebirth and have no further contact with it. Thus, though they are gods, they are not gods who can assist those who continue on the rounds of rebirth. Instead, they are models who have walked the path of enlightenment and who are to be emulated.

— STRUCTURE

There are two basic groups within Jainism, as there are in most religious traditions. These are the ascetics and the laypersons. Those willing to take upon themselves the vows which withdraw them from normal life are always few in number when compared to the laypersons, but because of that willingness, they are highly respected by the laity. In this section, we will examine the two groups in the Jain context.

MONKS AND NUNS

Those men who enter the ascetic, withdrawn life are known as monks, while the women are known as nuns. Among the Sky Clads, there are only monks, while all other forms of Jainism have both monks and nuns. Monks have historically been the scholars and teachers, while nuns have been more involved in explaining the faith and its precepts to laypersons. Neither group will use vehicles for transportation, and thus they walk everywhere. In this way, they do far less damage to life. To understand this, all we need to do is to look at the grille of our cars after a road trip to see the violence done to multiple insects. The primary aim of monks and nuns is to purify themselves sufficiently to gain release from the rounds of rebirth. According to figures gathered in 1995, out of about 4.2 million Jains, there were 2,327 monks and 8,248 nuns,[6] thus underlining the small proportion of ascetics found in most religions.

Monks and nuns take five vows, which we will examine. The first vow is the following: "I renounce all killing of living beings, whether movable or immovable. Nor shall I myself kill living beings nor cause others to do it, nor consent to it. As long as I live I confess, and blame, and exempt myself of these sins, in mind, speech and body."[7] This is an all-encompassing vow of nonviolence, and it touches every area of the lives of monks and nuns. For example, they carry the peacock feather duster to clear the path or a seat of life-forms in order not to hurt them. They walk with eyes downcast, so that they do not step on life-forms. They do not drink water or eat after dark for fear of imbibing some living organism unknowingly. They do not pick fruit off a tree, for that would be the taking of life, but given that, how do they eat? They receive food from laypersons, but only under certain conditions.

Notice in the vow that monks and nuns cannot cause another to take life, so they cannot cause persons to prepare a meal for them, for that would make the monks and nuns direct participants in the violence necessary to create the food. In other words, laypeople cannot whip up a meal for the monks or nuns when they see them coming down the street. All they can do is offer them the leftovers from their own meal, thereby exempting the ascetics from direct participation in violence. Of course, there is indirect participation, but the ascetics remove themselves as far from it as they can because in a world of violence, someone needs to stand against it as much as is possible. Someone needs to exemplify a nonviolent lifestyle.

The concept of nonviolence does not stop with the body. Notice that violence is eschewed in mind and speech as well. Where does violence originate? In the mind, and it often first manifests itself through speech. I would suggest that children can be hurt more severely by words said to them, which can reach their very soul, than they are by a physical blow. This sounds much like Jesus' admonition in the Sermon on the Mount:

> Ye have heard that it was said by them of old time, Thou shalt not kill; and whosoever shall kill shall be in danger of the judgment: but I say unto you, That whosoever is angry with his brother without a cause shall be in danger of the judgment: and whosoever shall say to his brother, Raca, shall be in danger of the council: but whosoever shall say, Thou Fool, shall be in danger of hell fire. (Matthew 5:21–22)

The second vow is this: "I renounce all vices of lying speech arising from anger or greed or fear or mirth. I shall neither myself speak lies, nor cause others to speak lies, nor consent to the speaking of lies by others."[8] What is the issue with lying? Basically, it breaks two fundamental principles of Jainism—nonviolence and asceticism. We usually lie to get ourselves out of trouble. If we were seriously practicing asceticism or nonattachment, it would not matter what people thought about us, thereby making the lie unnecessary. On the other hand, we lie about our younger brother basically to get the little blighter into trouble, a clear violation of nonviolence, since we are trying to get him spanked or worse. Lying reveals our inner natures for what they really are.

The third vow runs as follows: "I renounce all taking of anything not given, either in a village or a town or a wood, either of little or much, of great or small, of living or lifeless things. I shall neither take myself what is not given, nor cause others to take it, nor consent to their taking it."[9] This vow adds an additional dimension to life, especially when considering what Jain monks and nuns may eat. It is obvious that ascetics cannot take life, and so they could not pick an apple off a tree or a tomato off a vine. However, suppose the apple had fallen off the tree and was simply lying on the ground. Could it then be taken and eaten? Not according to this vow, for what ascetics eat or use must be offered to them. Somebody must give it to them, which underlines the symbiotic relationship between the ascetics and the laity. Laypeople gain merit by assisting the ascetics, who respond by teaching the Jain way. Neither ascetics nor laity can survive in a meaningful way without the other.

The fourth vow is the following: "I renounce all sexual pleasure. I shall not give way to sensuality, nor cause others to do so, nor consent to it in others."[10] Human sexuality is probably one of the strongest ties to the world and shows the difference between the Jain view of the world and the general Christian, Jewish, and Islamic attitude toward it. For Jains, things of the world are bad because the material things of life must be left behind. Christians, Jews, and Muslims usually affirm the value of the material world because God created it and pronounced it good and will make all things new materially at the time of the Resurrection. For the Jains, however, the material is antithetical to human destiny and therefore must be escaped. Thus, all sensuality must be avoided.

The fifth vow is as follows: "I renounce all attachments, whether to little or much, small or great, living or lifeless things; neither shall I myself form such attachments, nor cause others to do so, nor consent to their doing so."[11] This last vow is a summation of all that Jainism requires of persons, and so ascetics wander constantly so they do not form attachments to people, places, or things. They cannot have friends, fixed ideas or opinions, or certainly any possessions. Everything of the world will be left behind for the realm of the spiritual. In the end, these five vows define a difficult, very ascetic way of life for those who choose to assume the role of monk or nun.

LAYMEN AND LAYWOMEN

Active laymen and laywomen are firmly committed to the Jain life and commit themselves to certain daily religious practices.

They perform morning recitations remembering the twenty-four Ford Finders who have conquered the rounds of rebirth, and they will worship before an image of one of the twenty-four. They decide on a renunciation they will practice that day, one favorite being that they will neither eat nor drink for forty-eight hours during daylight hours.[12] Jains are to make a living without hurting life, and they should be liberal with their income. One suggestion is that 50 percent should go toward household expenses, 25 percent should be saved, and 25 percent should go to charitable causes. Few actually meet this goal, however.

Laypersons take vows as do the monks and nuns, but there is greater latitude to accommodate everyday life. Male and female laypersons take twelve vows, which are as follows:

1. Never knowingly to take the life of a sentient creature.
2. Never to lie.
3. Never to steal, or take what is not given.
4. Never to be unchaste.
5. To check greed, by placing a limit upon one's wealth and giving away any excess.
6. To avoid temptation to sin by, for example, refraining from unnecessary travel.
7. To limit the number of things in daily use.
8. To be on guard against evils that can be avoided.
9. To keep stated periods for meditation.
10. To observe special periods of self-denial.
11. To spend occasional days as a monk.
12. To give alms, especially in support of ascetics.[13]

As is clear, the principles of nonviolence and nonattachment drive the vows of the laypersons as well as those of the monks and nuns. The first vow of nonviolence is not as strict for laypersons as it is for ascetics, but even so, it has a major impact on choices of vocation and the way business is carried out. There is a movie entitled *Ahimsa: Non-Violence*[14] in which the implications of this vow are made clear. The narrator states that while the Jains make up about one-half of 1 percent of the Indian population, at the time of the making of the film in the 1980s, they might constitute as much as 50 percent of the tax base. If true, it is a direct result of this first vow because, while most of India makes its living farming, persons trying to follow nonviolence would normally not choose that vocation if they had a choice. Farming simply destroys too many life-forms. Consequently, Jains choose business, banking, computers, medicine, government, law, and other high-income vocations.

An example of a business choice is given in the film, which focuses on a man who owns a newspaper. He and his colleagues were looking for ways to diversify, and with the growth of the tourist industry in India, owning a hotel chain looked like a good investment. They then realized that to make a hotel profitable, they would have to have a restaurant, and for the restaurant to be profitable, it would have to serve meat. They felt it would be wrong to make money directly from such an enterprise and considered having someone else run the restaurant. However, they would still be making money from the sale of meat. This was too much at variance with their faith, so they gave up the idea. In other words, the concept of nonviolence shapes every Jain's life.

Lying was dealt with sufficiently under the vows of ascetics. Laypersons are not to steal, and thus they are to pay for what they receive. Sexual relations are to be had only within the context of marriage. Jains are known for their philanthropy, which is a direct result of giving away excess income. They avoid temptation by staying where they are known, and many limit possessions (e.g., sleeping on a reed mat instead of using a bed). The last four vows move laypersons closer and closer to the ascetic life, which at some time in this life or a future life they all must assume, if they are to gain release from the rounds of rebirth. In summary, all Jains, lay or ascetic, practice the three pillars of Jainism—nonviolence, nonattachment, and relative pluralism—to varying degrees.

— WORSHIP IN JAINISM

There are a variety of rituals in Jainism. For both Sky Clads and White Clads, the principal ritual centers on veneration of the Ford Finders. Veneration involves going to the temple in the morning while fasting and then worshiping the image by reciting the names of the twenty-four Ford Finders, singing hymns, listening to recitations, and meditating in a way detached from the things of the world.[15] Additional practices can include anointing the image of the Ford Finder with a paste made of saffron and sandalwood, performing the waving of lamps before the image, and offering flowers or fruits.[16]

But who do Jains worship? The Ford Finders have gone beyond and cannot respond to prayers for help and assistance, yet they can inspire. Thus, it is toward these that worship is directed for inspiration. Jains know that they are responsible for their own karmic contamination and that they must remove it themselves. However, worshipers desire to model themselves after the Ford Finder before them in the temple. To respond to the very human need for more assistance than this in daily life, many at the lay level worship celestial beings, most of whom have been drawn from Hindu life. Statues of these beings may be found in out-of-the-way places in a Jain temple.

A person worshiping in a Jain temple before a Ford Finder will sit quietly in meditation. The meditation focuses on the life and practice of the Ford Finder, which serves to inspire the practitioner on his or her path. They therefore recommit themselves to following the path and to reducing their karmic bondage which they alone have created.[17]

— WOMEN

Women in Jainism are equal to men among the White Clad Jains and almost equal among the Sky Clads. According to White Clads, men and women are equally capable of gaining release from the rounds of rebirth. Both must assume the lives of ascetics and follow the rigid discipline of the ascetic life. But neither is more susceptible to enlightenment than the other. Sky Clads, on the other hand, believe women cannot achieve release as women because they cannot practice complete nonattachment. They cannot wander naked, and nakedness is essential to gaining release, for it demonstrates complete nonattachment to things of the material world. Women must come back as men to gain their final release. Otherwise, men and women are essentially equal. Women still have charge of the home, but nothing prevents a Jain woman from assuming a job with leadership or executive responsibilities in the community.

— CONCLUSION

To Latter-day Saints, Jainism is probably the least familiar of the religions in this book. However, it can remind us how fleeting and unimportant the things of this world are. In a world fraught with violence, materialism, and sensuality, it is important that someone remind us that these things are not eternal and that they separate us from that which is ultimate.

— NOTES

1. "Major Religions of the World Ranked by Number of Adherents," Adherents.com, last modified August 9, 2007, http://www.adherents.com/Religions_By_Adherents.html.
2. Vastupal Parikh, *Jainism and the New Spirituality* (Toronto, Canada: Peace Publications, 2002), 168.
3. Robert E. Van Voorst, *Anthology of World Scriptures*, 6th ed. (Mason, OH: Cengage Learning, 2008), 113.
4. What follows is indebted to Natubhai Shah, *Jainism: The World of Conquerors* (Portland, OR: Sussex Academic, 1998), 1:108–14.
5. *History of the Church of Jesus Christ of Latter-day Saints*, ed. B. H. Roberts, 2nd ed. rev. (Salt Lake City: Deseret Book, 1951), 2:71–72.
6. Shah, *Jainism*, 1:139.
7. David S. Noss and John B. Noss, *A History of the World's Religions*, 9th ed. (New York: Macmillan College, 1994), 170.
8. Noss and Noss, *History*, 170.
9. Noss and Noss, *History*, 170–71.
10. Noss and Noss, *History*, 171.
11. Noss and Noss, *History*, 171.
12. Shah, *Jainism*, 1:152.
13. Noss and Noss, *History*, 171.
14. Michael Tobias, *Ahimsa: Non-Violence*, KRMA-TV Denver (Los Angeles: Direct Cinema, 1987).
15. Shah, *Jainism*, 1:178.
16. Parikh, *Jainism*, 35.
17. Parikh, *Jainism*, 56.

Buddhist temple, Ayutthaya, Thailand. The temple is a place where persons may show devotion to the three refuges: the Buddha, Dharma (teachings of the Buddha), and Sangha (the Buddhist Order). © Val Brinkerhoff.

CHAPTER 4

BUDDHISM

As one Zen master put it, "To come to Self-realization you must directly experience yourself and the universe as one." Reality is not captured by thoughts. In enlightenment, a person experiences reality as it is.

Buddhism is a non-Vedic tradition like Jainism. Both religions moved beyond dependence on Brahmin priests, their sacrificial rituals, and the authority of the Veda. Like Jainism, Buddhism denies the relevance of caste. The story of the Buddha will sound much like the story of Mahavira, but unlike Jainism, Buddhism has spread across the world and is 376 million strong.[1] Many Americans are adopting various forms of Buddhism as their own faith, perhaps in part because there is a strong sense of compassion that runs through Buddhism, making it attractive in a world of violence and exploitation. There are three major schools of Buddhism. The first and oldest is Theravada Buddhism, or the "Tradition of the Elders." It is found in south Asia in Sri Lanka, Burma, Cambodia, and Thailand. The second tradition is Mahayana Buddhism, or the "Great Vehicle," which is found in east Asia in Vietnam, Taiwan, Japan, Korea, and China. The third school is Vajrayana, or the "Vehicle of the Thunderbolt," found in Tibet and Mongolia. As we progress through this chapter, we will look at each of these forms. Each believes that its traditions were taught by the Buddha.

— ORIGINS

FOUNDER

The founder of Buddhism was a noble by the name of Siddhartha Gautama. He was born in 563 BCE in present-day Nepal and died in 483 BCE. Siddhartha was raised in luxurious surroundings. According to legend, at his birth, a wise man appeared and told Siddhartha's father that if Siddhartha never saw four sights, he would be a great ruler of India, but if he saw them, he would be a great ascetic. The four sights were old age, illness, death, and an ascetic. Needless to say, Siddhartha's father wanted him to be a great ruler of India, so he surrounded his son with young people and prevented him from seeing the harder side of life.

Eventually, Siddhartha married and had a son. Having fulfilled his obligations as a householder, he was free to follow his inclinations according to the four stages of Hindu life, but at this point, the Legend of the Four Sights returns to the story. After having his son, Siddhartha wanted to see what was outside the palace walls. He had been out before, since the family had three palaces (a summer palace, a winter palace, and a rainy season palace). As royalty, it was possible to travel between these in isolation from the countryside, so Siddhartha had never experienced anything other than court life. Since Siddhartha was almost thirty, it was hard for his father to deny his desire to go beyond the palace, so Siddhartha was permitted to venture out. Before he left the palace, however, his father sent servants to see that all old, ill, and dying persons were removed from the way along which Siddhartha would travel and that they were replaced by attractive young people. Thus, Siddhartha started off.

As his chariot moved along, suddenly an old man appeared beside the road. This was probably a god in the guise of old age, since the gods had the same problem that all other living beings had (i.e., they were trapped on the rounds of rebirth). They had been waiting for Siddhartha to come, gain enlightenment, and then teach the way so they could gain release. It would appear from the story that they wished to speed up the process. At any rate, Siddhartha brought the chariot to a halt and asked what he was seeing, saying that it looked like a man but was all shriveled and shrunken. In response, he learned the mystery of old age.

A bit further along (or on subsequent trips), he encountered a man writhing in pain on the ground, and he learned the mystery of illness. As they continued, he encountered a funeral cortege and learned the mystery of death. Shaken by the pain and suffering which he had witnessed, he encountered a holy man who seemed to have found internal peace in the face of all the pain Siddhartha had seen. Siddhartha wanted to be like him. Thus, he returned to the palace, and in the middle of the night, without saying good-bye to his wife or son, he left the palace. He avoided saying good-bye because he knew that were he to do so, he could not leave them. Thus, we are given a little insight into the emotions of Siddhartha and the difficulty of his decision, which we do not get in the story of Mahavira.

Upon leaving the palace, Siddhartha turned sequentially to two Brahmin priests for instruction. Neither, however, helped him over-come desire, and so he left the Brahmin way and embarked on a five-year period of extreme asceticism much the same as did Mahavira.

Siddhartha's ascetic practices were so severe—eating a grain of rice a day, for example—that five other ascetics began to follow him as the ultimate ascetic model. After five years of these extremities, Siddhartha was on the verge of death, and the statues and paintings of him at this time portray him as nothing but skin and bones. He realized, however, that were he to die, he would not achieve release from the rounds of rebirth in his current condition, so when a young girl offered him a bowl of rice, he accepted it. Seeing this, the five ascetics left him. After all, a bowl of rice in five years clearly made Siddhartha a glutton and a fallen prophet. However, having renewed his strength, Siddhartha sat down under a tree and that night came to enlightenment, but not without opposition. Mara, the demonic figure of Buddhism, tried to thwart Siddhartha by sending his daughters to seduce him, and when that did not work, he sent an army from hell, whose arrows and spears turned into flowers as they were launched at Siddhartha. Upon attaining enlightenment, Siddhartha became the *Buddha* (i.e., one who is fully awake).

Following his enlightenment, the Buddha stayed at Bodh Gaya, in the area of the tree, wrapped in the incredible enlightenment experience, but he also had a decision to make. In Hindu tradition, once a person gains enlightenment, or has one's calling and election made sure, so to speak, it would be perfectly appropriate to wander into the forest and let the flame go out—in other words, to die. However, out of compassion for the rest of suffering humanity, the Buddha decided to teach others what he had discovered, and therein lies the profound compassion of Buddhism.

Having made this decision, the Buddha left Bodh Gaya and walked to the deer park at Sarnath, near current-day Varanasi, and found the five ascetics who had left him. They saw him coming and debated among themselves whether they should let him sit down. They decided that they would, and when the Buddha sat down and began to teach them, the five realized that he had come to enlightenment. Thus they became the first five members of the Buddhist Order.

As with Mahavira, the Buddha's enlightenment destroyed the Brahmin argument that only Brahmin males were sufficiently advanced spiritually to gain enlightenment. Once again, a noble had reached this state, and as with Jainism, this opened possibilities for persons regardless of sex and caste. However, the way was not as difficult as that of Jainism, for the Buddha had realized that extremes of any kind did not necessarily lead to enlightenment. He had to step back from extreme asceticism before enlightenment came. Thus, Buddhism became known as the "middle way," the way between extreme luxury and extreme asceticism, both of which the Buddha had experienced. Consequently, Buddhism became very attractive in India and challenged the supremacy of Hinduism. The Brahmin response to the challenge was to validate the third way, the way of devotion, which also cut across caste and sex lines but which still encouraged the worship of familiar gods through the Vedic rituals that depended on the Brahmins and their knowledge. Hence, because of this Brahmin response, Buddhism gradually left India to cover the rest of Asia, and to this day it has very little presence in the land of its birth.

The Buddha taught for forty-five years after his enlightenment, which occurred around age thirty-five. Thus, he lived until he was eighty, when he died from eating spoiled pork. According to Buddhist tradition, he knew the food would kill him, but out of respect for the

Buddha at Bodh Gaya. It was here that Siddhartha Gautama reached enlightenment.

person who offered the food in good faith, the Buddha ate it. His last words to his disciples as he was dying were "Behold now, brothers, I exhort you, saying, 'Decay is inherent in all component things! Work out your salvation with diligence!'"[2] We will examine the first part of this statement later, but the last part makes it clear that the Buddha's Buddhism was a do-it-yourself religion in which no gods were available to give assistance.

THE BUDDHIST ORDER

As noted above, the Buddhist Order encompasses monks, nuns, and laypersons. For the ascetics in southern Buddhism or the Theravada form, there are four marks of the Order: the yellow or saffron robe, the receiving or begging bowl, the shaved head, and meditation. They all reflect humility and withdrawal from the world.

All Buddhists take five basic vows, four of which will sound very much like the vows of the Jain monks and nuns.[3]

1. *I take upon myself the discipline of abstaining from harming sentient beings.* A sentient being is one that possesses sense perception, meaning all moving life. Buddhists do not practice nonviolence to the degree that Jains do, but those trying to live a fully Buddhist life will be vegetarian. Buddhists farm, and in Mahayana Buddhism, monasteries may have gardens in which monks and nuns work as part of

their day and discipline. There is great variety in how Buddhists carry out this vow. Those living near the sea may fish and eat fish as part of their diet. Thus, there is some latitude for the practitioner.

2. *I take upon myself the discipline of abstaining from taking that which is not offered.* This vow is quite straightforward. For the layperson, it means paying for what one receives, but for the monks or nuns, it means that their livelihood is dependent upon the laypeople. For the southern Buddhist monk, it means daily begging rounds to collect his food for the day.

3. *I take upon myself the discipline of abstaining from sexual misconduct.* For laypersons, this means that sexual relations are to be had within the context of marriage. For the monks and nuns, the rule of celibacy is in force. If they break this vow, they will be ejected from the Order for life.

4. *I take upon myself the discipline of abstaining from false speech.* We have looked at this vow in Jainism and have seen that lying violates either the ascetic principles or that of nonviolence.

5. *I take upon myself the discipline of abstaining from stupefying drink.* This fifth vow is different from Jainism, where the last vow is one of nonattachment, but if we look at the vow in the light of the goal of Buddhism, it makes great sense. The goal is to become a Buddha, one who is fully awake, and persons who use alcohol or drugs blur the mind rather than making it awake and clear.

All the above vows are taken by all active members of the Order—monks, nuns, and laypersons. All of these vows can be carried out without entering the withdrawn life, although for the monks and nuns, there is clearly an augmentation to the basic vow. In addition to these vows, there are five more which summarize the additional weight assumed by monks and nuns. However, as we have seen, Buddhism is viewed as the middle way. This is a good test of that precept, so readers may want to ask themselves whether these additional vows define a less rigid asceticism than that which we have seen in Jainism, for example. These five are the Discipline in its simplest form,[4] which is designed to give guidance and rules for monks and nuns.

1. *Not to eat after midday.* In southern Buddhism, monks go out on early-morning begging rounds. They go to homes where they know householders will give them food, or they just stop at homes

A monk and novices with shaved heads.

and wait a few moments. If no one brings out food, they move on. After collecting their food, they return to the monastery, eat about half of what they collected, and then go about their morning chores or study. Shortly before noon, they eat the remainder of the food and then fast until the next morning. Liquids may be taken, but not food. This vow underlines the spiritual dimension of Buddhism—from noon until the next morning, monks fast with the intent of elevating the spiritual over the physical.

2. *Not to watch secular entertainments.* This vow removes monks and nuns from any kind of secular entertainment such as dance, songs, plays, movies, and so on. The point is that monks and nuns are living a withdrawn life, although they are not totally isolated from the population. They should not involve themselves in things that would draw them back to worldly attachments.

3. *Not to use perfumes or ornaments.* This is very similar to the previous and following vows. Do not use the things of the world: in this case, jewelry, perfumes, and aftershaves.

4. *Not to use high couches or beds.* Once again, these would be signs of worldly indulgence. These are what the wealthy use, and monks and nuns are not to indulge themselves in this manner.

5. *Not to handle gold or silver.* This is a ban against involvement in business. The laypeople provide everything the monks or nuns need.

Sometimes the monks will go out with a young boy who will buy a few necessities for the monks, but the monks do not involve themselves in the commercial transaction. Again, it is a recognition that the ascetic has stepped back from the world.

As we look at these additional vows, one may ask whether they reflect a middle path or an extreme asceticism. As we can see, while there is definitely a withdrawal from the world, it is not severe. Monks and nuns eat adequately and regularly. Some live in community. They spend part of their time in work and study and part of their time in spiritual disciplines. They interact with people daily, even conducting schools. Their lifestyles, however, generate humility and internal peace.

The Buddhist community had early decisions to make. The laity provided what the ascetics needed, including groves, parks, and monasteries. They also provided some very rich bolts of cloth, and one of the Buddha's closest disciples came to him to ask what they should do with them. After all, they were ascetics, and up to this time the monks had been sewing together rags for their robes! The Buddha responded that they should cut up the cloth and then sew it back together. It thus lost its commercial value and therefore could be used. Even today, the orange robes of southern Buddhist monks are sewn together rather than being of one piece.

Another issue was the role of women. As a man of his day, the Buddha looked upon women as temptations to ascetics. Their normal role was that of wife and mother, and only the White Clad Jains seem to have allowed women into an ascetic role. Ultimately the Buddha permitted this too, although senior nuns must still bow to the lowliest monks. The lineage of ordination for women in southern Buddhism has been lost, so there are no formally ordained nuns among the Theravada, although there are women who live the ascetic life, as do nuns in the other two Buddhist traditions.

THE SPREAD OF BUDDHISM

Buddhism spread rather slowly. At first, the Buddha and his disciples wandered, teaching what the Buddha had discovered in his enlightenment. After the Buddha's death, this practice continued until the reign of King Asoka (ca. 272–231 BCE). Asoka was the first ruler to conquer virtually all of India, but he did it through fifteen years of very bloody warfare. At the end of this period, he discovered Buddhism and became a lay practitioner. His commitment was such that he set up stone pillars around India with inscriptions encouraging people to live the Buddhist principles of compassion and kindness to one another as well as to other forms of life. Asoka sent missionaries as far west as Greece and Egypt, but Buddhism did not take root in that environment. The missionaries who went to the south and east, however, found fertile ground. Theravada Buddhism took root in Sri Lanka as well as in the south Asian countries of Burma, Cambodia, and Thailand.

Around the time of Christ, Theravada missionaries went north through the Himalayas and followed the Silk Route to China. The Chinese enjoyed life and families, and so the Theravada form, which required the ascetic life, was not especially attractive to them. However, a bit later, Mahayana missionaries arrived, and since persons could practice Mahayana with the help of heavenly figures and could remain in the midst of life as a practitioner, this was the form that took root in China.

From China, Buddhism moved to Manchuria and then into Korea. In the sixth century CE, the king of Paekche, one of the three kingdoms in Korea, sent an image of the Buddha, some Buddhist texts, and a letter to the emperor of Japan stating that the Koreans had found a religious faith that provided great benefits to its adherents and suggesting that Japan should explore it. Unfortunately, at the same time these articles arrived, so did a plague. The foreign gods were blamed, and the Buddha image was thrown into a canal. This happened again, but when the plague did not end after the Buddha image was again thrown into a canal, it was decided that perhaps it was the Buddhist deities who were angry at how they had been received.[5] Thus, late in the sixth century, a member of the royal family became a Buddhist, and the religion spread through the nobility and beyond.

In the seventh century, Mahayana Buddhism spread into Tibet, where it encountered an indigenous religion called Bon, which had many similarities to Buddhism. Thus, the Buddhism of Tibet is Mahayana blended with Bon. It is known as Vajrayana Buddhism, or the "Vehicle of the Thunderbolt." When the Mongols conquered Tibet in the thirteenth century and Kublai Khan accepted the faith, Vajrayana Buddhism became the dominant faith of the Mongols. Thus, over a period of 1,800 years, Buddhism covered most of Asia.

BUDDHIST SCRIPTURES

Each of the divisions within Buddhism has its own canon, but there is significant overlap between them. The foundational text is the Tripitaka, the "Three Baskets," and is the text of Theravada Buddhism. As its name suggests, it contains three divisions. The first contains the rules for monastic life. The second contains the teachings of the Buddha, as well as stories about his prior lives. The third basket contains philosophical texts covering "advanced topics." The Mahayana canon is not separated into categories, as is the Theravada, but there is significant commonality, with various additions used by schools within the Mahayana realm. Likewise, the Vajrayana Buddhists have their own canon, having sent people to India to copy scripture. It is somewhat different from that of the other two groups, but it contains material on monastic discipline and the teachings of the Buddha common to all.[6] Both Mahayana and Vajrayana Buddhism have many additional texts unique to themselves and to the various groups within their frameworks.

— THERAVADA PHILOSOPHY

THE FOUR NOBLE TRUTHS

The heart of the Buddha's enlightenment is captured in what are known as the Four Noble Truths. They are as follows:

1. Life is suffering.
2. Suffering is caused by desire.
3. Suffering will cease when desire ceases.
4. Desire will cease by following the Eightfold Path.

The first Noble Truth refers to life on the rounds of rebirth. The word used for suffering carries the sense of a wheel out of round. It goes bump, bump, bump, and becomes uncomfortable and disturbing. This is the way with life. By clutching at things that are constantly changing, we create suffering for ourselves, because the things of the world slip out of our grasp. This is the import of the first part of the Buddha's final words to his disciples. He said, "Decay is inherent in all component things."[7] Nothing is permanent. Trying to hold on to the transient can only cause pain and suffering, because we are bound to lose that for which we reach. Thus there is sickness, death, divorce, grief, and sorrow in life. This does not mean that Buddhism is a sad religion. It is not. Rather, it is highly pragmatic and realistic, noting that permanent happiness cannot be found when immersed in the transitory character of the world. Buddhism thus invites people to go beyond the moment.

The above leads logically to the second Noble Truth: suffering is caused by desire or grasping. Again, grasping for that which disappears creates pain. We grasp for and try to hold on to all sorts of things—objects, ideas, opinions, rites, rituals, and especially the "I." Every one of them slips away, including the "I," which is, as are all things, impermanent.

The third Noble Truth affirms that when grasping ceases, suffering will cease, and it is certainly the logical consequence of the first two assumptions. Finally, desire or grasping will cease if persons follow the Eightfold Path.

THE EIGHTFOLD PATH

Theravada Buddhists expect people to walk the eight steps of this path one at a time. The first five steps can be done as laypeople without the necessity of withdrawing from the world. The sixth step can be begun as laypersons but also bridges into the seventh step, which must be accomplished as part of the ascetic or withdrawn life.

The first two steps may be grouped under the heading of *study* and are (1) right view and (2) right attitude. Right view means that a person understands the Four Noble Truths and realizes that reality is different from the way it is usually perceived. Right attitude requires persons to be free from hate, anger, or confusion, which cloud perception. People must lay aside their usual attitudes of judgment and classification and be open to new and different possibilities.

The next steps are classified under *conduct* and constitute the ethical norms of Buddhism. These are (3) right speech, (4) right action, (5) right livelihood, and (6) right effort. Right speech means that people's speech is first and foremost helpful and compassionate. It is free of gossiping, lying, backbiting, and so on. Right action means people's actions are helpful and compassionate (i.e., they do not kill, steal, or have sexual relations outside of marriage). Right livelihood defines the parameters within which vocations should be carried out. As above, persons in their vocations should be helpful and compassionate and should embody the previous principles. Buddhists would not normally be sellers of slaves or animals for slaughter, soldiers, drug dealers, butchers, fishermen, or hunters, nor should they accept a vocation involving deceit. There is, however, a great deal of variation in the way this step is carried out among Buddhists. They certainly farm, which entails taking a certain amount of life. Those who live by the sea may fish, since it is their only source of food or income. In Buddhist countries, some serve in the armed forces. Finally, right effort means to overcome those things which are holding people back spiritually and to develop those things that move them further along the path of spirituality, all of which involves significant self-examination.

The final two steps are (7) right mindfulness, and (8) right concentration. Right mindfulness is the ability to be aware of what is going on around oneself and see reality as it is. In reality, most of us wander through life on autopilot, never seeing the beauty and intricacy of life. We are always going somewhere and are rarely fully present in the moment. Our eyes are not open. We see little or nothing. Our spouses deserve us to be present with them mentally as well as physically. We should not be at the office or in the classroom or designing a project or worrying about the children when we are on a date or sitting down to dinner. The goal of Buddhism is not to be mesmerized by the things of the world, but rather to be fully awake, to be present in the moment, and to see things as they are at any given instant.

Right concentration means to be able to focus on one thing to the exclusion of all other competing elements. This is accomplished through proper meditation, the goal of which is to stop the "monkey mind" from bounding from one thought to another like a monkey bounds from tree to tree, with no specific plan. For all of the religions at which we have been looking, the mind gets in the way of knowing reality, which can be found only through an encounter with it, not by thinking about it. Right concentration is the path to that encounter.

According to Theravada Buddhism, if one walks the entire Eightfold Path step by step, that person will be led to enlightenment. It will take multiple lifetimes to travel the whole distance, but enlightenment should be the goal.

KARMA

Since Buddhism arises from the soil of Hinduism, the basic principles are much the same. There is the concept of karma, but it is not the karma matter of Jainism; rather, it is the cosmic, nonmaterial karma of Hinduism. All karma will one day come to fruition, giving consequences to prior actions. Similarly, the idea of reincarnation is very present. Persons live multiple lifetimes and may live in multiple life-forms before they find release from the rounds of rebirth.

In the previous religions, reincarnation takes place through the process of transmigration, in which souls move from one life to the next. But suppose that a religion does not believe in the reality of a soul. Can reincarnation take place? The offhand answer is usually "Of course not." Yet Buddhists do not believe that there is a soul, and they still believe in reincarnation. How can this be?

SKANDHAS

The answer lies in a concept known as the *skandhas*, which are the five temporary constituents of being, or as Jack Kornfield calls them, the collection of "five changing processes."[8] The five elements are a physical body, feelings, perceptions, responses, and a flow of consciousness. It is these that make me who I am at any moment, but everyone knows that they are constantly changing and that they ultimately fall apart. Those of us who are aging know we are in flux as we watch our chests slide somewhere around our waists, our hair thin, and wrinkles appear, or as we need lifts in our shoes and find ourselves replacing various body parts. In the end, if our bodies were just buried and then dug up a year later, it would be obvious that we had fallen apart. The doctrine of the skandhas is highly pragmatic.

It recognizes that nothing is permanent and that all things are in the process of change.

REINCARNATION

But what about reincarnation? Many of us have either played with or seen sealing wax. We know that it can be melted and then have a seal pressed into it to leave a visible image. Buddhists ask in this illustration whether anything has transmigrated from the seal to the wax, and the obvious answer is that it has not. Yet there is a clear impression in the wax. Reincarnation is similar. After death, if the things which keep persons on the wheel have not been eliminated, individuals will return. Thus, a puddle of unformed skandhas appears. It contains a generic body, for it is unknown what form it will take. It could be a human, a deer, or a rabbit, all of which the Buddha experienced, according to the stories of the Buddha's previous lives. In addition, unformed feelings, perceptions, responses, and flow of consciousness are added. They are stamped with my impression accumulated over hundreds and perhaps thousands of lifetimes, and once again I reappear. What stamps the skandhas? It is my karma, accrued over all my lifetimes. Remember that karma is not material in Buddhism but cosmic in nature. Because it is my karma, I am the one who is reborn. Thus Buddhism has a doctrine of no soul, but still the doctrine of reincarnation is present.

NO SOUL

This doctrine of "no soul" or emptiness is captured by the word *shunyata*, which may be translated as "emptiness" and is a doctrine most fully developed in Mahayana Buddhism. This doctrine does not mean, according to the Buddha, that reality does not exist. It does exist, but it is "transparent to analysis."[9] This means that no matter how much we may analyze various phenomena or ourselves, we can never nail down the underlying reality. We cannot find it. It is much like being in a room. We know it contains space, but we can never find it, define it, or identify it; yet we know it exists. So it is with ultimate reality. Roger Corless states that reality for Buddhists is more like the concept of space than of particles and is thus indescribable. Consequently, the word *shunyata* has a variety of translations—"emptiness" or "transparency"—but the one which best captures what we have just said is the Chinese "spaciousness."

Atomic physics has certainly shown us that everything which we consider to be solid is really more space than substance. There are immense spaces between the atoms that make up material life, but for the Latter-day Saints, there is concrete reality that continues eternally. This is different from the Buddhist view of things. For Latter-day Saints, matter, energy, and intelligence are eternal. The spirit composed of "finer matter" with which the Father clothes our intelligence will continue through mortality into the eternities. There is nothing impermanent about it. So also the body, which is temporarily laid down at death, will be raised, and is at a minimum immortal, never to die again no matter what degree of glory it may occupy. Thus, a major difference in perspective between Latter-day Saints and Buddhists would be over the issue of transiency versus permanence.

— MAHAYANA PHILOSOPHY

Most of what has been discussed above has been part of Theravada Buddhism, the Buddhism of south Asia. Mahayana Buddhism, by contrast, is the Buddhism of east Asia. The principle difference between Mahayana Buddhism and Theravada Buddhism is that the former has a number of helping beings from whom practitioners can receive aid in gaining release from the rounds of rebirth. But how is that Buddhism, if Theravada is what the Buddha taught? The answer from a Buddhist perspective is that, while it is true that the Buddha taught the Theravada way, he also taught the Mahayana way to those who were prepared for a higher path. In a sense, it is like Jesus, who preached a public message to the crowds in the synoptic Gospels (Matthew, Mark, and Luke) but gave additional knowledge to his inner circle of disciples in the Gospel of John. Likewise, both ways arise from the Buddha.

BODHISATTVAS

The concept of the *bodhisattva* is central to Mahayana Buddhism. The first point of contact with the idea is at the individual level. It says, "Take the challenge to unlock the Buddha nature within you desiring to become a Buddha, and when you do, you become a bodhisattva, a Buddha to be, a compassionate being." In Mahayana Buddhism the purpose for attaining Buddhahood and release from the rounds of rebirth is so that the individual may turn back and help all life find release. Essentially, the "Buddha to be" takes a vow of eternal compassion or eternal helping. But persons do not need to wait until some future life to help people. That service can begin here and now, and it is no accident that many Buddhists involve themselves in all kinds of compassionate service, such as hospice or hospital volunteering.

In addition, Mahayana also offers a cloud of already-enlightened heavenly beings that are committed to helping persons on earth through their profound compassion. There are two categories of these: (1) cosmic Buddhas and (2) cosmic bodhisattvas.

Cosmic Buddhas. At each of the major compass points, there exists a heavenly land, and a cosmic Buddha presides over each of these four lands. Amitabha or Amida presides over the western paradise, with others over each of the other three lands. In the center is Vairocana, the generator of the four others. Hence, there are only five cosmic Buddhas, four of whom preside over heavenly paradises.

Cosmic bodhisattvas. Perhaps because the cosmic Buddhas appear somewhat exalted and distant from us, there are cosmic bodhisattvas who bridge the gap between them and us. They fill a role somewhat akin to that of the saints in Roman Catholicism, and each has taken the eternal vow of compassion to help sentient life. Each of the Four Lords of Lands has a number of cosmic bodhisattvas surrounding him, but it is the Lord of the Western Land who receives the major attention. The structure of the other lands is similar to that of the west, and it is the west that we will explore here.

The principal cosmic bodhisattva associated with Amida is Avalokitesvara, who was created by a ray of light from the third eye, or eye of enlightenment, of Amida. Avalokitesvara is one of the most popular compassionate figures, especially in his feminine form as Kannon (Japan and Korea) or Kwan Yin (China). The statues of Kannon or Kwan Yin, who is known as the Madonna of Buddhism, are lovely and graceful. She is usually shown with multiple heads, implying that she misses nothing, and with multiple arms, since nothing escapes her safety net. Women and children often turn to

Amida, cosmic Buddha who presides over the western paradise.

Kannon for assistance with problems ranging from exams for children to childbirth or family problems for adults. Kannon is near and is profoundly compassionate to those in need.

Usually, there is a third figure presiding over the western land. This third personage in addition to Amida and Kannon is usually Maitreya, the cosmic bodhisattva who will come at the end of the age. All of these Buddhas and bodhisattvas may be accessed through prayer, and they may aid a petitioner. In Tibetan Buddhism, Avalokitesvara's compassion is so great that he descends and dwells among us as the Dalai Lama, head of Tibetan Buddhism, who is currently in exile in India. For his work on behalf of Tibet and Tibetans, the Dalai Lama has been awarded the Nobel Peace Prize.

SCHOOLS OF MAHAYANA BUDDHISM

Pure Land and True Pure Land sects. The Pure Land and True Pure Land sects in Japan worship Amida, Lord of the Western Paradise or the Pure Land. The founder of the Pure Land sect, Honen (1133–1212), held that to show one's faith in Amida's power to release persons from the rounds of rebirth, one should pronounce the name of Amida as many times as possible during the day. Honen would pronounce the name sixty to seventy thousand times daily. One of his followers, Shinran (1173–1262), founded the True Pure Land sect believing that it was necessary to call on Amida only once in a lifetime, because there was nothing that any person could do to save himself or herself. Humanity was so depraved that even faith was a gift, so having received it, persons could not fall out of grace. They were guaranteed salvation at death. Thus, in both sects, salvation comes through faith in Amida. The founders would have agreed with Martin Luther that "by faith alone are you saved," but this did not excuse a person from a life of good works for any of the above. In the cases of Honen and Shinran, one had to live a life acceptable to Amida, just as the life of a disciple is expected from those who profess faith in Jesus Christ as Lutherans or Latter-day Saints.

— ZEN BUDDHISM

Since we have talked all through these first three religions about meditation, we will spend some time with Zen and examine what the meditative life actually involves. Zen Buddhism, while a Mahayana school, returns to the self-help Buddhism seen in Theravada. Zen has become quite attractive to Americans looking for something they have not found in traditional Christianity. There are no divine figures from whom one can gain assistance, although the bodhisattva of wisdom, Manjushri, serves as a model of the insight one is seeking. The founding of Zen is usually attributed to Bodhidharma (ca. third to fourth century CE), an Indian. It is said that Bodhidharma meditated facing a cliff for nine years until he came to enlightenment. Having attained this goal, he decided to take his knowledge to China and to teach the monks. Upon arriving in China, he found the monks physically unfit for the rigors of meditation, so after watching animals, he developed a series of exercises to get the monks in shape.

These exercises form the foundation of the techniques of karate today. But for Bodhidharma, they were not the end of the path, only the beginning. They prepared the monks for the spiritual dimension of life, and too many karate instructors have either forgotten this or never knew it. The black belt is not an end but a beginning. The tradition that Bodhidharma developed is known as Ch'an Buddhism in China and Zen Buddhism in Japan.

The focus of Zen is sitting meditation, which takes place in a meditation hall. Various forms of meditation occupy the attention of the monks or nuns. One tradition chooses to simply focus on the breath as it enters and leaves the nostrils. We learn to be present in each moment, and therefore while sitting, one is just sitting and aware of it, and when one breathes, one is just breathing and aware of it. Awareness leads to seeing the world as it truly is.

Around the interior of the meditation hall is a raised platform, about five feet wide and a foot and a half above the floor, upon which people place their sitting cushions. The cushions are placed on the platform so that persons meditating are facing the wall—like Bodhidharma did his cliff—to limit distractions, since meditation is done with the eyes open. In addition to the sitting meditation, there are many activities during the day in a monastery, and every activity is a form of meditation. Whether one is working, eating, studying, sitting, or walking, all activities are to be done mindfully. Periodically, a gong may ring, and persons stop what they are doing in the garden, in the kitchen, or on other work sites to come back to the breath and refocus. Even at meals, persons are to continue in the meditative state and contemplate how their food arrived on their plates. If one takes this exercise seriously, it leads to an understanding that there is no existence in isolation. Everything is connected and part of a larger whole. Think of the hands all over the world that harvested the grain, made the equipment, made the boxes, shipped the food, and so on. It does not take long to see that all things are linked. This larger whole is like a fishing net. If I cut a knot out of it, the knot has no meaning separated from the other knots in the net. So it is with human beings, who have meaning only as we are united with the universe and each other. Seeing ourselves as one with the universe is a partial definition of enlightenment.

A regular part of monastery life is to talk with the head of the monastery (the Abbot) sitting on cushions knee to knee. The topic may be any aspect of life, and the purpose is to allow the Abbot to guide the student. Another practice is to participate in a concentrated period of meditation, which runs five to seven days. The day begins at 5:00 a.m. and ends at 9:00 p.m., and the entire time is spent in the meditation hall except for trips to the restroom. All meals are taken in the hall in a highly stylized manner which emphasizes mindfulness. Sitting meditation is dominant, but it is broken by lectures, slow walking meditation, and meals. The first objective is once again to quiet the monkey mind, which may take three or four days before it is quiet enough that other things can begin to happen. It is in this concentrated period that someone often comes to enlightenment, the reality of which is weighed and validated by the Abbot.

The essence of enlightenment is the loss of our individuality into the oneness with the cosmos. As one Zen master put it, "To come to Self-realization you must directly experience yourself and the universe as one."[10] Reality is not captured by thoughts. In enlightenment, a person experiences reality as it is.

As we have seen, meditation in Buddhism is primarily aimed at quieting the monkey mind, which bounds from thought to thought to thought. If Latter-day Saints could do that, it would undoubtedly improve their prayer life. But meditation in Latter-day Saint terms focuses more on scriptural content or on the person of the Father or the Son. Meditation on any of these is mental knowledge about scriptural passages or understanding of the Father and the Son and their work. But if we push meditation further, it can lead to a deepened *relationship* with the Father and Son through openness to the Holy Ghost. In the end, this should be the goal of meditation, for as in Buddhism, real knowledge is experiential, not intellectual. We may know much *about* God, but the ultimate challenge is to *know him* through the Spirit, so that his mind and will are ours. This is more than intellectual understanding. Perhaps persons who have become enlightened in other traditions have experienced something akin to this union of the human spirit with the Holy Ghost. It would certainly be in harmony with Elder Dallin Oaks's assertion that manifestations of the Holy Ghost are available to persons who are not Latter-day Saints.[11]

—VAJRAYANA PHILOSOPHY

Vajrayana Buddhism, or the "Vehicle of the Thunderbolt," is the Buddhism of Tibet and Mongolia. It builds on Theravada and Mahayana Buddhism and, like Mahayana, views itself as established by the Buddha for those ready for the highest way. It compares the three forms of Buddhism to the three forms of the Buddha. His human form is comparable to Theravada Buddhism. His divine form is comparable to Mahayana, and his formlessness is comparable to Vajrayana.

There are some unique elements in Tibetan Buddhism. One is the concept of terma. Terma are hidden treasures of various kinds, but most especially texts. Terma were hidden in the past for a future generation. These texts are written in unknown languages. The person who finds and translates them is called a terton. As noted, the message was for a future day and time and was hidden away to await the appointed age. Not only can tertons translate these hidden texts, but they may also receive texts directly with no intervening medium. Such texts are considered as sacred as are those that came through some physical medium.

The concepts of terma and terton may send chills up the backs of Latter-day Saints, for terma sound remarkably like what the Book of Mormon is—an ancient text hidden in the past for our specific time. That would, of course, make Joseph Smith a terton—one who has the gift to translate the hidden text, as well as the ability to bring new texts to light without any physical medium. The latter would be comparable, for example, to the story of Enoch in Moses or the many other revelations received by Joseph.

The heart of Tibetan meditation is the practice of visualization. Persons seek to identify with a cosmic Buddha or bodhisattva, making the heavenly figure's attributes their own. This is done through mental and physical practices, since individuals may identify with the heavenly being through body, speech, and mind. Identity with a heavenly figure like Avalokitesvara (the bodhisattva of compassion) moves individuals to think beyond themselves and expands their kindness, compassion, intelligence, and wisdom, because they take upon themselves those attributes from the deity. Thus, they see the needs of others more clearly and can communicate with them and help them as would the deity. Latter-day Saints living in close harmony with the Spirit experience these very qualities.

Bodily identification with a deity is accomplished through various hand positions, each of which has a specific symbolic meaning. For example, the right hand on the left in a meditative posture is the hand position of compassion.

Identification in speech is through chanted sounds that connect a person with a heavenly figure. The syllables may or may not have meaning, but that is not the point. At the vibrational level the sound is the deity. Thus, the chant *Om mani padme hum* ("Ohm manny padmay hoom") is Avalokitesvara in sound.[12] The mantra has power as it is chanted.

Persons identify with the mind of a deity by remembering and accurately performing the hand positions and chants. Both hand positions and chants have power in themselves, but that power is enhanced immeasurably when done with remembrance.

Another tool in visualization is sand paintings. A sand painting portrays a world not captured in the rounds of rebirth. Its two-dimensional picture is actually a three-dimensional sphere that encloses and protects the three-dimensional palace, at the center of which is a deity. Students must memorize minutely the sand painting, which they can then visualize at any later time. This practice is called "deity yoga," and one acts as if he or she is the deity, reflecting as suggested above all the deity's wisdom, compassion, and other attributes.[13] Thus, the Vajrayana practitioner operates as if he or she has attained the goal of unity with the visualized heavenly figure, while other forms of Buddhism are paths leading to that goal.

It may seem as if there is no connection between sand paintings and the Latter-day Saints. However, a sand painting is the home of a deity. The goal is to be fully identified with that figure. The temple of the Latter-day Saints is in a sense a sand painting because it requires, as does a Buddhist sand painting, that practitioners pass by the gods who are guardians to reach the highest realm in which one can dwell with the ultimate of all realities. There are actions and words in the temple which help the Latter-day Saint identify with the Father and his Son and which are highly symbolic. In the end, the worshiper dwells in the presence of the Father, and in a similar way the Vajrayana Buddhist encounters the deity of the sand painting.

——WORSHIP AND RITUAL————————————

There are many rituals in Buddhism, but they differ dependent upon whether one is talking about Theravada, Mahayana, or
Vajrayana Buddhism. The basic rituals in Theravada Buddhism
focus on what are known as the three refuges: "I take refuge in the
Buddha," "I take refuge in the Dharma" (teaching of the Buddha),
and "I take refuge in the Sangha" (the Buddhist Order). When
chanted, these are repeated three times and are believed to purify,
uplift, and strengthen the heart. Taking refuge in the Buddha
means that persons take the Buddha as the ultimate model for what
persons may become. Refuge in the teachings in short form would
be to follow the Eightfold Path, and refuge in the Order would be
to take guidance, support, and direction from others following the
path. In Mahayana Buddhism, refuge in the Buddha can include
refuge in the cosmic Buddhas and bodhisattvas, such as Amitabha
or Avalokitesvara. In Zen the refuges are internalized. Thus, to take
refuge in the Buddha means to turn to one's own Buddha nature and
to find enlightenment there. The teaching is truth, and the Order is
purity.[14] In Tibetan or Vajrayana Buddhism, there are additional
refuges. The first is taking refuge in one's teacher or lama, who is
believed to be the embodiment of the refuges. One then enters into
the three refuges already mentioned under the teacher's guidance.
The next refuge would be the personal deity that the person will
worship and visualize. Further, there will be purification rituals,
the most strenuous one being the grand prostration, which begins
with persons standing, then going to their knees, and then completing the prostration by extending themselves fully on the floor
facedown. This is done one hundred thousand times, and after the
physical pains are transcended, there is joy.

The use of images is common to all forms of Buddhism. In
Theravada Buddhism, the image of the historical Buddha or a symbol
of him reminds persons of the various spiritual qualities that are necessary for them to gain. While this is also true for Mahayana and
Vajrayana Buddhism, there is an added dimension in which the spirit
and power of the deity represented are present in the image.[15]

The temple is a place where persons may show devotion to the
refuges. The Buddha is represented by a statue, a stupa (a dome-shaped

*Pagoda with a golden stupa. At the temple, persons may show
devotion to the refuges of Buddhism. © Val Brinkerhoff.*

structure), or the tree under which the Buddha was enlightened. The
teaching is present through sermons or informal teaching, and the
Order is visibly present in the monks and nuns themselves. Often,
temples are circled clockwise as an act of reverence. Apart from the
temple, the home plays a principal role in the lives of Buddhist laypeople. There, worship is carried out, the goal of which is to reverence and honor the three refuges. Normally, bowing before an altar,
which may contain symbols or statues of the Buddha, is prominent.
The bows are normally done three times out of respect for the three
refuges and may be acts of repentance. Offerings of flowers may also
be given, and chants may be performed.

Other aids to worship are incense, which symbolizes the odor of sanctity about the Buddha; light using small lamps, symbolizing the Buddha's enlightened state; and chanting, which aids the memory, holds persons' interest, and creates joy and calm in the practitioners. Rosaries may be used to count the chants. Pilgrimage has also been popular among Buddhists, with sites related to the life of Siddhartha Gautama being especially favored.

Two festivals are directly tied to the Buddha. The first celebrates the Buddha's birth, enlightenment, and taking of nirvana (i.e., his death) and occurs on the night of the full moon in May. It is a joyous time, and homes are decorated. The second festival remembers the Buddha's renunciation of family and society and his first sermon, and it is also the beginning of the rainy season, which begins in July in south Asia. During this season, monks remain in the monasteries, and many laypersons take temporary ordination and withdraw to monasteries for about three months.[16]

Finally, devotion plays a major role in Mahayana Buddhism, and two principal figures receive the majority of that worship. They are Avalokitesvara and Amida. Avalokitesvara, the bodhisattva of compassion, will immediately respond to anyone who turns to him in faith. Common in the worship of these figures is the prayer wheel, which may be a small handheld one or a huge one that is mounted in a temple for Avalokitesvara or his female manifestation, Kwan Yin or Kannon. On its outside, the prayer wheel has a chant reflecting the divine figure, and inside is the same chant written multiple times on a piece of paper that is then folded and inserted into the wheel. The large wheel at a temple has the chant written on numerous pieces of paper, and thus the chant appears thousands of times. One turn of the wheel is equivalent to reciting the chant the number of times it appears both on and in the wheel. Goodness and power are gained as the prayer wheel is turned.[17]

The other figure who receives faith and prayers is Amitabha or Amida, who is the Lord of the Western Land or Paradise. Essentially, a person purifies his or her mind by thinking on Amida or by reciting his name or chant. Since a chant is primarily the deity manifest in sound, the sounds *are* Amida. Reciting the syllables awakens faith in Amida and rids one of egoistic power in exchange for the power of Amida.[18]

— WOMEN

Buddhism is a patriarchal faith in practice, although there is nothing male or female about the teaching of the Buddha. The Buddha held that both males and females could gain enlightenment and release but resisted letting women into the Order, saying that if he did not admit them, the Order would last for a thousand years. If he did admit them, it would last for only five hundred years. Finally, he admitted women to the Order, but with prescribed constraints. The principal restrictions defined nuns as always subordinate to monks. Even the most senior nun, no matter how old or how long ordained, must bow before the newest and most junior monk, even if he is only eight years old. Secondly, no nun may teach men.

With these restrictions, an order of nuns was established, and nuns were present in all the Theravada countries, as well as in the Mahayana and Vajrayana ones. The lineage for Theravada nuns was lost in the fifth century CE, but it still exists in China, Korea, and Vietnam and could be reestablished in the Theravada countries. Powerful monks have resisted its reestablishment, though the Dalai Lama supports its renewal.

Unfortunately, nuns are not as highly regarded as monks, especially ascetic women in Theravada countries. The laity tend not to support ascetic Buddhist women in the way they do men, and perhaps that is due to the lack of formal ordination in the Theravada countries. By contrast, women who become Buddhists in Western countries are usually articulate and well educated and are good teachers of the dharma. They may bring respect to the female practitioners of Buddhism that has been lacking to this point.

— CONCLUSION

Buddhism, while having its own distinctive worldview which is quite different from that of the Latter-day Saints, forces Latter-day Saints to think seriously about the things they presume to be ultimate reality. In the end, there is permanence in the elements of the universe in the Latter-day Saint view that is not present in Buddhism. Also, Buddhism has no concept of an ultimate deity, for all things are in flux.

—NOTES

1. "Major Religions of the World Ranked by Number of Adherents," Adherents.com, last modified August 9, 2007, http://www.adherents.com/Religions_By_Adherents.html.
2. Robert E. Van Voorst, *Anthology of World Scriptures*, 6th ed. (Mason, OH: Cengage Learning, 2008), 79.
3. Roger J. Corless, *Vision of Buddhism: The Space under the Tree* (New York: Paragon House, 1989), 77.
4. Corless, *Vision of Buddhism*, 102.
5. David S. Noss and John B. Noss, *A History of the World's Religions*, 9th ed. (New York: Macmillan College, 1994), 216.
6. Van Voorst, *Anthology*, 67–70.
7. Van Voorst, *Anthology*, 79.
8. Jack Kornfield, *A Path with Heart* (New York: Bantam Books, 1993), 199.
9. Corless, *Vision of Buddhism*, 20.
10. Philip Kapleau, comp. and ed., *Three Pillars of Zen* (Boston: Beacon, 1965), 106.
11. Dallin H. Oaks, "Always Have His Spirit," in Conference Report, October 1996, 79–80.
12. Corless, *Vision of Buddhism*, 263.
13. Corless, *Vision of Buddhism*, 264.
14. Peter Harvey, "Buddhism," in *Worship*, ed. Jean Holm with John Bowker (New York: Pinter, 1994), 11–12.
15. Harvey, "Buddhism," 15–16.
16. Harvey, "Buddhism," 28–30.
17. Harvey, "Buddhism," 22–25.
18. Harvey, "Buddhism," 25–26.

A Sikh family walks past the Golden Temple at Amritsar, India.

CHAPTER 5

SIKHISM

Sikhism is an impressive religious tradition with which Latter-day Saints can find a sense of kinship. There is a strong sense that human beings are related to God and that he loves us.

Sikhism differs from Hinduism, Jainism, and Buddhism in that it believes in only one God. At the same time, the religion retains the concepts of karma, reincarnation, and release from the rounds of rebirth. Sikhism has a more positive attitude toward the world than the other faiths but, like them, is not a missionary faith, since it sees all other religions as leading to the same place that Sikhism does—namely, to God. Sikhs live predominantly in the Punjab region of India (i.e., in the northwest of India). Their primary vocation is farming, but because of certain tenets of their faith, they are often found in military or police positions all over the British Commonwealth. There are about twenty-three million Sikhs in the world today, with the majority living in India.[1]

ORIGINS

FOUNDER

The founder of Sikhism was Guru Nanak, who was born in 1469 CE in the village of Talwandi, which is in present-day Pakistan about thirty miles outside Lahore. Nanak died in 1538 CE. His father was an accountant and farmer from a mercantile caste. The village in which Nanak lived was governed by a man named Rai Bular, who had converted from Hinduism to Islam and had an interest in seeing the two faiths live peacefully together. Sikhism is often explained as an effort to reconcile Hinduism and Islam, but Sikhism connects strongly to Hinduism through the devotional and inner paths to God. In addition, Sikhism retains much of the fundamental philosophy of Hinduism. In other words, the presence of Islam is unnecessary to explain the doctrines of Sikhism, and Nanak was not trying to amalgamate the two faiths. Rather, he was attempting to be true to the mission he received when he was taken into the presence of God and commissioned.

Nanak was an interesting child. He preferred sitting in meditation to playing with the other children. He went to school for one day, came home saying that they had nothing they could teach him, and refused to return. In harmony with traditional Hindu practice, Nanak's father arranged a marriage for him. It seems to have been a happy one, and he had two sons. In his late teens, Nanak gained a post in the district capitol and did very well. His deepest love, however, was reserved for God. Each evening Nanak would praise God and pray. Gradually a group of seekers began to gather around him. Each morning Nanak would bathe in the river before sunrise, and on one of these mornings, he disappeared into the river. His companions believed he had drowned, but according to his account, he was taken into the presence of God and commissioned. A probable account of the experience, since he was a poet and musician, appears in poetic form and is as follows:

I was a minstrel out of work; The Lord gave me employment.
The Mighty One instructed me: "Night and day, sing my praise!"
The Lord did summon this minstrel to his High Court;
On me He bestowed the robe of honor of those who exalt Him.
On me He bestowed the Nectar in a Cup, the Nectar of His true and Holy Name.[2]

In other words, God commissioned Nanak to make known the one God, much as he did Abraham. After three days, Nanak reappeared but sat in silence for twenty-four hours, and then the first words he said were, "There is neither Hindu nor Muslim." What he meant—and this idea underlies all Sikh thought about other faith traditions—is that there is one God. This one God makes himself known in many ways, in many places, and under many names. Thus, all those who worship God, no matter what they may choose to call him, are all worshiping the same deity. The Sikhs call this God "True Name" or Vahiguru (which means "the wonderful sovereign"), since no name is adequate for God. Others may call him Shiva or Vishnu or Allah, yet all are worshiping the one God. Therefore, there are neither Hindus nor Muslims, nor, for that matter, Jews, Christians, Buddhists, or others, for all human beings who worship God are brothers and sisters before God. There is no reason for interfaith tensions. Hence, Sikhism is not a missionary faith but one that sees all faiths as leading to the same place (i.e., to the presence of God) when followed well.

Upon returning from his visionary experience, Nanak began what were to be several trips to spread his message. To *visually* communicate his message, Nanak dressed partly as a Hindu and partly as a Muslim.[3] Nanak would sing his message to the accompaniment of a stringed instrument played by his Muslim companion, Mardana, who never became a Sikh, thus exemplifying further the inclusiveness of his message. His first trip took him through central India. A second trip carried him as far south as Sri Lanka. The third trip took him to Tibet and the fourth to Mecca and Medina in Arabia, as well as to Baghdad in present-day Iraq.

There is a story associated with his visit to Mecca that further underlines the inclusive nature of his theology. According to tradition, when he was lying down for the night in a mosque, his feet were pointed toward the niche in the wall that indicates to the worshiper the direction of the central shrine of Muslim religious piety. A Muslim, seeing what he discerned to be disrespect, kicked Nanak's legs and told him to point his feet away from God. In return, Nanak asked him to point his feet where God was not, indicating that God is not limited by shrines and sacred places.

Despite all the travel, Nanak's principal success came at home in the Punjab region of India. There, groups of Sikhs (disciples) began to gather around him. As he neared the end of his life, Nanak appointed his successor, so that there would be no doubt about who should succeed him.

The man appointed was Lehna, a close associate who became known as Guru Angad. Interestingly, Nanak did not appoint either of his sons, whom he considered to be unworthy of the position, although they protested the decision and caused some trouble following Nanak's death.

The story surrounding Guru Nanak's death supports the basic idea that nothing should cause religious division. According to tradition, as Nanak approached death, his Hindu followers wanted to cremate his body as was their custom. His Muslim followers, however, according to their tradition, wanted to bury his body. Nanak told both groups to bring fresh flowers and place them on either side of him. Whichever group's flowers were in bloom in the morning could have his body. He then pulled the sheet over his head and became quiet. In the morning, both sets of flowers were in bloom and Nanak's body had vanished. Thus, even with his death, unity was maintained.

SCRIPTURES

According to Gurinder Singh Mann,[4] the Sikh scriptures (the Guru Granth Sahib) were compiled over an extended period of time, with portions being contributed by six of the ten human Gurus. The first part of the scriptures comes from Guru Nanak, and this was followed by writings of the next four Gurus. Guru Arjan is usually credited with compiling the Granth, but each Guru contributed to the growing collection during his Guruship. The last Guru to add his writings was the ninth one, Tegh Bahadur. Following the section of the scriptures composed by the above six Gurus, there is a section containing the works of various Sikh religious poets. The scriptures end with a section from a number of non-Sikh religious persons of both the Hindu and Muslim faiths, demonstrating clearly the religious inclusiveness of Sikhism. The tenth Guru, Guru Gobind Singh, declared the book to be his successor, and thus the Guru Granth Sahib is given the place of honor in all Sikh places of worship.

— BASIC DOCTRINES

GOD

The center of Nanak's teachings was the one God, known sometimes as "True Name" or more regularly as Vahiguru.[5] As suggested earlier, God is beyond names, so the best that can be done is simply

Granthi reading the scriptures. The scriptures of Sikhism are
known as the Guru Granth Sahib, the living Guru of Sikhism.

to call him by a word that expresses an attribute or quality of God. To place anything in the place of God, be it persons, material wealth, a job, or something else, is to live a life of illusion, since the only true life is that which has God at its center. What the Sikhs call illusion would probably be called idolatry by many others.

Mann notes that God is also beyond form.[6] He is transcendent, yet he is involved in the world. He expresses his justice by destroying evil and supporting good, often through earthly rulers. This reflects the "Father" side of God, while the side of mercy and forgiveness reflects the maternal side of deity. God is loving and extends his grace to humankind, but persons need to be prepared to receive that grace.[7] Grace is not imposed on them without their cooperation.

Of all the religions we have examined thus far, Latter-day Saints will likely feel the most comfortable with Sikhism because of its belief in one God. The multiple gods of Hinduism or the lack of a supreme deity in Jainism and Buddhism may feel uncomfortable to a Latter-day Saint, but in Sikhism there is the belief in one supreme deity with human beings bearing a spark of his divinity. Humans seek a profound union with this God. There is, however, an openness in Sikhism to other faiths that may be a bit unfamiliar to Latter-day Saints. Sikhism does not see itself as the only valid religion, as we have already seen.

The openness of Asian religions to traditions other than their own makes Latter-day Saint missionaries shake their heads. They will find a person, teach the restored gospel, and get affirmations that the person believes that Joseph is a prophet, that the Book of Mormon is true, and that the current President of the LDS Church is a true and living prophet; but when the missionaries press the person to accept baptism, the reaction is often something like, "Convert? How narrow can you be? I will just add what you have taught me to what I already know to be true."

CREATION

Unlike in Hinduism, in Sikhism there is a clear beginning to the created order and to human beings. Mann records a creation hymn from the Guru Granth Sahib which sounds very much like Christian, Jewish, and Islamic theologies of creation:

> For endless eons, there was only darkness.
> Nothing except the hukam existed.
> No day or night, no moon or sun;
> Vahiguru alone sat in a primal stance. . . .
> When Vahiguru so willed, creation came into being. . . .
> Without any support Vahiguru erected the universe. . . .
> The Unmanifested One revealed itself in the creation.[8]

This would appear to approach the doctrine of "creation from nothing." The *hukam* is the divine will, or the divine command. Human beings were created simultaneously with the world, and Vahiguru is very much involved in the daily management of the world and its inhabitants. He is anything but a distant God.

HUMAN BEINGS

Human beings are central to God's creation. According to Mann, their "goal is to attain liberation, which is to be one with Vahiguru by having a respectful place in the divine court."[9] Other Sikhs see a direct connection between God and the human being in that the human contains a spark of the divine, and the goal is for that spark to return to its origin in God, much like a spark returning to the bonfire. In this view there may be a loss of individuality envisioned. Humanity's primary purpose is to rid itself of ego so that people can recognize their place in the divine creation and in relationship to deity.

Human beings are to recognize two fundamental poles to life—their relationships with God and those with one another. Sikhism is first concerned with the relationship between the human being and God, and then it is concerned with the relationship between humans. There is no solitary dimension to Sikhism. Salvation involves not merely individuals but also families, communities, and ultimately the world community.[10] This principle sounds familiar to Latter-day Saints, who believe that families may be eternal and that husband and wife are bound together for eternity if sealed through the authority of the priesthood.

Sikhs consider human beings to be princes and princesses of a heavenly ruler but separated from God by their egos. Thus, humankind should develop their godly aspects and realize the image of God (defined as his attributes) in which they have been created and recapture their true selves. In the end, religion should transform people, and all religions bring their adherents to the same place. But humans are not to deny the material world. The spiritual and the material are not necessarily antithetical to one another. Therefore, there is not an officially recognized ascetic order among Sikhs. The material world is to be used wisely by spiritually enlightened persons.

Similarly, from the Jewish, Christian, or Islamic perspective, everything that God has made is good. "And God saw every thing that he had made, and, behold, it was very good" (Genesis 1:31). As one person put it, "God don't make no junk!" While the grammar is a bit suspect, the sentiment is true. For the Sikh it is also true. As with the other monotheistic faiths, this world is to be used and enjoyed within the bounds of good stewardship. We are not to waste it or destroy it, but to be stewards of all that God has given us. Thus, the married state, for example, with its physical pleasures, as well as the other things of the world, is given to us by God. We should not, however, make the material things our goal. We are to use the world's materials for the betterment of humankind in general. Sikhs, like Latter-day Saints, are to live in the midst of the things of the world without letting those things capture them.

GETTING NEARER TO GOD

The community of Sikhs is guided by three golden rules. The first rule is that persons should remember God through meditation, but this is not the type of meditation that we find in Zen. There persons empty their minds and simply focus on the breath. Here meditation may be on God or the scriptures, so there is content to the meditation, much as among Latter-day Saints. Secondly, Sikhs are to earn their livelihood honestly. A guidebook of India that the author once used suggested that if persons needed automobile or motorcycle repairs, they should look for a "Mr. Singh," a name taken by male Sikhs at the time of baptism. What this guidebook meant was that persons needing assistance should find a Sikh because he or she would treat the customer honestly, which is not to say that persons of other faiths would not do the same. Rather, this statement is an interesting affirmation of the integrity of Sikhs as a whole from the guidebook's perspective. Finally, Sikhs are to share with the needy. If a person is lost, hungry, and in need of shelter, he or she can go to a Sikh place of worship and find food and a place to sleep.

Overlapping the golden rules are the three ways to get closer to God. First is service to people, and Sikhs seek various opportunities to serve. As noted above, a communal meal is available at the Sikh worship centers, and anyone is welcome. A wonderful example of this desire to serve occurred at the World Parliament of Religions held in Barcelona, Spain, in the summer of 2004. The Sikhs from all over Europe, and particularly from England, gathered with the primary motive of serving the four thousand people who attended the conference. The Sikhs erected a tent which served as a worship center, and there they served a free community meal each day to any of the participants who wanted to eat. People would sit on the floor in long lines and be served. No one sat higher than anyone else because all are equal. In addition, as the author came out of one lunch, he noticed an anonymous act of service—an elderly Sikh cleaning the shoes that had been left outside the tent.

Meditation, addressed above, is the second way to get closer to God. The third way is to belong to a community of believers who need each other to draw and stretch them to a deeper faith commitment. As already noted, a Sikh is not a person of faith in isolation from the human family.

KARMA AND REINCARNATION

Karma and reincarnation are a part of Sikh thought. Sikh karma is like that of Hinduism (i.e., the cosmic karma that has no form or materiality). While considered part of the theological conversation, karma is transcended by the omnipotence of God. God can forgive all that is past, and thus karma among Sikhs is more like sin among Christians. It is something that through his mercy God can overcome. Reincarnation is a reminder that people can be less than God created humans to be, but it does not have the grinding effect on human life that it might in other religious traditions.

RITUAL AND RELIGION

Nanak denounced ritual. Ritual did not bring one into union with God and was therefore unnecessary. One finds in the Guru Granth Sahib the following statement from God to Nanak:

> Religion consisteth not in a patched coat, or in a Yogin's staff, or in ashes smeared over the body; Religion consisteth not in earrings worn, or a shaven head, or in the blowing of horns. . . . Religion consisteth not in wanderings to tombs or places of cremation, or sitting in attitudes of contemplation. Religion consisteth not in wandering in foreign countries, or in bathing at places of pilgrimage.[11]

If ritual is not religion, then what is? Once more, the answer is given in the Guru Granth Sahib:

Let compassion be thy mosque, Let faith be thy prayer mat, Let honest living be thy Koran, Let modesty be the rules of observance, Let piety be the fasts thou keepest; In such wise strive to be a Muslim; Right conduct the Ka'aba; Truth the Prophet; Good deeds thy prayer; Submission to the Lord's Will thy rosary; Nanak, if this thou do, the Lord will be thy Protector.[12]

It is clear that, to the Sikhs, real religion concerns inner attitude and spirituality. Religion is, therefore, compassion, faith, honest living, modesty, piety, right conduct, good deeds, and submission to the Lord's will. Any religious person would be hard-pressed to find a better list of what it means to be religious. Anybody can put on the outward trappings of religion, but only truly religious people embody religion at the level of attributes. The Sikh is challenged by God through Guru Nanak to make these attributes a part of his or her daily life.

SIKHS IN THE WORLD

Because God is good, there should be no despair before the world. The world and its people, which he created, are good. Thus, Sikhs are to have fellowship with persons of all castes and levels of society. They are to seek knowledge, love their spouses, and not violate their marriage bonds. They are not to be argumentative or arrogant. They are to avoid

The Golden Temple at Amritsar built by Guru Arjan Dev. Courtesy of Oleg Yunakov.

persons that would lead them into evil ways. In the end, Sikhs are to be conciliatory and peaceful, and if persons attack them three times, God will fight for them the fourth time. Through the first five Gurus, the Sikhs were pacifists living out Nanak's vision for them. However, things changed in the transition from the fifth to the sixth Guru.

— POLITICAL HISTORY AND THE GURUS

Much of Sikh life and thought arise out of their political history and the succession of ten Gurus, who shaped Sikh life. This section will examine some of the successors to Guru Nanak. As noted above, with the fifth Guru, a change occurred in Sikhs' attitudes toward violence.

THE THIRD GURU: GURU AMAR DAS

Amar Das came from a Hindu family which worshiped Vishnu. He was born in 1479 and died in 1574, becoming Guru in 1552. Once he was Guru, he established the communal kitchen with its communal meal. Anyone seeking to have an audience with Guru Amar Das had to sit on the floor with the community and eat the meal. This even held true when the Emperor Akbar wanted to see Guru Amar Das. Perhaps the measure of Akbar's greatness is that he sat on the floor with everybody else and participated in the communal meal, after which the Guru visited with him.

Guru Amar Das lived in a day and time when women could not remarry when their husbands died. Their lot in life after the death of their husbands was often extremely hard, and Amar Das disapproved of them remaining unmarried, which was a significant departure from Hindu practice. Amar Das added to the collection of writings begun by Nanak and also collected writings from Hindu holy men. He had all of the writings translated into Punjabi, the language of the average Sikh, again breaking with traditional Hinduism, in which the sacred language was Sanskrit.

THE FIFTH GURU: GURU ARJAN DEV

Guru Arjan Dev was born in 1563 and was the youngest son of Guru Ramdas, the fourth Guru. He was appointed Guru in 1581 and died in 1606. He is known for two principal accomplishments. First, he built the Golden Temple at Amritsar. His predecessor had already dug the lake in which the temple sat, and this glorious building is especially sacred to Sikhs today.

Secondly, Guru Arjan compiled the Adi Granth, or "first book," which ultimately became the Sikh scriptures. This compilation was the product of an elder brother's jealousy and duplicity. His brother, Prithi Chand, was composing his own hymns and passing them off as the compositions of Guru Nanak. Guru Arjan Dev realized that he needed to preserve the authentic stream from the Gurus, so he continued the collection of the Gurus' hymns begun by his predecessors. To their work he added his own, and he also collected the hymns of Hindu and Muslim holy men whose works reflected the glory of God. His collection, which first appeared in 1604, was called the Adi Granth, and with the addition of Guru Tegh Bahadur's writings, it is today known as the Guru Granth Sahib. True to Sikh egalitarianism, anyone could read the book, regardless of sex or caste or faith. Guru Arjan sent a copy of it to the Muslim Emperor Akbar, who thought it was well done. However, in 1605, Akbar died and was succeeded by Jehangir. Unfortunately, the new emperor was morally lax and sought to please the Muslim clerics. They did not approve of the Adi Granth and wanted parts of it changed, something which Arjan Dev refused to do. Thus, to please the clerics, Jehangir demanded that Arjan present himself to the court.

Before going, Guru Arjan Dev named his son, Hargobind, the next Guru. He then presented himself before the emperor, who turned him over to a man named Murtaza Khan, who tortured him for refusing to modify the Adi Granth. Guru Arjan was forced to sit on a red hot sheet of iron, had burning sand poured over his body, and was immersed in boiling water. Finally, on May 30, 1606, Arjan asked for permission to bathe in the river. Repeating the words, "Sweet is your will, O God; the gift of your Name alone I seek," he walked into the river and was swept to his death.[13]

THE SIXTH GURU: GURU HARGOBIND

Guru Hargobind was born in 1595, became Guru on May 25, 1606, and died in 1644. Because of the way his father died, Hargobind moved in a more militant direction with the purpose of protecting the faith. He wore two swords, one of secular power called Miri, and the other of devotion which was called Piri. It was Hargobind who transformed the Sikhs from a pacifist community to one of saint-soldiers. He wore the royal robes of a king and encouraged the Sikhs to be involved in physical training, horsemanship, and training in arms. Interestingly, even though he had numerous battles with the Muslims, because of his charm and holiness, he became friends with the emperor Jehangir, who had sent Hargobind's father to his death. Hargobind even saved the emperor's life when he was threatened by a tiger.

THE EIGHTH GURU: GURU HAR KISHEN

Guru Har Kishen was born in 1656, was appointed Guru in 1661, and died in 1664. His appointment at such a young age offers an opportunity to consider the meaning of Guruship. When God, or the Divine Light, rests upon a Guru, all the knowledge and wisdom that are necessary to fill his role are embodied in him, regardless of age. Har Kishen had great spiritual power, and "the answer to the spiritual power of the young Guru lies in the understanding that the Guru, though human in body, is Divine in Spirit."[14]

When the emperor Aurengzeb succeeded Jehangir, he wanted Har Kishen to come to the court for the purpose of destroying Sikhism and converting all Hindus and others to Islam. Because his father had forbidden him to see the emperor, Har Kishen refused but later was enticed to go to Delhi by other Sikhs. In Delhi, cholera and small-pox were everywhere, and the Guru contracted them, understanding the diseases to be God's will for him. A Sikh explanation states, "The Guru out of human compassion took the small-pox to himself and absolved the inhabitants of Delhi of it. Raja Jai Singh got a tank [a manmade lake] excavated. The Guru dipped his feet in the water of the tank and after that whosoever took bath with that water, was cured from small-pox."[15]

Har Kishen died at age eight from the diseases, but his last words according to one tradition were "Baba Bakala," meaning that the next Guru would be found in the town of Bakala, but no one knew who it was.

THE NINTH GURU: GURU TEGH BAHADUR

According to the above tradition, Sikhs went to Bakala but found several persons claiming the right to be Guru. Meanwhile, there was a merchant who had ships at sea, and he promised God that if they arrived safely, he would give five hundred gold pieces to the Guru. When they reached port, he went immediately to Bakala to pay his debt, but he found no identified Guru. He decided to test claimants and give each two gold pieces, believing that the real Guru would ask for the rest. After giving each of the pretenders two gold coins and having none of them ask for the remainder, he asked if there were no other holy men in Bakala. He was told that Tegh Bahadur, the youngest son of Guru Hargobind, lived there. When he presented Tegh Bahadur with the two coins, Bahadur asked where the remainder of the coins were. The merchant ran outside shouting that he had found the Guru.

Tegh Bahadur was born in 1621 and was appointed Guru in 1664. He died in 1675. He was primarily interested in the meditative life, but once he became the Guru, he traveled and established community kitchens, had wells dug, and promoted honest work and charity for the poor.

In 1675, Hindus came to Guru Tegh Bahadur asking him to intercede on their behalf with the Emperor Aurengzeb, who was persecuting the Hindus and demanding that they become Muslims or lose their lives. Seeing that something was troubling Tegh Bahadur, Gobind Rai, his nine-year-old son, asked his father what was wrong. Teg Bahadur explained to him the plight of the Hindus and told him that unless a holy man were willing lay down his life for the Hindus, they would be slaughtered. Gobind Rai asked who was better suited for that than his father. Tegh Bahadur simply stated that he was concerned that his son was too young to take over the Guruship. Gobind Rai told him to leave that to God and to protect the Hindus.

Tegh Bahadur then told the Hindus to inform the emperor that if he could convert Tegh Bahadur, they would all convert. He then appointed his son to succeed him and left to see the emperor. When Tegh Bahadur arrived at court, he castigated the emperor for his narrowness, his bigotry, and his intolerance. In response, Aurengzeb had him arrested, tortured, and finally beheaded on November 11, 1675. All day the body lay in the street because no Sikh had the courage to show himself. Finally, after dark, Sikhs collected the body and placed it in a nearby house which they burned down, thereby cremating the corpse. The head was retrieved during a rain storm and Gobind Rai cremated it. In doing so, however, he swore that Sikhs would never be able to hide again.

THE TENTH GURU: GURU GOBIND SINGH

Under Guru Gobind Rai, the Sikhs consolidated their strength. When he was thirty-three, the Guru went to a spring festival known as Baisakhi, set up his tent, and remained out of sight until people had gathered. Suddenly, the Guru came out of his tent with his sword in his hand and asked for a Sikh willing to give his head for the faith. Finally, a man came forward and was taken into the tent, where a thud was heard, and then the Guru reappeared with a bloody sword in his hand. He asked for a second person who went into the tent, a thud was heard, and Gobind Rai returned with a bloody sword. He did this five times, and the people were becoming horrified. At last, the Guru threw back the door of the tent, and there were the five, dressed in royal robes. Some Sikhs hold that the Guru actually decapitated the five and by his divine power made them whole, holding that the Guru had the power to raise the dead. Other authors state that there were five decapitated goats lying in the back of the tent. Regardless of which account is accurate, all five men went into the tent believing they were going to die. These five became known as the "Five Beloved" and became the foundation of the Khalsa (The Pure Ones), which the Guru proceeded to establish.

At that time, the Khalsa was the community of baptized Sikhs. To create the Khalsa, Guru Gobind Rai took a large steel kettle, poured water into it, and stirred it with a double-edged sword. While some stories are amplified, tradition says that he then took a sparrow and gave it two drops of the water. The sparrow immediately defeated the Guru's hawk. Seeing this, the Guru's wife poured some sugar into the water, saying that with strength there should also be sweetness. This sweetened water, known as amrit, was put in a basin from which the Guru had all five of the men drink, and then he sprinkled amrit in the eyes and hair of the five. All the men were from different castes, so drinking from a common vessel, in the Hindu context, totally destroyed any caste distinctions. Then Gobind Rai asked them to initiate him, for he was no better than they. As part of the initiatory ritual, he had each of the men and himself add the name Singh (meaning "lion") to their names, and thus Guru Gobind Rai became Guru Gobind Singh, or Gobind the Lion. Women add the name Kaur (meaning "princess") to their names.

We should now remember that the Guru had promised upon the death of his father that no Sikh would be able to hide in the future. Thus, in addition to the initiation ceremony, Gobind Singh gave himself and the initiates the five marks of the Khalsa, known as the "five Ks." All Sikhs were to wear these as a sign of their initiation into the Khalsa and their commitment to its principles. The Ks are as follows, and both men and women wear them.

Kesh. The kesh is long uncut hair and beard. Neither men nor women cut their hair, nor men their beards. Sometimes it appears that a man has trimmed his beard, but if one looks closely, one can see that he has probably separated it and tied it on top of his head. Women do not shave body hair, and many women will have extremely long, loose hair. To some, the kesh signifies spirituality and living out God's purposes and will naturally.

Kangha. The kangha is a small comb that holds the hair in place. It is particularly important for men, whose very long hair needs to be wrapped up before a turban can be put on. Women often wear the kangha as a decorative item in their hair. The kangha is said by some to symbolize mental discipline.

Kacch. The kacch is a pair of short underdrawers which symbolize sexual purity.

Kara. The kara is a steel bracelet which symbolizes control of a person's actions and the remembrance of God. It is usually worn on the right hand if right-handed, or on the left if left-handed.

Kirpan. The kirpan is a short dagger or "sword" and is a religious symbol which represents a Sikh's willingness to stand against injustice and oppression committed against anyone. Sikhs have died in defense not only of their own faith but also of Hindus, as did Tegh Bahadur, as well as of Muslims.

In addition to the five Ks, Khalsa members commit themselves to certain practices in life. They are to worship only one God, to honor the Guru Granth Sahib, and to honor the Gurus. They are to deny

Sikh men with the five Ks, including uncut hair and the short daggers.

caste and other ritual practices, both Hindu and Muslim, and any person is welcome. They are to wash, pray, and chant the scriptures at the beginning of each day. They may not use drugs or alcohol, nor may they smoke, steal, or gamble; and they may not make holes in their noses or ears. Finally, Sikhs are expected to contribute one-tenth of their income to charity. Some of this will go to the worship center, but some may also be contributed to hospitals, schools, or other enterprises to support the less fortunate. Thus, these are highly principled saint-soldiers.

As can be seen, Latter-day Saints and Sikhs hold comparable values. Neither believes in the use of alcohol or drugs. Both value chastity, and sexual relations are to be had only within the bonds of marriage. Both value truth. Both give 10 percent of their income to charitable causes. Both try to apply their faith to daily life.

Sikhs are conscious, however, that different Sikhs live by a variety of standards. Thus, Amritdhari (nectar-bearing) Sikhs are those who have been baptized. Keshdhari (hair bearing) Sikhs are those who maintain the long hair but have not yet been baptized. A third group has arisen who follow Nanak's precepts and disciplines but who have shaved their hair and beards. Most of these individuals live outside India and have adapted themselves to new cultures. According to Mann, an acceptable term for them has not been found.[16]

Gobind Singh swore that no Sikh would be able to hide after the death of his father, Tegh Bahadur, because no Sikh had the courage to reveal himself and collect Tegh Bahadur's body after he was beheaded. The author remembers standing outside a Gurdwara in Old Delhi talking to a couple of Sikh gentlemen and having one of them say, "I can't tell whether you are English, American, German, or Dutch, but you look at me, and you know who I am." The five Ks clearly mark Sikhs, and endowed Latter-day Saints are also marked. They wear a temple garment which identifies them. It is not visible to the world the way the five Ks are, but it bears markings that remind Latter-day Saints of covenants they have made, thereby reminding them whose they are. They are children of God who have made agreements with their Heavenly Father to live a life different from that of the surrounding world. So also does an Amritdhari Sikh live similar commitments, although for him or her, the signs of those commitments are external rather than hidden. But the signs are equally real to the faithful Sikh or Latter-day Saint.

The tenth Guru, Gobind Singh, died as the result of an attempted assassination in which he was wounded. The Muslim Shah of his area sent his doctors to attend the wound, which they were able to sew up, and the prospects looked good for a full recovery. However, after a time, feeling that he was healed, the Guru decided to see how far he could throw a spear. The effort tore the wound open, and a week later he was dead. Before his death, he declared that there would be no more human Gurus, and the eleventh Guru would be the sacred scriptures. Thus, these texts are known today as the Guru Granth Sahib.

—Worship and Rituals

The Gurdwara

The Sikh worship center, known as a Gurdwara, is the center of Sikh religious and social life. In the center of it are the Sikh scriptures, the Guru Granth Sahib, which are constantly being read by a Granthi through the day. Persons come to the worship center first and foremost to hear the Guru Granth Sahib read (or sometimes sung), and all persons are welcome. Sikhs bow before the book but never before people, for no person is better than another before God. The worship center has four entrances facing each of the cardinal directions, inviting the world to enter. Persons must take off their shoes and cover their heads, but no one is excluded if they meet these simple requirements. Communal meals are provided at the worship centers, and again all are welcome.

RITUAL

There is very little ritual among the Sikhs largely because of the negative response that Nanak provided when considering rituals. As noted above, real rituals for Nanak were not outward activities like making pilgrimages and bathing in the river, but rather were the reflections of religion such as compassion, justice, and mercy. Thus, even though there are some rituals among Sikhs today, they are minimal.

The most important ritual is that of initiation into the Khalsa. As we noted earlier, Guru Gobind Singh initiated the Five Beloved by splashing amrit into their eyes and onto their hair and then having them drink amrit from a common vessel. This still happens today, with the Five Beloved represented by any five baptized Sikhs, either male or female. Once initiated, persons are given the five Ks, and they are also given the Guru Mantra (chant), which is whispered into their ears. The chant is "Vahiguru," the principal name used for God. In a Sikh meeting, if the volume begins to rise too high, someone will often begin to quietly say "Vahiguru, Vahiguru," and

Langar at a Langar hall and Gurdwara. Courtesy of Hari Singh.

a neighbor will pick it up until it has traveled throughout the room and reverence is reestablished.

A second ritual relates to the Guru Granth Sahib, the sacred text. In the worship centers, the Granth is treated as royalty, with an attendant waving a fan to keep it cool and to keep bugs away from it during the day. At the end of the day, the Granth is ceremoniously carried in procession and put in an actual bed. In the morning it is awakened and ceremoniously returned to its "throne" in the Gurdwara as if it were a king.

Third, upon entering the Gurdwara, Sikhs will bow before the Granth. The Granth is the living Guru in their midst, the channel through which God is present in the community, and is thereby worthy of reverence. At a wedding, the only ritual is that of the bride and groom together walking around the Granth. As an extension of this activity before the Granth, a Sikh will occasionally be seen kissing the steps of the worship center. This is a symbol of respect for the community. In Indian society, younger persons will often greet parents or grandparents or other respected elders by touching their feet as a symbol of honor and respect. In Sikhism, the community as a whole deserves this respect.

Near many worship centers is a tank or manmade lake. Sikhs will dip themselves in these tanks as a symbol of immersion in the ocean of divinity. We need to remember that the ultimate goal of Sikhs is to find union with God and bliss in that union. This is what is symbolized as Sikhs immerse themselves in the water.

The Sikh greeting is "Sat Sri Akal," meaning "God is true." The author's experience has been that Sikhs appreciate being greeted with these words, for it is the heart of their faith, and as a Latter-day Saint, I believe the affirmation is correct.

Even though the above is a relatively small collection of rituals, how did rituals develop at all, given Nanak's attitude toward them? The answer lies in continuing revelation, for Sikhs believe that each Guru brought God's presence into the midst of the real world. What was correct in Nanak's day, which he perceived as being fraught with rituals that took the place of real religion, was gradually changed over time by later Gurus as they encountered new needs in the community. Religion is not static but alive. Even today, the Guru Granth Sahib speaks to new situations as the world changes.

— WOMEN

Women are absolutely equal to men in Sikhism. There is nothing a man can do that a woman cannot, though they may not choose to do all things in a given community. Women can be Granthis, reading from the Guru Granth Sahib, and can participate in the initiation ceremony, even giving the Guru mantra to the new initiate. Sikh women are also a much more public presence than Hindu or Muslim women tend to be. Since men and women are equal in marriage and in the faith, Sikhs recommend that Sikhs marry Sikhs, for to do otherwise dilutes the faith and does not enable husband and wife to share the deepest spiritual experiences of life.

Latter-day Saints and Sikhs both believe that men and women are equal to one another; yet at the same time, Sikhs in practice may demonstrate that women are a bit more equal than Latter-day Saints believe. There is no question in either faith that men and women are equal before God. They are. However, women in Sikhism can do *anything* that a man can do. This is not true in The Church of Jesus Christ of Latter-day Saints, for though equal, men and women have different roles in this life. Men hold the priesthood, and women do not. As a convert to Mormonism, the author is convinced that this latter practice is divinely inspired, for it gives men a clear role to fulfill and teaches them service, which the world ordinarily does not value. Most women already know that life is service, and while they may not hold the priesthood, they are not excluded from leadership in the church. As my wife said, "I have done everything as a Relief Society president that I ever hoped to do as a Methodist minister." For Latter-day Saint men and women, there is not only equality but equality with diversity.

— CONCLUSION

Sikhism is an impressive religious tradition with which Latter-day Saints can find a sense of kinship. God and his holiness stand at the center of both traditions, and there is a strong sense that human beings are related to this God and that he loves us. We seek in the end to be with him and to share in his life. Because of that, we share common values and common lifestyles. Sikhism is a good example of how God works among all his children.

— Notes ————————————————

1. "Major Religions of the World Ranked by Number of Adherents," Adherents.com, last modified August 9, 2007, http://www.adherents .com/Religions_By_Adherents.html.
2. David S. Noss and John B. Noss, *A History of the World's Religions*, 9th ed. (New York: Macmillan College, 1994), 262.
3. Noss and Noss, *History*, 262.
4. Gurinder Singh Mann, *Sikhism* (Upper Saddle Ridge, NJ: Prentice Hall, 2004), 15.
5. Mann, *Sikhism*, 72–75.
6. Mann, *Sikhism*, 79.
7. Mann, *Sikhism*, 79.
8. Mann, *Sikhism*, 80.
9. Mann, *Sikhism*, 81.
10. Mann, *Sikhism*, 81–82.
11. Quoted in Noss and Noss, *History*, 265.
12. Quoted in Noss and Noss, *History*, 265.
13. The story of Arjan Dev is found in *Sikh Religion* (Detroit, MI: Sikh Missionary Center, 1990), 116–21.
14. *Sikh Religion*, 162.
15. *Sikh Religion*, 164.
16. Mann, *Sikhism*, 100.

EAST ASIA

Lungshan, Taipei, Taiwan. Religious Taoist temples can be very confusing because at first, visitors are not sure whether they are in a Confucian, Buddhist, or Taoist temple. The answer is yes—you are in all three. Courtesy of Allen Timothy Chang.

CHAPTER 6

ANCIENT CHINESE RELIGION

The veil between the living and the dead has always been thin in the Asian world. The two are interdependent.

Confucianism and Taoism did not arise in a spiritual vacuum. There was an entire religious world into which Confucius and Lao Tzu entered and whose principles they used and tailored to their own needs. In what follows, we will examine briefly some of the major principles and practices of ancient China. By doing so, it will be come apparent how these were adapted to the thought of the great Chinese sages Confucius and Lao Tzu.

It is almost impossible in the Chinese world to separate Confucianism, Taoism, and Buddhism. Thus, those individuals practicing "Chinese traditional religion" today number 394 million and include all three of the religions in China and Taiwan.[1]

— YIN AND YANG

Yin and yang are the complementary energy modes of the universe. They arise as a product of examining the natural order of the world. Yang is the male energy mode and is characterized by being active, warm, dry, bright, procreative, and positive. Yin is fertile and breeding, dark, cold, wet, mysterious, secret, and negative.[2] First, these are *complementary* opposites, neither one being better than the other. They reflect the natural balance of the universe. Thus, we are not dealing with good and evil but rather with balance and imbalance. Therefore, the terms *positive* and *negative* are not loaded as are the words *good* and *bad*. These are the positives and negatives of physics. The positive pole of a battery is neither better nor worse than the negative pole. Both poles are essential to the proper functioning of any battery, just as neither is better or worse in a chemical solution composed of positive and negative ions. Applying this to contemporary life, this would mean that men really can run vacuum cleaners, change diapers, and do dishes and laundry—all those things that some men want to think are "women's work." Similarly, women are perfectly capable of assuming all the roles that some men would like to believe are their unique province, like executives, judges, governors, prime ministers, and other heads of state. By contrast, one author states, "They [men and women] show differing proportions of the qualities of each activity-mode, men being heavenly (that is, predominantly yang) and of great worth, whereas women are earthly (predominantly yin) and of less account."[3] While this may sadly be the reality in some of the Asian world today, it is contrary to the intent of the complementarity of yin and yang.

If we look at nature, we can see these opposites in operation. For example, masculinity and femininity are obviously yang and yin respectively. Similarly, light would be yang and darkness yin. Heat would clearly be yang, while cold would clearly be yin. Dryness is yang and wetness yin. Equally clearly, the sun would be yang, with the moon being yin.

A bit less clear might be the contrast between sky and earth, with sky being yang, because it is bright and dry, while the earth, which gives birth to life, is yin. Similarly, the south side of a hill, which receives the sunlight at the height of the day, is the yang side of the hill, while just over the ridge to the north is the yin, or shaded side. It is on the yin side that vegetation is usually found, while the yang side is often barren of most vegetation because of the heat. Other pairs which are less obvious, but are clear as one thinks about them, are listed here in yin-yang order: lovable/capable, beautiful/powerful, creative/methodical, intuitive/intelligent, and merciful/just. Many other pairs could be made and are probably somewhat subjective in the eye of the beholder. Once again, the purpose of all this is that there is a harmonious balance in the universe oriented around these complementary opposites.

To illustrate a further point, let us ask ourselves what energy mode a log lying in the forest might be. Clearly, it would be yin. But suppose we take that same log and put it in the fireplace. Very quickly it is yang as flames arise from it. This exemplifies the reality that all things contain within themselves their opposite. The symbol for yin and yang is two complementary, interlocking shapes: one bright in color (yang) and the other dark (yin). In the bright side there is a dark dot, and in the dark side there is a bright dot, signifying that even at the height of winter the seeds of summer are present, and vice versa.

Tao

The concept of Tao (pronounced "Dao") was present in early China. It was understood as being that which gives harmony and order to the universe and from which all things arise. Things in harmony with it follow a natural, regular process and tend toward peace, prosperity, and health. The harmony with Tao is not forced, but mystical. Just as one has to set a radio dial to the frequency on which the transmitter is broadcasting, so also persons have to be in mystical harmony with the Tao, according to ancient Chinese thought.

Divination

The desire to know the future is very much a part of human beings. Divination is a technique to answer questions about present or future needs in many cultures. We kid about reading the tea leaves, but when this activity is taken seriously, it is a form of divination through which one plumbs the future. Some cultures read the entrails of a bird or animal to determine whether a propitious time has come for a particular task. Perhaps they examine the spots on the liver to discern patterns. In China, the under shell of a turtle has been used as a divining device. A hole was partially drilled through the shell (after the turtle had been turned into soup!) and then hot lead was poured into the hole, causing cracks to radiate from the site. A shell could also be heated to create cracks, and then a diviner would read the cracks and tell his client

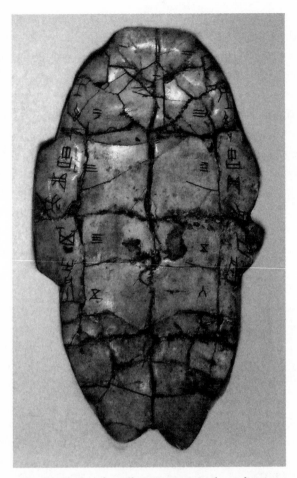

*Tortoise plastron from Shang Dynasty used as a divining
device. Courtesy of BabelStone.*

whether it was a good time to marry off his daughter, go on a trip, start a business, or enter into a trade relationship. The scapula bones of sheep and cattle were also used for this purpose.

However, a stylized divining device called the Pa Kua (Ba Gua) came into use. In the center of an octagon is a symbol of the complementary opposites, yin and yang. Around the edges are broken and unbroken lines in each of the eight sides. Using probably the most ancient book in China, the *I Ching* (Yi Jing), a diviner deciphers the lines for people and can tell them whether they should embark upon the project they are considering. This practice is still in use today.

— SPIRITS

All of life is filled with spirits. The heavens, the earth, and the lower regions all contain spirits. Some are good, some are malevolent, and some are in between; but if persons know how to treat them properly, they can be very beneficial. Sacrifices are made to all these spirits either to keep them away or to keep them on the side of those who sacrifice. In almost any Chinese restaurant, there will be a small table with incense, an orange, and a bowl of rice as an offering to the spirits. A close and important spirit even today is the Kitchen God, whose image is hung in the kitchen in Chinese households. He reports annually to the Jade Emperor. A family will sometimes try to bribe him by smearing sugar on his mouth to encourage him to give a good report. His image is burned yearly to enable him to ascend and make his report.

There are many more deities, such as the village deity. The hierarchy of deities in heaven mirrors the hierarchy of offices in the royal court. Thus, there are many gradations among the gods.

— ANCESTORS

The veil between the living and the dead has always been thin in the Asian world. The two are interdependent. "Prayers kept their [the ancestors'] memory alive, and sacrifices provided them with the food they needed."[4] As noted above, sacrifices are food offerings to the ancestors, as well as to spirits. The essence of these sacrifices is consumed by the ancestors, but not the material part which those who offer sacrifices may later consume, although the claim is made that it does not taste as good after the ancestors have had their portion. The ancestors may also be provided with articles for the afterlife by burning paper replicas of money, clothing, houses, or other essentials. Twice a year, in spring and in autumn, families visit the graves of their ancestors to leave sacrifices and offerings to them. In the spring, the graves are normally cleaned as well. If these acts of respect are not performed, the ancestors can become angry and cause problems for their family members or others.

The author was told in all seriousness about a busy intersection in Taipei, Taiwan. Accidents happened constantly. To help with the problem, the authorities erected four-way stop signs, but this created no change. They then put in stoplights, which still did not help. Finally, in desperation, they summoned a diviner who determined that there was a spirit present who had been improperly buried and had been trying to get someone's attention. As a result, the remains of the person were reburied in a more propitious place, and the accidents stopped. Such a scenario would be fully commensurate with Chinese beliefs about the relationship between the living and the dead.

— EMPEROR

The emperor was the person in China who kept the relationship between heaven and earth in harmony. Annually at the winter solstice, he would offer sacrifices to heaven on behalf of the entire nation. When the capitol came to Beijing, these offerings were done at the Altar of Heaven. If the emperor were to fail in his duties, the balance between heaven and earth would be upset, and disaster could befall China.

— CONCLUSION

This is the backdrop against which we must understand Confucianism and Taoism (Daoism). Many of the concepts we have seen here will reappear in slightly different guises as we examine these two great Chinese religious traditions.

Forbidden City, Beijing, China. Surrounding the Forbidden City were four major shrines at which the emperor worshiped and made sacrifices on behalf of himself and the nation.

---NOTES--

1. "Major Religions of the World Ranked by Number of Adherents," Adherents.com, last modified August 9, 2007, http://www.adherents .com/Religions_By_Adherents.html.
2. David S. Noss and John B. Noss, *A History of the World's Religions*, 9th ed. (New York: Macmillan College, 1994), 277–78.
3. Noss and Noss, *History*, 278.
4. Noss and Noss, *History*, 283.

Roger Keller standing in front of the tomb of Confucius in Qufu, China. Confucius is the founder of Confucianism.

Chapter 7

Confucianism

Confucianism's emphasis on a disciplined life and the centrality of the family makes it feel quite comfortable to Latter-day Saints.

No tradition has influenced China more than Confucianism. For two millennia, the teachings of Confucius served as the foundation for civil service examinations. The Chinese ethos is permeated with the thought of Confucius. Even the Cultural Revolution from 1966 to 1976 was unable to remove its influence, and so today Chinese proudly see Confucius as a great figure of their history. His tomb is in a lovely, well-cared-for area in Qufu, and the Confucian temple there is beautifully restored and maintained. While many people in China and other Asian countries may not claim to be "Confucianists," the values and relationships of the Confucian ethic are maintained. Confucius and his teachings have practically been transmitted in the DNA. He is simply part of them. Today there are in the world 394 million[1] practitioners of what one website calls Chinese traditional religion. Included in this category is Confucianism, but no matter what other religion Chinese persons and other Asians may claim, they usually live the Confucian values. It is the author's belief that Confucianism impacts far more people than the above number suggests.

—— ORIGINS ——

FOUNDER

Confucius was born in 551 BCE and died in 479 BCE. He came from a poor but respected family. His father, Shu-liang He, a soldier and district steward in Lu, died when Confucius was three.[2] After her husband's death, Confucius's widowed mother did everything she could to keep them alive, taking in laundry and doing other odd jobs. She wanted Confucius to be a gentleman and did what she could to see that he was educated. It is not clear whether she was able to pay for formal education, but somehow he gained knowledge through interacting with people around him. At age fifteen, Confucius made the decision to become a great scholar. At the age of eighteen, Confucius was married and had a son and later a daughter.[3] About the same time, he began a career in government, beginning with some accounting and looking after livestock. From there, he gradually moved up.[4]

In Confucius's early twenties, his mother died, and he went into three years of mourning. The power of this account is that the extended mourning period is exactly what Confucius would have done based on his philosophy of life, and we will examine this later as we look at his basic precepts. Following the mourning period, Confucius in his midtwenties began his teaching career.

Confucius taught a wide variety of subjects, something much easier to do in his day than now, because his library consisted of what are known as the Five Classics. Based on these, Confucius taught history, poetry, government, moral conduct, and music. The goal of all this teaching was to enable his students to become government officials, since in Confucius's mind this was a privilege for those trained in the values of a Confucian society, not something simply inherited by birth. Government would not change unless his students assumed governmental posts, for they would bring the values required to govern.

Lest one think that Confucius was merely a bookworm, we should note that he loved hunting and fishing, and it is said that he could knock down a duck in flight with a bow and arrow. Many cannot do

Confucius's goal was to train students to become moral government officials.

that with a shotgun! Basically, Confucius enjoyed life and probably would have been pleasant company.

Confucius's students were primarily from royal or wealthy families because they could pay for their children's education. Confucius had to live. But if a student really wanted to learn, whether he could pay or not, Confucius would accept him, perhaps reflecting his own desire to learn as a young man but being thwarted from formal education because of his poverty. Fundamentally, Confucius believed that anyone who wanted to learn should be permitted to do so. Thus, 2,500 years ago, he believed in universal public education, something which first occurred in the twentieth century in the United States with the growth of public school systems, community colleges, and state universities.

A divergence in the story occurs when Confucius is approximately fifty years old. Some accounts say that although Confucius sought all his life for a government position for himself, he never found one. Thus, at the end of his life, he felt that he had failed in his life mission.

The other tradition, represented by Annping Chin, holds that at age fifty, Confucius gained the major position of Minister of Crime in the government of Lu.[5] Some ancient writers paint the five years that Confucius held this position as almost a golden age, but that is probably overdrawn, since Confucius was forced after five years to flee Lu due to court intrigue and perhaps his own involvement in a plot to change the power structure of Lu.[6] Much of that attempt may have been due to his belief in "moral government." Sadly, to both ancient and modern ears, that may sound like an oxymoron. Probably the idea of moral government was no more popular 2,500 years ago than it is today, and to suggest that a ruler should rule for all his subjects and not for just a few may have caused Confucius to have to leave Lu. According to this tradition, Confucius wandered for thirteen years, teaching here and there and looking for a government position. Finally through the good offices of one of his students, he was invited to return to Lu. There he lived the last three years of his life teaching a little and giving occasional counsel to the duke. He died, however, feeling that he had failed.

How does one determine which of these two stories is historically correct? What creates a sense of failure? From the author's perspective, it is failure in a job, rather than never having it, that creates this sense. Suppose a person wanted to be president of an organization, submitted his or her résumé, but never received a call back. That certainly need not cause a sense of failure. One can just say the organization did not know what it was missing and go on with life. If one gained the position, however, and then failed to lead others to catch his or her vision, that would create a sense that one had failed. It is the author's belief that this is what happened to Confucius. Confucius truly believed that one Confucian gentleman in the midst of a barbarian society, merely by his presence, could change that society. If Confucius was Minister of Crime and was forced out of office through court intrigue, that would create a strong sense of failure, given his belief in the influence of the Confucian gentleman. In both accounts, he had to leave Lu around the age of fifty-five. The first account has no reason to explain this, while the second does. Thus it seems most likely that Confucius did have an opportunity to serve in government between the ages of fifty and fifty-five but failed to create the environment he had hoped to create. Hence, his life ended with a feeling that he had not succeeded as he had hoped he would.

AFTER CONFUCIUS

Confucius, however, did not live long enough to see his dreams realized. After his death, China entered what is called the Period of the Warring States, which lasted from 480 to 221 BCE. During this period, a pivotal figure was born who prepared the way for stabilization in China. The name of this person was Mencius (Meng-zi), who lived from 370 to 286 BCE. Mencius's story is somewhat like Confucius's. According to the traditional account of Mencius's life, his father died when Mencius was quite young, and his mother exemplified the ideal of motherhood. Initially, they lived near a cemetery. When Mencius's mother discovered that he was reenacting the funeral rituals which he watched, she decided to move near a market, but then Mencius showed an inordinate interest in buying and selling. To avoid this, she moved near a school, hoping that he would copy the behavior of the teachers and students, and this seems ultimately to have led to Mencius becoming a great scholar like his model, Confucius. He firmly believed in the goodness of human beings and their ability to follow the good when they saw it in others because he believed each person is predisposed to that which is good. He also believed, like Confucius, that he was following the guidance of heaven in his teaching.

During the reign of emperor Wu Di (156–87 BCE), Dong Zhong-shu, a Confucian scholar, encouraged the emperor to look closely at the principles of Confucianism in order to end confusion among the people concerning what school or standard they should follow. The emperor agreed and established an academy for the teaching of Confucian values. From this point until the fall of the Manchu-Ching dynasty in 1912 CE, Confucianism was the philosophy that guided China.

SCRIPTURES

As noted earlier, Confucius's teaching was based primarily on the Five Classics, texts from ancient Chinese thinkers and philosophers.

Tradition says that Confucius edited these, and they are as follows, beginning with the oldest. The first is the *Classic of Changes* and is used by diviners to determine whether persons should do things at certain times. Confucius recommended it for finding moral and metaphysical meaning in life. The second book is the *Classic of History* and contains material from the early Chou dynasty (1100–1000 BCE), which Confucius held to be the golden age in China. The third book is the *Classic of Poetry*, containing about three hundred poems all set to music. The fourth book is the *Spring and Autumn Annals*, which contains a chronology of events in the principality of Lu, Confucius's home province, from 720 to 480 BCE. Finally, there is the *Classic of Rites*, which contains an account of rituals that were both public and private.

In addition to the Five Classics, there are also the Four Books. Most of these postdate Confucius, and the first of the books is the *Analects*, the sayings of Confucius. While loosely organized, the *Analects* capture the essence of Confucius's thought on relationships, what is proper, the true man, and so on. Second is the *Book of Mencius*, which is well organized and about twice as long as the *Analects*.[7] Third is the *Great Learning*, which was a chapter in the *Classic of Rites*. The introductory chapter is considered to be from Confucius, with the following ten chapters being commentaries on the first by Tseng-tzu. The focus is on the moral ruler as an example for his people. Finally is the *Doctrine of the Mean*, also a chapter in the *Classic of Rites*, which teaches that persons should avoid going to the extremes in any aspect of life.[8]

— CONFUCIAN PHILOSOPHY

HISTORY

As we have seen, the period from 1100 to 1000 BCE was China's golden age in Confucius's eyes. His model ruler was the Duke of Chou, who ruled in this time frame. Thus, the place to look for the values that had been lost from China, whose loss had led the country to the edge of the Warring States Period, was the discipline of history. History was not some irrelevant discipline but rather the very heart of insight into the future, which explains Confucius's love of the Five Classics.

MODEL

According to Confucius, persons cannot teach until they embody that which they teach. It is not good enough to say "Do as I say, but not as I do." In the end, learning should lead to self-improvement, and only then does a person have the right to teach, rule, or guide others.

VIRTUES THAT FOSTER COMMUNITY

Li ("observing ritual propriety"). Li is the foundational principle of Confucianism. It is the glue which holds society together. Failing to practice Li is much like having a stack of canned corn in a grocery store. Someone decides to pull out a bottom can, and the whole structure tumbles down. So it is with Li. If Li is not practiced, society will disintegrate and fall apart. Confucius puts it this way:

> What I have learned is this, that of all the things that people live by, *li* is the greatest. Without *li* we do not know how to conduct a proper worship of the spirits of the universe; or how to establish the proper status of the king and the ministers, the ruler and the ruled, and the elders and the juniors; or how to establish the moral relationships between the sexes; between parents and children, and between brothers; or how to distinguish the different degrees of relationships in the family. That is why a gentleman holds *li* in such high regard.[9]

The word *Li* originally meant "sacrifice," and then it was used for "ritual." In Confucius's hands, it came to mean observing ritual propriety, politeness, or good form and was related to the five relationships that Confucius believed were foundational to society. These five relationships are the following:

Ruler-Subject
Husband-Wife
Father-Son
Elder Brother-Younger Brother
Friend-Friend

It is within actual relationships that Li functions. Each person understands how a relationship is to take place, for Li defines the role of each partner. For example, I may be a subject of a ruler who calls me into his presence, and we both know the script. I do not speak until spoken to. When the sovereign addresses me, he does so in very condescending language. In response, I must use language that exalts him and minimizes me. As I leave, I never turn my back on the ruler. Returned missionaries from Asian countries report the reality of this situation. When they are out on the street, local people will talk to them using the forms of address for cats, dogs, and little children. The missionaries are on the bottom of the totem pole. However, on Wednesday night, the missionaries teach an English class, and all of a sudden they are teachers, the most respected vocation in a Confucian society! Now the language used in relationship to them is from below to above. They are in the position of "the rulers," and the whole structure of language switches, but to underline their position as servants of the people, they have been asked by mission presidents not to receive the exalted terminology of a superior.

In the husband-wife relationship, the husband is to treat his wife with righteousness and provide for and support her. She in return is to show righteous behavior before him and be obedient to his will, but it is not a harsh relationship. Similarly, a father is to teach and guide his son. The son in return is to be obedient to his father and respect him, meaning that he would do nothing that would bring shame to his father or the family.

The relationship between brothers in a Confucian society is more formal than that in the West. The eldest brother has the responsibility of caring for his younger siblings, and therefore the younger brothers and sisters are to respect and obey him. As we went over this in class one day, an Asian-American student put up her hand and said that she finally understood her father and her uncle. She had never understood why her father was so formal to his brother. Of course, the brother was the elder of the two, and her father gave the prescribed deference to him, which would puzzle most Western persons. Finally, in the friend-friend relationship, if there is a difference in age, the older one takes the lead and the younger one follows behind, figuratively speaking. Thus, as with brothers, age plays a role. These five relationships can also be applied to women, with age being a major determinant in how the relationship proceeds. In the end, Li governs all life.

> *Li* is based on heaven, patterned on earth, deals with the worship of the spirits, and is extended to the rites and ceremonies of funerals, sacrifices to ancestors, archery, carriage driving, "capping" [the ceremony of putting a cap on a boy when he is considered to have entered manhood], marriage, and court audience, or exchange of diplomatic visits. Therefore the Sage shows the people this principle of a rationalized social order (*li*) and through it everything becomes right in the family, the state and the world.[10]

Latter-day Saints certainly do not have anything that is as formal as Li, but there are expected proprieties within the church. For example, respect is shown for seniority in various councils of the church. The President of the church always precedes his First Counselor, who is then followed by the Second Counselor. Likewise, in the Quorum of Twelve, the Apostles sit in order of seniority at general conference and in meetings. While not demanded in the church handbooks, it is normal for priesthood holders to wear white shirts as a symbol of purity when performing sacred duties. Males who serve in leadership positions or in the temple normally do not have mustaches or beards. Thus there are certain "proper" things to do in the church, but human relationships are generally not defined as they are with Li.

Jen (Ren) ("humaneness"). The danger of Li is that persons may go through the ritual motions but have no real concern for the other. This is where the supreme virtue of Jen enters the stage, for Jen is a virtue of reciprocity. It takes what potentially could be very stale and meaningless Li and makes it a virtue filled with concern for the other. Jen is the supreme human virtue and is such that no one, not even Confucius or the Duke of Chou, fully realized it.

> I have not seen a person who loved virtue, or one who hated what was not virtuous. He who loved virtue would esteem nothing above it. He who hated what is not virtuous would practice virtue in such a way that he would not allow anything that is not virtuous to approach his person.

Is any one able for one day to apply his strength to virtue? I have not seen the case in which his strength would be sufficient. If there might be any such case, I have not seen it.[11]

Despite this assessment, Jen is still the goal, as is perfection for Latter-day Saints, and is the ideal to be manifest. There are several translations of the word Jen—goodness, humaneness, humanness, and love. Jen recognizes that all of us are facing similar conditions and that we should make life better for each other. By doing so, we make life better for ourselves, since the wants and needs of others are also our wants and needs.

As noted, Jen humanizes Li because it is a virtue of inclusion and concern for other people. In Latter-day Saint terms, it is charity or love, meaning the pure love of Christ. It captures very well the idea of the Golden Rule (i.e., "Do unto others as you would have them do unto you"). The pure love of Christ means that all people have value and that we should be willing to sacrifice ourselves on their behalf. There should be no self-interest, for that was how Christ loved us. He gave himself, without a thought for himself, that we might have life.

Hsiao ("filial responsibility"). Hsiao is "filial responsibility," or obligations to parents and ancestors. It was the loss of Hsiao, along with other virtues, that created the cultural slide from the golden age to Confucius's day with its political anarchy. The Master said, "If the son for three years [after his father's death] does not alter from the way of his father, he may be called filial."[12] If the descendants of the Duke of Chou had done this, the virtues practiced by him would have been passed on. Sadly, from Confucius's point of view, they did not imbibe this virtue and changed the moral value of society. In this vein, mourning for one's parents, as did Confucius for his mother, means that for three years the children do not change the way the parent did things in business, in government, or in the home. Not to follow this admonition is a violation of both Hsiao and of Li. The following passage gives a sense of how Hsiao would work itself out in daily life:

While his parents are both alive, at their regular meals, morning and evening, the eldest son and his wife will encourage them to eat everything. They themselves will eat what is left. When the father is dead, and the mother still alive, the eldest son should wait upon her at her meals. The wives of the other sons will do with what is left as in the former case. The children should have the sweet, soft, and oily things that are left.[13]

Underlining the importance of the respect for parents and ancestors was a poll that was taken a decade ago of which the author was told. Asians and Westerners were asked the question "If you, your wife, and your mother-in-law fell off a ferry and you could only save one of them, who would it be?" The universal answer for Westerners was the wife, while the answer for Asians was the mother-in-law. Older people have a very special place in Confucian society.

Given this, there is certainly nothing more central to Latter-day Saint theology than the family. There is usually clear respect for the patriarchs and matriarchs when families gather. The authority of parents is affirmed by the church, but any kind of abuse of that authority is strongly condemned. The authority must be tempered with love in the same way that Li is tempered by Jen. Ancestors are especially important when it comes to temple work, for the ordinances of the temple bind generation after generation together. Those imbued with Confucian values should find the message of the temple very exciting because most of these persons have ancestral lineages that go back numerous generations. To know that they can be bound to these ancestors for eternity through the temple ordinances is very comforting to Asian peoples who accept the fullness of the gospel.

Cheng Ming ("rectification of names"). The translation of Cheng Ming is "rectification of names." In other words, persons should be what they are called. Names should correspond to realities. If people are peasants, they should be good peasants. If they are rulers, they should be good rulers. If they are merchants, they should be good merchants. The doctrine is not, however, to keep the huddled masses in their places. This is not a doctrine of castes, because there is mobility in a Confucian society. Mobility is accomplished through education. Persons may be born peasants, but through education they can become officials in the government. After all, this is why Confucius was teaching young men, and we should remember that he would take a promising student, even if that student could not pay. Thus, Cheng Ming identifies people by their role in society.

Chung Yung ("the golden mean"). Chung Yung is often translated as "the golden mean." It is the concept that persons should not go to extremes in any aspect of life. In our language, it would mean that we should not be too conservative or too liberal; too poor or too rich; too slow or too fast; too strict or too permissive. There should simply be moderation in all that individuals and groups do.

Chun Tzu ("the superior man"). A final concept is that of the Chun Tzu, the "superior man" or the Confucian gentleman. This is precisely what Confucius is seeking to create—a man who embodies all the virtues listed above so that he can rule with integrity and morality. Ruling is not a matter of birth or right but rather of nobility of spirit and righteousness, hardly items which are sought in the political arenas of today in any country. The Confucian virtues have all too often been replaced by wealth, power, and cynicism, to the detriment of societies.

GOVERNMENT

Confucius's goal was to bring harmony to a Chinese society that was on the verge of 260 years of chaos. As we have seen, it was the failure on the part of China's rulers for the better part of five hundred years to maintain the virtues of the golden age that had led, in Confucius's view, to this sorry state of affairs.

Confucius believed that just and moral government would lead to the respect, loyalty, and support of the people, and this would certainly be so, if it were possible to find one. Mencius articulates what such a government might look like:

> By benevolence the three dynasties gained the empire, and by not being benevolent they lost it. By the same means are determined the decaying and flourishing, the preservation and perishing, of states. If the emperor is not benevolent, he cannot preserve the empire from passing from him. If the sovereign of a state is not benevolent, he cannot preserve his kingdom. If a high noble or great officer is not benevolent, he cannot preserve his ancestral temple. . . . Therefore, an intelligent ruler will

regulate the livelihood of the people, so as to make sure that they shall have enough to serve their parents, and enough to support their wives and children. He ensures that in good years they shall always be abundantly satisfied, and that in bad years they shall escape the danger of perishing. Then he may urge them to what is good, and they will do it, for in this case the people will follow after the good with ease.[14]

Thus, according to Confucius and Mencius, government was for the people. The ruler was to see that the littlest peasant was well fed, well housed, well clothed, and happy. He was to rule for all his people, not just for his cronies or the wealthy and powerful in society. To rule poorly was sufficient for the Mandate of Heaven to be withdrawn from the ruler and for the people to revolt against his rule. In addition, the ruler was to consult with his people to determine what they wanted and needed. For that day and time, and even today in many places in the world, this was and would be a radical thought. So while government was to be for the people and in consultation with them, Confucius left it to Abraham Lincoln to say "by the people" because he did not believe this. Government was to be carried out by the superior man or the Confucian gentleman schooled in Confucian ethics, virtues, and morality. No one had a right to rule. Rather, the privilege was earned through study of the Confucian classics and finally through an examination on them. Then one could embark upon rulership.

NEO-CONFUCIANISM

Because traditional Confucianism does not contain a transcendent element, Confucianism has usually been held in combination with another religion. Persons may be Confucian and Buddhist. They may be Confucian and Taoist. They may be Confucian, Shinto, and Buddhist. They add to Confucianism a religion or religions which deal with elements beyond the social and which provide the missing transcendent dimension. This is still the way Confucianism functions in today's world, for the most part. However, historically, some Confucian scholars tried to address the issues raised by Buddhists and Taoists and gave rise to what is termed "Neo-Confucianism."

There are two principal figures in this movement: (1) Chu Hsi (1130–1200 CE) and (2) Wang Yang-ming (1473–1529). Chu Hsi

Hall of prayer for good harvest located on the Temple of Heaven compound, where the emperor came to worship and make sacrifices.

believed that nature contained the laws and principles of the universe. He held that there was the Great Ultimate, which was the law or rational principle of the universe. It was the rational principle Li elevated to the cosmic level, and while he did not personify it, Chu Hsi did say that it was like a universal ordering will. The Great Ultimate impelled the Universal Vital Force, which seems to generate matter and to cause movement and change in that matter, thereby bringing into being yin and yang and the five elements.

Thus Chu Hsi saw something outside the human being as producing the world of reality. While exploring the transcendent dimension of life, Chu Hsi denied what most Chinese held as absolutely sacred, that the souls of one's ancestors continue to exist beyond death. The rituals honoring them were still appropriate acts of respect, but there was no reality to them after death. Finally, he incorporated meditation into his Confucianism, but it was self-examination to evaluate his own moral situation.[15]

Wang Yang-ming held a contrasting view. Wang held that reason was not external to human beings but rather resided in the mind, thereby giving order and reality to the world and objects in it. This reason was moral reason and was born with us, meaning that humans are good. He, like Chu Hsi, practiced a form of meditation he called "tranquil repose" that was similar to Zen and thus in reality quite different from Chu Hsi's meditation.

— WORSHIP AND RITUALS

As noted earlier, it is very hard to separate Confucianism, Taoism (which we will treat in the next chapter), and Buddhism from one another in the Chinese world. A single individual may practice all three simultaneously. Thus in this section we will look at rites and rituals that are closest to Confucian emphases, and reserve other rites and rituals for the Taoism chapter.

OFFICIAL RITUALS

Worship may be categorized as official or popular.[16] Official worship fits with Confucianism, while popular worship will be reserved for the Taoism chapter. Official worship has fixed times and places as well as fixed gods or ancestors. The center of formal worship in China became Beijing, where the emperor resided. Surrounding the Forbidden City were four major shrines at which the emperor worshiped and made sacrifices on behalf of himself and the nation.[17] The most important of these was the Altar of Heaven located to the south of the Forbidden City. Here the emperor came on the winter solstice to offer sacrifices to Shang Ti ("Sovereign on High" or "High Lord") or to T'ien ("Heaven"). As he did so, he sought help to avoid droughts, the blight of insects, or the scourge of invasion. On the other hand, he sought Heaven's blessing for a good harvest, peace within the land, and permission to rule. Besides the offerings, music, dance, and the reading of prayer documents were part of the service, and only the emperor could perform these acts. The Altar of Heaven was round, focusing on the infinite, and was associated with the yang principle. On the summer solstice, the emperor went to the Altar of the Earth, where he offered sacrifices to the earth. The architecture was square, in contrast to the Altar of Heaven, symbolizing finitude, yin, and the five elements.

To the east was the Temple of Ancestors. Once again, the emperor would perform annual sacrifices to the royal ancestors, offering a bull, a sheep, a pig, vegetable products, and crops from the field to them. He also provided wine for the earth. Divinations were performed in the presence of the imperial ancestors. The enthronement of a new emperor was announced here, as well as imperial marriages and states of war.[18] To the west were the Altars of Land and Grain, to which the emperor came twice yearly. In the spring he would offer sacrifices for a good harvest, and in the fall he would offer sacrifices of thanksgiving. Confucius would have wholeheartedly approved of all these sacrifices, for if they were not done, Li would be violated, harmony broken, and the nation endangered.

CONFUCIUS

It may surprise many, since Confucius simply does not tell us about his personal religious beliefs, that he himself became an object of worship, apparently beginning among his disciples shortly after his death. With the rise of the Han dynasty (206 BCE to 9 CE), Confucianism became the guiding philosophy with Confucius being worshiped at a state level. By the seventh century CE, he was worshiped as the greatest teacher and the perfect moral model for ten thousand generations, and sacrifices were made to him. Many Confucian temples were established across East Asia, but the most important was the one in his hometown of Qufu in today's Shandong Province. Annually, the emperor went there to honor Confucius. Xinzhong Yao notes that "in many of these temples there was an inscription: 'He forms a triad with Heaven and Earth.'"[19] The "he," of course, is Confucius.

At this point I add a Latter-day Saint reflection because Latter-day Saints are sometimes mistakenly believed to worship Joseph Smith. Latter-day Saints, however, understand that there is a difference between worship of a person and reverence for what that person did and was. This is the case with Joseph. Latter-day Saints revere him because he was God's chosen vessel to restore, at this time in history, the very same gospel that had been given to Adam and Eve. D&C 135:3, written by John Taylor shortly after Joseph's martyrdom, says, "Joseph Smith, the Prophet and Seer of the Lord, has done more, save Jesus only, for the salvation of men in this world, than any other man that ever lived in it." To some, this may sound almost blasphemous, but when we consider what Joseph did, if his message is true, then it is just a simple statement of fact. Through Joseph, God made available all the effects of the Atonement of Christ to every member of the human race who has lived on this earth—past, present, or future. Without Joseph or someone like him, what Jesus did for us would have been available to only a few persons who lived when he was on the earth. With Joseph, however, the keys of the authority were restored to him to bind in heaven the saving ordinances of the gospel done on earth. Those ordinances could be done both for the living and the dead, thereby extending the Atonement of Christ to the entirety of this earth's human family. It is little wonder that Latter-day Saints *reverence* Joseph, but they *worship* their Heavenly Father through Jesus Christ, whom they also worship.

RITES OF PASSAGE

As already noted, rituals of all kinds were exceptionally important to Confucius because they were manifestations of Li. They reflected the binding principle of society without which the very foundations of the social order were endangered. Thus rites of passage are appropriate to the Confucian chapter.

Birth rites reflect the union of yin and yang and the production of an heir, if the child is male. Celebrations occur on the third,

*Entrance to the temple of Confucius and his tomb
located in his hometown, Qufu.*

thirtieth, and one hundredth days after the birth, as well as the year anniversary. They are joyous rites, although perhaps a bit muted for a girl. Offerings and reports are made to the ancestors. The only negative aspect of birth arises from the polluting character of the birth blood, which makes the mother ritually impure for a month. She is thus isolated from all but her husband and other women. Xinzhong Yao suggests that the practical aspect of this was to protect her from disease.[20]

The rite of passage into adulthood was "capping" or "hairdo or coiffure," the former for boys and the latter for girls. As with so many rituals or acts in Chinese society, the propitious time for the transition to adulthood is determined through divination. There is disagreement about the age of maturity, some indicating that it is sixteen, while others assert that it should be eighteen or even twenty. The boy is capped three times as blessings are sought from heaven, the earth, and the water under the world. A new name is also given, symbolizing the attainment of maturity. The formula used at the capping ceremony is instructive:

> In this auspicious month and on this lucky day, we endue you with the cap for the first time. Put away your childish thoughts from now on, and see that you keep guard upon the virtues of your manhood. Then shall your years all be fair, and your good fortune grow from more to more.[21]

Marriage is the next rite of passage. It is a bond between families and is arranged by a go-between or matchmaker. It begins with a request for the girl's "eight characters," meaning the year, month, day, and time of her birth. If the girl's family provides these, they indicate that they would look upon the union favorably. These eight characters are balanced with the male's eight characters to see if the match would be a good one. One gets a little sense of what this is about by looking at the Chinese zodiac on a restaurant place mat. Some combinations are fortuitous while others are seen as problematic. Upon marriage, the wife moves in with the husband's family.[22]

The final rites relate to death. The mourning period upon death may be only three days, ninety days as in Taiwan, or up to three years. The latter was what Confucius practiced, and for him to do less would have been to fail in practicing filial responsibility. Traditionally, coarse, white clothing was worn as a symbol of mourning, and thus a white wedding dress in the West would cause some confusion for a person from the Chinese culture. Today, black clothing may also be worn as a sign of mourning. The things that will be needed in the afterlife were buried with the body, such as clothing and paper money, which is special money to be used at funerals. It is also burned to send it to the world of the ancestors, who are kept fully informed of the events through reports, sacrifices, and offerings.[23]

— WOMEN

The Confucian society was definitely patriarchal. Women played a secondary role to men but found their role in the bearing of children, particularly male children, who would become the heirs of the family resources. According to Confucius, a man was to treat his wife with righteousness and was to support her and care for her. She in return was to support her husband and be obedient to him. But with the family being central, she had a powerful position, although she was always more in the background than was her husband. These values still hold, although Western values are causing the two roles to be equalized.

Among Latter-day Saints, men and women are equal before God, but in daily life they may have different responsibilities. "The Family: A Proclamation to the World" makes this statement:

> By divine design, fathers are to preside over their families in love and righteousness and are responsible to provide the necessities of life and protection for their families. Mothers are primarily responsible for the nurture of their children. In these sacred responsibilities, fathers and mothers are obligated to help one another as equal partners.[24]

Thus, there are differences in roles in life with the husband being the provider while the wife cares for the home and children. Some outside the Latter-day Saint community see the woman's role as demeaning, but from the Latter-day Saint perspective, this is the way God designed the world to be. There is simply no greater role in life than raising the next generation, and as the Proclamation states, this is the responsibility of both the father and the mother "as equal partners." Perhaps the terms "partner" and "companion" capture best the Latter-day Saint understanding of the relationship between husband and wife.

— CONCLUSION

Confucianism is a powerful philosophy for regulating society and has more influence on Chinese and Chinese-influenced cultures than does any other system. Its emphasis on a disciplined life and the centrality of the family makes it feel quite comfortable to Latter-day Saints.

— NOTES

1. "Major Religions of the World Ranked by Number of Adherents," Adherents.com, last modified August 9, 2007, http://www.adherents .com/Religions_By_Adherents.html.
2. Annping Chin, *The Authentic Confucius: A Life of Thought and Politics* (New York: Scribner, 2007), 24–25.
3. Chin, *Authentic Confucius*, 25.
4. Chin, *Authentic Confucius*, 25.
5. Chin, *Authentic Confucius*, 26.
6. Chin, *Authentic Confucius*, 28–29.
7. Robert E. Van Voorst, *Anthology of World Scriptures*, 6th ed. (Mason, OH: Cengage Learning, 2008), 141.
8. Van Voorst, *Anthology*, 141.
9. David S. Noss and John B. Noss, *A History of the World's Religions*, 9th ed. (New York: Macmillan College, 1994), 320.
10. Noss and Noss, *History*, 321.
11. Van Voorst, *Anthology*, 148.
12. Van Voorst, *Anthology*, 150.
13. Van Voorst, *Anthology*, 149.
14. Van Voorst, *Anthology*, 153–54.
15. Noss and Noss, *History*, 342–44.
16. Xinzhong Yao, "Chinese Religions," in *Worship*, ed. Jean Holm with John Bowker (New York: Pinter, 1994), 159–60.
17. Xinzhong Yao, "Chinese Religions," in *Sacred Place*, ed. Jean Holm with John Bowker (New York: Pinter, 1994), 176–77.
18. Yao, *Sacred Place*, 180.
19. Yao, *Worship*, 168.

20. Xinzhong Yao, "Chinese Religions," in *Rites of Passage*, ed. Jean Holm with John Bowker (New York: Pinter, 1994), 159–60.

21. Yao, *Rites of Passage*, 162.

22. Yao, *Rites of Passage*, 163–64.

23. Yao, *Rites of Passage*, 166–67.

24. The First Presidency and Council of the Twelve Apostles of The Church of Jesus Christ of Latter-day Saints, "The Family: A Proclamation to the World," *Ensign*, October 1995, http://www.lds.org/library/display /0,4945,161-1-11-1,00.html.

Chi Nan Temple, Muzha, Taiwan. A temple may be dedicated to one god, in this case Lü Dongbin, one of the Eight Immortals, but also include figures of the Yellow Emperor, Confucius, Buddha, and Lao Tzu, as well as others.
Courtesy of Kasuga Huang.

CHAPTER 8

TAOISM

*Taoism has in its philosophical form profound similarities
with the Spirit-guided life which Latter-day Saints seek to live.*

Taoism (Daoism) comes in two basic forms—philosophical
Taoism and religious Taoism. We will treat both but will begin
with philosophical. The kind of Taoism practiced in the world
today is religious Taoism, a form closely allied with ancient Chinese
religious life and somewhat foreign to Latter-day Saint experience.
Philosophical Taoism, on the other hand, has several aspects which
will feel familiar to members of The Church of Jesus Christ of Latter-
day Saints.

— ORIGINS

FOUNDER

Among scholars there is debate about the founder of philosophical Taoism to the extent that some question whether Lao Tzu,
the traditional founding figure, even existed. Interestingly, modern
scholars of religion have become more and more skeptical about
knowing anything about the religious figures of the past. This is true

even of Jesus, many scholars claiming that the Gospels contain no historically accurate information about him. It is the sense of the current author that this "doubting Thomas" attitude has gone too far. Thus for the purposes of this chapter, we will accept Lao Tzu as the founder of the philosophical Taoist school, and we will accept him as the author of the foundational text, the *Tao Te Ching* (or *Dao de Jing*).

According to tradition, Lao Tzu was born in 604 BCE. It seems that Lao Tzu held a government position, perhaps keeper of the royal archives. However, he became discouraged with society and decided to leave. As we have seen with Confucius, who was a slightly younger contemporary of Lao Tzu, China in the sixth century BCE stood on the verge of the Period of the Warring States. Thus, China was bordering on anarchy, and it seems to be this state of affairs with which Lao Tzu became disenchanted. Tradition holds that Lao Tzu mounted his black ox and left the city. As he arrived at the western pass, the gatekeeper stopped him, and when he discovered that Lao Tzu was leaving, he asked him to write down his thoughts. In five thousand Chinese characters and eighty-one chapters, Lao Tzu wrote the *Tao Te Ching*, climbed back on his black ox, and disappeared into the sunset, never to be heard from again. Thus, there is no death date for him.

Lao Tzu had a disciple who lived about three hundred years after him by the name of Chuang Tzu (died 275 BCE). Chuang Tzu, who wrote the *Chuang Tzu*, is usually credited with being the best interpreter of the *Tao Te Ching*. In this chapter, we will use parts of the *Tao Te Ching* as well as parts of the *Chuang Tzu* to come to an understanding of philosophical Taoism. One of the reasons to treat Taoism after Confucianism is that Chuang Tzu liked to poke fun at the Confucianists, and if we reversed the order, we would miss some of his jokes.

As we will see, the *Tao Te Ching* is not always easy to understand, but in a very real sense it is not to be "understood," at least with the mind. As we have already noted, Eastern religions do not see reality as something that can be comprehended intellectually. Ultimate reality is to be experienced, not thought about in the abstract. We will also discover that some of the *Tao Te Ching* may seem contradictory to Western ears. In reality, it is not contradictory at all but rather *complementary*.

Lao Tzu, who was disenchanted with society, wrote the Tao Te Ching *and departed, never to be heard of again. Courtesy of Tommy Wong.*

If we remember that yin and yang are complementary opposites and that everything contains within itself its opposite, then we will understand the *Tao Te Ching*. Some literary statements contain within themselves these opposites, and they have a name—"reversions." Thus, if the Taoist statements seem confusing, we should relax, not worry if we do not understand every word, and let the essence of philosophical Taoism seep into our hearts. With philosophical Taoism, as with Zen Buddhism, we need to be prepared for a new experience.

—— PRINCIPLES OF PHILOSOPHICAL TAOISM ——

THE TAO

Not too surprisingly, the Tao is the center of Taoism, but as we shall see, it is indefinable. We get a sense of this from the first chapter of the *Tao Te Ching*.

Tao called Tao is not Tao.

Names can name no lasting name.

Nameless: the origin of heaven and earth.
Naming: the mother of ten thousand things.

Empty of desire, perceive mystery.
Filled with desire, perceive manifestations.

These have the same source, but different names.
   Call them both deep—
      Deep and again deep:
The gateway to all mystery.[1]

The above is, of course, crystal clear, but in the off chance that something has been missed, we will look at Chuang Tzu's commentary on the passage. As will be noted, Chuang Tzu often comments in story form.

Ether asked Infinite, "Do you know Tao?"

"I don't know," replied Infinite.

He asked No-action the same question and No-action replied, "I know Tao."

"So you know Tao. Can you specify?"

"Certainly. I know that Tao can be high, can be low, can be centered and can be dispersed. These are some of the specifications that I know."

Ether told No-beginning of No-action's words and asked, "Thus Infinite says he does not know and No-action says he knows. Who is right?"

"The one who thinks he does not know is profound, and the one who thinks he knows is shallow. The former deals with the inner reality, the latter with appearance."

Ether raised his head and sighed: "Then one who does not know really knows, and one who knows really does not know. Who knows this knowledge without knowing?"[2]

Once again, in the event that something has been lost in translation, we will turn to another source for clarity. This is something even I can understand, because it gets down to the level where I live. The commentator in this case is Winnie the Pooh.

"We've come to wish you a Very Happy Thursday," said Pooh, when he had gone in and out once or twice just to make sure that he *could* get out again.

"Why, what's going to happen on Thursday?" asked Rabbit, and when Pooh had explained, and Rabbit, whose life was made up of Important Things, said, "Oh, I thought you'd really come about something," they sat down for a little, . . . and by-and-by Pooh and Piglet went on again. The wind was behind them now, so they didn't have to shout.

"Rabbit's clever," said Pooh thoughtfully.

"Yes," said Piglet, "Rabbit's clever."

"And he has Brain."

"Yes," said Piglet, "Rabbit has Brain."

There was a long silence.

"I suppose," said Pooh, "that that's why he never understands anything."[3]

From the above, several things should be clear. From the first passage, we should be able to see that names cannot capture the Tao. It is in and behind all things but is indefinable. When we do try to put names to it, all we do is name phenomena that arise from it. The Tao is a mystery. From the *Chuang Tzu* passage and from Winnie the Pooh, we learn that reality is not captured by the intellect. Tao is something that transcends all definitions. Rabbit never understands anything because he is trying to capture it with "Brain." So, likewise, we need to experience reality rather than trying to think about it. A further passage gives a bit more insight into the Tao.

Tao is empty—
    Its use never exhausted.
Bottomless—
    The origin of all things.

It blunts sharp edges,
    Unties knots,
    Softens glare,
    Becomes one with the dusty world.

Deeply subsistent—
I don't know whose child it is.

It is older than the Ancestor.[4]

Here I would suggest as the meaning of this passage that we learn that all things arise from the Tao but that it is not sharp, complicated, or brilliant. It is close to us where we live. It has no origin of its own. It is self-subsistent. Lin Yutang says this about the Tao:

> The Tao of the Taoist is the divine intelligence of the universe, the source of things, the life-giving principle; it informs and transforms all things; it is impersonal, impartial, and has little regard for individuals. . . . Above all, the one important message of Taoism is the oneness and spirituality of the material universe.[5]

WU-WEI

A central concept in philosophical Taoism is that of *wu-wei*, a term which means "inaction" or "nonaction." It is not, however, what it seems at first blush. A working definition might be as follows (and notice this is a reversion): wu-wei means inaction or nonaction, which is the Taoist action by which all things are accomplished and the world is conquered. We can learn more about wu-wei from chapter 22 of the *Tao Te Ching*:

Crippled becomes whole,
Crooked becomes straight,
Hollow becomes full,
Worn becomes new,
Little becomes more,
Much becomes delusion.

Therefore Sages cling to the One
    And take care of this world;
Do not display themselves
    And therefore shine.
Do not assert themselves
    And therefore stand out.
Do not praise themselves
    And therefore succeed.
Are not complacent
    And therefore endure;

Do not contend

And therefore no one under heaven

Can contend with them.[6]

As we seek to understand wu-wei, we will begin with the portion which recommends noncontention. As we do, we should ask the question "How many people does it take to make a fight?" Obviously, it takes two, and if we will not participate in fights, there can be none.

During a father-son overnight outing, I was not paying too much attention to what was going on with the boys. Suddenly, I realized that people were flying off the top of a nearby dirt pile. I looked and discovered that the boys were playing King of the Mountain with my son on top, and the rest of the boys were trying to get him off. My son today is a fifth-degree black belt in Kenpo Karate, and at that point he was pretty well advanced. As I watched, all he was doing was using his hands to pass the force of the other boys' rushes on by him so that he just helped them go where their momentum would naturally take them—flying off the top of the hill. This was wu-wei—not meeting force with force but rather letting things take their natural course, which was clearly to his advantage.

Another question we might ask is "How many great people do we know who have to tell us they are great?" True greatness just naturally shows. Sages "do not praise themselves and therefore succeed." A Hindu Guru naturally draws people to him because they see qualities of spirituality that they want for themselves. He never has to hang out a sign. So it is with the holy men and women of virtually any faith. Greatness is evident. This is wu-wei.

One final example of wu-wei in the above passage is found in the words "crooked becomes straight." Anyone who has ever traveled in the Far East knows that scaffolding is usually made from bamboo and not from steel or aluminum. Why? Because bamboo bends. In a typhoon, bamboo bends before the wind but does not break, whereas steel or aluminum would bend permanently and henceforth be useless. But as the natural force of the wind subsides, the bamboo straightens and is once more useful. This is wu-wei.

We see the power of wu-wei in the following passage on world peace.

Tao endures without a name,
Yet nothing is left undone.
If kings and lords could possess it,
All beings would transform themselves.

Transformed, they desire to create;
I quiet them through nameless simplicity.
Then there is no desire.

No desire is serenity,

And the world settles of itself.[7]

Imagine that you are standing by a stream and someone drops a huge boulder into it. What does the water do? It simply flows around the boulder. But what happens when someone drops a boulder into our stream? We are Westerners. We have to make deserts blossom like a rose, so we haul out the dynamite, the pickax, and the shovel and go to work on it. Yet we cannot move it. It is too big and permanent. So are many things that are in our lives. No matter how badly we want them to go away—the divorce of our parents, the death of a friend or sibling, the failed class, the child that has gone astray—they are just simply there. We can either bang our heads against the problem until we have a headache, or we can be like the water, finding a creative way to flow around the problem. That is wu-wei.

Another passage from the *Tao Te Ching* teaches us that everything can be accomplished through wu-wei.

Pursue knowledge, gain daily.
Pursue Tao, lose daily.
Lose and again lose,
Arrive at non-doing.
Non-doing—and nothing not done.
Take the entire world as nothing.
Make the least effort,
And the world escapes you.[8]

This time, let us imagine a wide river. On one side of me is a Confucianist and on the other is a philosophical Taoist. Both want to get to the other side of the river; notice that for the Taoist, wu-wei does not mean that he or she does not have desires. In this case, the person just wants to get to the other side of a rather large river. So, how is the Confucianist going to swim this river? For a Confucianist, everything has to be done according to Li in the proper way. On top of this, he is a good Euclidian, and, remembering the first theorem he learned on the first day of geometry, he knows that the shortest distance between two points is a straight line. Thus, he dives in and swims straight across the river and flops on the opposite bank utterly exhausted from the effort.

How will the Taoist swim the river? By wu-wei, of course. She will wander into the river, letting the current catch her. She will paddle a bit with her hands and feet but not exert herself. In a little while she ends up two miles downstream, and she gets out, goes on her way refreshed, while the Confucianist is still lying on the bank upstream recovering. Remember that wu-wei may mean inaction or nonaction, but it is the Taoist *action*. Taoist action is nonegoistic and in natural harmony with the Tao. Nothing is ever forced, for force defeats itself. There is a natural flow and harmony to all things, and to be out of harmony with that flow is harmful. In true harmony with the flow, everything is possible.

We will end this section with a passage from *Chuang Tzu*.

[Says Chuang Tzu] By a man without passions I mean one who does not permit likes and dislikes to disturb his internal economy, but rather falls in line with nature and does not try to improve upon [the materials of] living.[9]

Once again, to our Western ears this sounds almost blasphemous! Not try to improve on the materials of life? What about the Protestant work ethic? Remember that the desert was supposed to blossom? But I wonder if these attitudes really capture the essence of life. I wonder if we in the West truly understand what happiness is. I hear students all the time making statements like the following: "I will be happy when I finish this rotten religion class." "I will be happy when I graduate."

"I will be happy when I get my first job." "I will be happy when I get married." If we live like this, we will never be happy because we are depending on things outside ourselves to make us happy. Happiness is something which we find within ourselves and which we carry with us. I pity the person who must be married to be happy, because the marriage likely will not last. The partners will always disappoint one another in some way. If persons want a successful marriage, they need to be happy single, and then there is a real possibility for being happy plural because they have found their own happiness inwardly.

Mistakenly, we tend to live as if we will live forever. We live as if we have forever to find happiness. We live in the search but rarely in the moment. It is to live in the moment that philosophical Taoism teaches us. The past is over. The future is not yet here. We can worry about neither, because they have little relevance to the contemporary moment. In reality, all we have is this little slice of the present moment. Are we present in it or lost somewhere wallowing in the past or hunkered down, scared to death of the future? Philosophical Taoism tells us that neither is helpful or real. We should open our eyes and travel with the natural harmony of the universe, for when we do, there is no fear in the moment. Perhaps Muhammad said it best: "Live in this life as if you live forever; live in this life as if you die tomorrow. The balance between the two is Islam."[10] So it is for all of us.

From a Latter-day Saint perspective, to comment on the Tao and wu-wei requires us to deal with the two terms together. As we have seen, the Tao is impersonal, yet people have a mystical relationship with it which ensures that life will flow properly. But suppose we were to personalize the Tao. Would it be like anything in Latter-day Saint thought? Yes—it would be very much like the Holy Ghost. Latter-day Saints talk a great deal about living by the Spirit, something that we all know is not easy. The basic idea, however, is that our goal should be to live so closely to the Spirit that we have the mind of God. We should be like Nephi in the book of Helaman, to whom God says, "I will make thee mighty in word and in deed, in faith and in works; yea, even that all things shall be done unto thee according to thy word, for thou shalt not ask that which is contrary to my will" (Helaman 10:5).

Think how closely one would have to walk with the Spirit to never ask amiss of the Lord. Nephi accomplished that. He had reached the goal that Jeremiah stated when he said:

> But this shall be the covenant that I will make with the house of Israel; After those days, saith the Lord, I will put my law in their inward parts, and write it in their hearts; and will be their God, and they shall be my people.
>
> And they shall teach no more every man his neighbour, and every man his brother, saying, Know the Lord: for they shall all know me, from the least of them unto the greatest of them, saith the Lord: for I will forgive their iniquity, and I will remember their sin no more. (Jeremiah 31:33–34)

Why will they no longer have to teach each other? Because they all possess the mind of God by walking with the Spirit! Is this not very similar to walking in harmony with the Tao? When persons do so, nothing can go wrong, for they are in harmony with the universe. This humble walk is wu-wei and is similar to what is required of the Latter-day Saints if they are to have the Spirit with them always. We cannot force that Spirit. Rather, we must be like little children in our humbleness and obedience if we are to be in harmony with that Spirit. Wu-wei in Latter-day Saint terms is to live by the Spirit.

GOVERNMENT

Lao Tzu was a slightly earlier contemporary of Confucius. Confucius's ultimate goal was to bring about a harmonious society because he was living on the eve of the Warring States Period. Similarly, people misread Lao Tzu if they believe him to be concerned solely with the individual's harmony with the Tao, because the last third of the *Tao Te Ching* is concerned with proper government. Lao Tzu sought the very same thing that Confucius sought, but they approached the problem with different tools. Confucius came at the problem with values like Li, Jen, and Hsiao, while the Taoists see these as artificial and attempting to force the Tao. Government should flow naturally and harmoniously and should not be bound by human principles, no matter how lofty they may appear. Thus, Lao Tzu says:

Use the expected to govern the country,
Use surprise to wage war,
Use non-action to win the world.
How do I know?

Like this!

The more prohibitions and rules,
    The poorer people become.
The sharper people's weapons,
    The more they riot.
The more skilled their techniques,
    The more grotesque their works.
The more elaborate the laws,
    The more they commit crimes.

Therefore the Sage says:
    I do nothing
And people transform themselves.
    I enjoy serenity
And people govern themselves.
    I cultivate emptiness
And people become prosperous.
    I have no desires
And people simplify themselves.[11]

Perhaps the above seems impossible, but I wonder. First, "I enjoy serenity and people govern themselves" sounds very much like Joseph Smith's "I teach them correct principles, and they govern themselves."[12] We are free to choose our path. In addition, and this author's commentary is a bit tongue-in-cheek, there is a little here for everyone of whatever political persuasion. For example, many people hold that government interference in small businesses makes it difficult for people to earn a living because of the "prohibitions and rules." For others, Lao Tzu acknowledges that weapons cause problems in society and that maybe there should be gun controls. However, we have seen that Taoists would not pass an ordinance, but rather they would model by their lives, harmony with the Tao. Some persons would undoubtedly agree that greater skill in art or music does create grotesque things (i.e., some modern art and contemporary music). Finally, I wonder if we have ever thought about all the laws that are passed and the consequences of doing so. Lao Tzu suggests that the more laws there are, the more there are to break, and thus we are automatically creating criminals. In other words, the more we force and legislate, the more trouble we create.

The last portion of the section quoted above seems to Western ears utterly irrelevant to contemporary life. However, from my personal experience, lack of force can provide positive results. In one of my previous "incarnations," I served as the administrative vice president of a small, church-related private college. My predecessor believed that it was his job to control every nickel that the institution spent, and thus he felt it was his job to determine how many fetal pigs the biology department needed, how much paint the art department could use, and how many test tubes the chemistry department should have. Needless to say, he was not loved by faculty, and when they had the opportunity to spend money, they did not always spend it wisely, in order to spite this person.

I came into the position from the faculty, so I had some of the feelings that my colleagues had. I was also convinced that the iron fist approach would not work. Thus, I told the faculty that it was not my call on the number of fetal pigs or test tubes, and I certainly had no idea of the amount of paint the art department needed. What I could tell them was how much money they had, and I could tell them when it was gone. It was, however, up to them how it was spent. In essence, I gave them both responsibility and authority. I enjoyed "serenity," and the faculty "governed themselves." At the end of the year, we had funds left over. This style of management has become more common in certain segments of the business world. Many years ago, Texas Instruments began "quality circles" in which management and labor were brought together to work out problems, thereby creating a more productive working environment. That is the wu-wei mode of governance. It brings people together to solve problems rather than imposing solutions from above.

Advice on how to solve problems is also given in the *Tao Te Ching*. We read:

The most difficult things in the world
Must be accomplished through the easiest.

The greatest things in the world
Must be accomplished through the smallest.
Therefore the Sage
Never attempts great things
And so accomplishes them.[13]

The point here is that if we never let problems get large, we have accomplished greatness. Imagine a world that had the wisdom to deal with nuclear proliferation in 1946. Today, the problem is so awful and looming that it may never be solvable. Consider marriage. Having done a good deal of marriage counseling, I know that people store up their hurts and woes until they finally just explode from some trifling stimulus. The sack into which they have been stuffing all their unspoken hurts and slights finally can hold no more. Suppose, however, that these couples dealt daily with the small bumps of life, lovingly saying what they felt and asking for equally loving responses. They would be great because they would never have to deal with great problems. In marriage, daily work conversations can be immensely helpful in preventing any problem from getting out of hand.

So what would the ideal philosophical Taoist society look like? Clearly, the ideal ruler over that society would be one who led by example and did not force ideas or legislation on the people. The next-to-last chapter of the *Tao Te Ching* gives us insight into this society:

Small country, few people—
Hundreds of devices,
But none are used.

People ponder on death
And don't travel far.
They have carriages and boats,
But no one goes on board;
Weapons and armor,

But no one brandishes them.
They use knotted cords for counting.

Sweet their food,
Beautiful their clothes,
Peaceful their homes,
Delightful their customs.

Neighboring countries are so close
You can hear their chickens and dogs.
But people grow old and die
Without needing to come and go.[14]

It would seem that this is a peaceful, prosperous people with all they could possibly need. It sounds much like we who live in the West, but somehow the peaceful part has escaped us, perhaps because we are never satisfied, no matter how much we have. We are constantly looking to see what is in other people's driveways. We covet their houses and playthings, be they big or small. Yet in the Taoist society, there is a quiet simplicity. They are not like the bear that has to go over the mountain merely to see what is on the other side. They determine time (sort of) by tying cords. They enjoy their food, clothing, homes, and customs, and they live in close harmony with their neighbors. They enjoy life and let it be natural. They are happy where they are planted. Who could ask for more?

Both Confucianism and Taoism were concerned with government and the stability of society. Confucianism was concerned that government be moral, which would be congruent with Latter-day Saint desires. We are often counseled to vote for those who best reflect the values we hold. Morality in government would certainly be one of those values. Confucianism, however, also wants to force life into little boxes, whereas Taoism seeks to find a government that will follow the Tao without force. Once again, this brings us back to living by the Spirit, which is the ultimate goal of the Latter-day Saint when he or she envisions the ideal government. This government will appear in the Millennium with the Savior at the head and with people living by the Spirit. Unfortunately, it is difficult to have a great deal of optimism about the nature of secular government, for the concepts of "moral" government or "living by the Spirit" are simply not part of the modern world.

HUMILITY

After wu-wei, humility is probably the most important virtue, and water is the principal symbol of humility. The *Tao Te Ching* states:

> Best to be like water,
> Which benefits the ten thousand things
> And does not contend.
> It pools where humans disdain to dwell,
> Close to the Tao.[15]

In essence, water flows to the lowest places, which are antithetical to normal human inclinations. We want to reside on mountaintops, not in the lowest places, but it is in those low places that one is closest to the Tao through humility. We also read:

> Nothing in the world is soft and weak as water.
> But when attacking the hard and strong
> Nothing can conquer so easily.
>
> Weak overcomes strong,
> Soft overcomes hard.
>
>> Everyone knows this,
>> No one attains it.
>
> Therefore the Sage says:
>> Accept a country's filth
>> And become master of its sacred soil.
>> Accept country's ill fortune
>> And become king under heaven.
>
> True words resemble their opposites.[16]

Arrogance and force accomplish little. The ability of water to flow around obstacles and to reach the low places gives it power. To be in harmony with the Tao, we must have the humility to live where we are placed. From there, through humility and wu-wei, the world will be conquered. Finally, ultimate humility is to have no egotistical interest in how things go, as the seventh chapter of the *Tao Te Ching* tells us:

Heaven is long, Earth enduring.

Long and enduring
Because they do not exist for themselves.

Therefore the Sage
    Steps back, but is always in front,
    Stays outside, but is always within.

No self-interest?
Self is fulfilled.[17]

The passage on humility in the *Tao Te Ching* sounds almost like Philippians 2:5–9:

Let this mind be in you, which was also in Christ Jesus:
    Who, being in the form of God, thought it not robbery to be equal with God:
    But made himself of no reputation, and took upon him the form of a servant, and was made in the likeness of men:
    And being found in fashion as a man, he humbled himself, and became obedient unto death, even the death of the cross.
    Wherefore God also hath highly exalted him, and given him a name which is above every name.

In this passage, Heavenly Father shows us the way to gain the celestial kingdom. We simply have to forget about it and give ourselves away in the service of others with no thought for ourselves, in precisely the same way Jesus did. He was God, yet he gave up all his glory to live a human life; to suffer our trials, temptations, and pains; and to suffer for our sins. For Latter-day Saint Christians, service and self-sacrifice with no thought for themselves are the path to the celestial kingdom, just as humility in harmony with the Tao is a product of "No self-interest? Self is fulfilled" in the *Tao Te Ching*.

— PRINCIPLES OF RELIGIOUS TAOISM —

One does not find philosophical Taoism practiced in China today. Certainly the Chinese have embodied some of its quiescence and peacefulness, but the form of Taoism that is practiced in

Taiwan and mainland China is religious Taoism. Religious Taoism has in a way always been in China, for it encompasses all the elements of the ancient Chinese religion that were treated earlier. It is here that we still have the multiplicity of gods, reverence for ancestors, and divination.

THE DIVINE HIERARCHY

The heavenly courts resemble that of the emperor on earth. There is a hierarchy, at the head of which stand the Three Pure Ones. The first of these is "the Celestial Worthy of Primordial Beginning." He is as close to the idea of God as one might find in the East, for he seems to have created everything out of primordial energy. The second is "the Celestial Worthy of Numinous Treasure" and is the source of scripture and knowledge. The third is "the Celestial Worthy of the Way and Its Power," who is identified as the deified Lao Tzu, who authored the *Tao Te Ching* and participated in the development of China.[18] These three deities seem rather distant, but under them are a myriad of other gods, many of whom are humans elevated to godhood. These other gods, however, are not supreme, for tricks can be played on them, they sometimes need rescuing, and they can be mocked.

At the top of this lower hierarchy stands the Jade Emperor, who controls the natural elements but is one deity that is sometimes mocked. In conjunction with him are Tao Chun, the ruler of yin and yang, and Lao Tzu again. Notice that Lao Tzu may be located in many places in the Taoist chart of divinities. Under these last three may be Huang Ti (the Yellow Emperor), who is considered to be the father of human knowledge and the ancestor of all peoples. With him is Kwan Yin, who actually is a figure from Buddhism—the bodhisattva of compassion in feminine form—and is probably the most popular of all divine figures in China. She is the goddess who rescues people in need; she even rescued the Jade Emperor on one occasion. The third person of this triangle is once again Lao Tzu, the wise guide, but he like others may be subject to ridicule. So, these are not gods that are all-powerful or all-knowing. They have their foibles and follies. The most senior god on earth is the Grand Emperor of the Eastern Peak, who resides on Mount Tai, or Tai Shan, which is the easternmost of the five sacred mountains. Under the earth are ten levels of hell, presided over by various deities.

The most popular figures at the lay level are the Eight Immortals. These are figures that seem to have one foot in the immortal world and one in the mortal. They assist some people and play tricks on others. Their stories are enjoyable to read and bring laughter to religion. All have been humans before becoming immortals.

SPIRIT AND ANCESTOR WORSHIP

As we have already seen, there are multiple spirits to worship in Chinese mythology. There are the gods of the earth or the village gods. There are also the family gods of the doors, wells, wealth, hearths, and kitchens. These can all be benevolent if treated properly with appropriate sacrificial offerings. As the emperor has official

Kwan Yin, the most popular member of the divine hierarchy.
Courtesy of Farm.

duties to his ancestors, so the average person has responsibility to his or her ancestors. While the emperor makes offerings at official shrines, the people may have ancestral temples or home altars where offerings may be made to ancestors. At the popular level, little has changed in three millennia.

SACRED MOUNTAINS

In China there are five sacred mountains, which are believed to hold up the dome of sky. On each mountain are various deities, immortals, and spirits. The most sacred of these is Mount Tai in the east, and emperors for centuries have climbed the mountain to offer sacrifices to the gods, since the mountaintop was as close to the heavenly realm as they could get. The other mountains are Mount Hua (west), Mount Heng (south), Mount Heng (north), and Mount Hsung (middle).[19]

TEMPLES

Religious Taoist temples can be very confusing because at first visitors are not sure whether they are in a Confucian, Buddhist, or Taoist temple. The answer is yes—you are in all three, for religious Taoism is very inclusive in its relationship to the other two religions. A temple may be dedicated to one god, like the god of war, who was a very successful general in life. But in that same temple, there may be figures of the Yellow Emperor, Confucius, Buddha, and Lao Tzu, as well as other less-known figures. Thus, if the temple seems inclusive, it is almost certainly a religious Taoist temple.

PRACTICES

The purpose of religious Taoism is the same as that of philosophical Taoism (i.e., harmony with the Tao). However, the methodologies to attain this harmony and its end result differ significantly. Philosophical Taoism focused primarily on the here and now, living life in harmony with the Tao through wu-wei. There is no forcing of the Tao, as we have seen. Religious Taoism, however, is concerned with health and longevity in this life, as well as with immortality in the next. It was believed that in the eastern sea there was an island called P'eng-lai where immortals dwelt and that there one could find

Mount Tai is the most sacred of the five sacred mountains.

the elixir of immortality produced from a sacred mushroom. Several expeditions were dispatched to find this island, but they were either lost at sea or returned without having found it.[20]

The principal difference between philosophical and religious Taoism is that religious Taoism tries through various practices to force harmony, and thus immortality, with the Tao. There were those who sought immortality through elixirs derived from various combinations of the five elements. Some used gymnastics to bring the body into harmony with the Tao, while others used breath control to quiet the body and bring themselves to the state of embryonic respiration (i.e., respiration like that of a baby within the womb). Still others followed hygiene practices under the belief that meat, wine, and the five grains caused the body to decay. Thus, these foods were avoided and replaced with fruits, berries, and roots and tubers.[21] Some practiced sexual exercises in which they sought to withhold semen at the moment of ejaculation so that the semen combined with breath would cleanse the brain or repair it.[22] Thus, religious Taoism is quite a different world from philosophical Taoism.

— WOMEN

Theoretically, a woman would be equal and complementary to a man in philosophical Taoism in the same way that yin and yang are complementary opposites. However, it is religious Taoism that predominates in the Chinese world. This tradition is predominantly patriarchal in nature and inculcates the values of Confucianism along with it. Thus a woman's position is below that of a man, as it would be in Confucianism.

— CONCLUSION

I like philosophical Taoism because it leads us to think about what it really means to live in harmony with the organizing principle of the universe. The concepts of Tao and wu-wei lead me to a deeper understanding of what it means to live by the Spirit. Religious Taoism, on the other hand, is further from my own religious experiences and has less to attract me as a Latter-day Saint.

After reading this last sentence, my colleague Dr. Alonzo Gaskill rightly pointed out that *on the surface*, there seem to be more connections between religious Taoism and Christianity than between philosophical Taoism and Christianity. To make his point, he provided the following chart:

— RELIGIOUS TAOISM —	— PHILOSOPHICAL TAOISM —
Belief in gods	Wu-wei and no gods
Dietary restrictions	No dietary restrictions
Divination or revelation	No revelation
Priests	No priests
Temples	No temples

It is worth examining these similarities because it provides an opportunity to talk about what is a similarity and what is a real parallel. It is true that there are "gods" in religious Taoism, but what does this mean? They are imperfect, capricious, and in need of help themselves, which is a far cry from what Heavenly Father, Jesus Christ, and the Holy Ghost are with all their perfections. There are also dietary restrictions, but these are to starve the worms (and thus the person) that live in various centers of the body in order to gain immortality. Latter-day Saint dietary laws are for our physical and spiritual health, not immortality, and they are certainly not designed to starve the body. Further, divination is not revelation and is profoundly condemned in Christian and Jewish scriptures. "A man also or woman that hath a familiar spirit, or that is a wizard, shall surely be put to death: they shall stone them with stones: their blood shall be upon them" (Leviticus 20:27). Revelation comes directly from God, not through an unauthorized medium who examines the entrails of animals or throws dice or sticks.

The fact that there are priests is a more legitimate parallel, for the priests do rituals similar to ordinances performed by priesthood authority in the Latter-day Saint community. For both traditions, the priesthood plays an essential role. For religious Taoists, temples are usually places of personal worship of one or more deities. There priests may perform rituals for the dead, such as the burning of paper funeral money or paper replicas of items believed to be needed in the afterlife. These same things can also be done in a home, so they are not limited to temples. Thus, there are a few points of legitimate contact between the Latter-day Saint faith and religious Taoism, especially when considering the priesthood. But all are done in the context of a very different understanding of the universe and the gods that inhabit it.

Philosophical Taoism, however, is in my view closer to the *goal* toward which Latter-day Saints should be moving. Granted, there are no gods, priests, or temples; but as we said earlier, if the Tao were personalized, it would be comparable to the Holy Ghost or to Heavenly Father. It is that which gives order to the universe and from which all things arise. If we are in harmony with it, we can never go wrong. I believe the day will come when all the external rules we currently live by will become obsolete because they will be written on our hearts. We will know what to do because we will walk with God and have his will within us. We will not try to bribe him with our good works;

rather, we will simply do them without thinking about them. All will flow smoothly and harmoniously because of our perfect harmony with the will of the Father through the Holy Ghost. It is of this kind of effortless harmony that philosophical Taoism speaks, so I return to my initial statement that more of the goal of my religious life is reflected in philosophical Taoism than in religious Taoism.

Taoism is interesting because it is so diverse. It does, however, have in its philosophical form profound similarities with the Spirit-guided life which Latter-day Saints should live. People live in harmony with the organizing principle of the universe, which for the philosophical Taoist is the Tao and for Latter-day Saints is the Holy Ghost. Religious Taoism is the form of Taoism one would encounter today in Taiwan and mainland China. It is distant from philosophical Taoism in that it depends on "methods" to bring persons into harmony with the Tao rather than relying on humility and "nonaction."

— NOTES

1. Lao Tzu, *Tao Te Ching*, trans. Stephen Addiss and Stanley Lombardo (Indianapolis, IN: Hackett, 1993), 1.
2. Lin Yutang, trans. and ed., *The Wisdom of Laotse* (New York: The Modern Library, 1948), 42–43.
3. Benjamin Hoff, *The Tao of Pooh* (New York: Penguin Books, 1983), 15.
4. Lao, *Tao Te Ching*, 4.
5. Lin, *Wisdom*, 15.
6. Lao, *Tao Te Ching*, 22.
7. Lao, *Tao Te Ching*, 37.
8. Lao, *Tao Te Ching*, 48.
9. Lin, *Wisdom*, 256.
10. "Islam, There Is No God but God," in *The Long Search*, video recording (New York: Time-Life Films, 1977).
11. Lao, *Tao Te Ching*, 57.
12. Quoted by John Taylor in "The Organization of the Church," *Millenial Star*, November 15, 1851, 339. Also quoted in "Leading in the Lord's Way," *Teachings of Presidents of the Church: Joseph Smith* (Salt Lake City: The Church of Jesus Christ of Latter-day Saints, 2007), 284.
13. Lao, *Tao Te Ching*, 63.
14. Lao, *Tao Te Ching*, 80.
15. Lao, *Tao Te Ching*, 8.
16. Lao, *Tao Te Ching*, 78.
17. Lao, *Tao Te Ching*, 7.

18. "San Qing: The Three Purities," White Cloud Monastery in Beijing, White Cloud Monastery, http://www2.kenyon.edu/Depts/Religion/Fac /Adler/Reln472/Purities.htm.

19. Xinzhong Yao, "Chinese Religions," in *Sacred Place*, ed. Jean Holm with John Bowker (New York: Pinter, 1994), 183.

20. David S. Noss and John B. Noss, *A History of the World's Religions*, 9th ed. (New York: Macmillan College, 1994), 299.

21. Noss and Noss, *History*, 302.

22. Noss and Noss, *History*, 302.

Hall of Dance at the Ise Grand Shrine. Ise Grand Shrine is dedicated to the worship of Amaterasu and is the most sacred Shinto shrine.

Chapter 9

Shinto

*We in the West could learn something from those of the
Shinto faith about the reverence for the land and water and
our responsibility for them.*

S hinto is a religion about Japan and its people, and it is practiced
by four million persons in Japan.[1] Because of its geographical
ties, it is rarely practiced outside Japan, although there are Shinto
temples where groups of Japanese have migrated (e.g., Taiwan, Hawaii,
and California).

— ORIGINS

Shinto is rooted in a myth which seeks to explain the origins of
the land of Japan as well as the origin of its people. The myth arose in
the form in which we will consider it about the sixth century CE as
Chinese influence was entering Japan. Buddhism was beginning to
take root. Confucian principles were accompanying it. Thus, while
things Chinese were attractive, what did it really mean to be Japanese?
This question was answered by bringing together the ancient strains
of Japanese history and mythology to create the myth that will be
examined below.

THE MYTH

Central to Shinto is the concept of *kami*, which is a life energy or self-creative life force that permeates everything, be it animate or inanimate. Kami constantly seeks to manifest itself and does so in multiple ways. It may be manifest in waterfalls, rocks, trees, mountains, hills, animals, and people. All contain this sacred energy, and nothing is without it. But what is universal in nature may also be individual, so there are divine figures that are manifestations of kami and are themselves called kami or gods. The name of the religion reflects this, for the word *Shinto* is derived from the two Chinese words *shen* and *Tao*. Shen are the good spirits or gods, and Tao means "way." Thus Shinto is the way of the gods, implying that life is to be lived in harmony with them. The Japanese name for the religion is Kami-no-michi, which also means "way of the gods," just as the Chinese does. So the practice of Shinto implies belief in the kami and a life lived in harmony with kami, meaning not just the "divine" figures but all of life, the world, and the universe.

Kami has some similarities with Latter-day Saint thought, but none are to be pressed too far, for they are similarities, not parallels. The most obvious point of similarity might be the Light of Christ, which permeates all space and which people bring with them into this world. However, kami is something that resides in a person and is his or her enlivening power, much like a soul. Since kami is eternal, it could be compared to an intelligence, which has no beginning and no end. This intelligence resides in a person and in all other life, but it is not an independent entity which seeks to manifest itself as humans, animals, or other life. Instead, it is something that our Heavenly Father clothes with spirit form, bringing us as spirit children into his presence in a premortal existence. Only then do we enter an earth life, so what seems similar to Latter-day Saint understandings of life at first is actually quite different. Kami is more appropriately compared to Brahman in Hinduism.

The foundational myth is found in two histories of Japan. The first history is the *Kojiki*, or "Record of Ancient Matters," written in 712 CE by Ono Yasumaro. This is the oldest surviving book in Japan. The second writing is the *Nihongi*, or *Nihonshoki*, the "Chronicles of Japan." It was written by a committee in 720 CE as a corrective to the

Kojiki, which the committee felt had overemphasized the imperial or Yamato clan and not sufficiently located Japan among the nation-states of Asia. It was written in Chinese. Both of these writings contain the basic myth of Shinto, but perhaps before we go further, we should ask what a myth is.

First, the term can have a variety of meanings. If I say, "Ah, that's just a myth," I am probably saying that something is not true. On the other hand, if I were to talk about the Creation myth in the book of Genesis, I would be talking about a literary genre. In literary terms, a myth is any story about gods without judgment of truth or falsity. In between these two uses of the term is the one we will use. A myth may simply be an attempt to explain something we observe using the building blocks at hand. Thus, if I were today trying to explain the origins of the Japanese islands, I would use the "mythic" language of plate tectonics and volcanology. However, in the seventh century CE, these tools were not available to the ancient inhabitants of Japan. Therefore, they explained their origins in their own way using the building blocks they had.

Izanagi and Izanami. According to the myth, the heavens were separated gradually from the lower world, which was unformed and chaotic. For seven generations, kami were born and resided in the heavens, but with the eighth generation, the kami decided it was time to create the land of Japan. To that end they sent Izanagi, the primal male and kami of the sky, and Izanami, the primal female and kami of the earth, to create the islands. First, Izanagi dipped his jeweled spear into the watery brine, and as he lifted it out, foam dripped from the tip and formed the great island of Japan. Then, Izanagi and Izanami discovered their sexual differences and had intercourse, which led to Izanami giving birth to various other islands of Japan, along with additional kami. The last kami to which she gave birth was the kami of fire, which burned her to death, thereby forcing her to go to the world of the dead.

Upon Izanami's death, Izanagi was brokenhearted and determined that he would follow her into the underworld and bring her back. After searching for her, Izanagi finally found Izanami, but since corruption had begun to set in, she told him not to look at her. He ignored this, looked, and was horrified at what had happened to her.

She, for her part, was intensely angry that he had seen her in this state, so she along with the other inhabitants of the underworld began to chase him. He fled, finally finding the exit, and escaped, slamming a rock over the entrance, and the two parted with something less than loving words.

Izanagi and Izanami play roles similar to those of Elohim and Jehovah on the one hand, and Adam and Eve on the other. Elohim and Jehovah created this world by organizing preexisting matter, much as did Izanagi when he dipped his spear into the primordial ocean. Adam has some similarity to Izanagi, also, in that he was a participant in the creation of this world as the premortal Michael, but his goal was to dwell here. That does not seem to be part of what Izanagi and Izanami envisaged. Adam and Eve, by contrast, are definitely the first parents of the entire human family, and while the entire Japanese people were viewed in the myth as descendants of the gods, it is not clear that any pair stands at the beginning of that family as do Adam and Eve. Thus there are some interesting contacts between the Latter-day Saint view of creation and that held in Shinto, but the parallels are not firm.

Amaterasu, Tsukiyomi, and Susano. Izanagi now found himself polluted with the corruption from the underworld, so he went to the River Hi and began to wash himself. As he washed his left eye, suddenly the sun goddess, Amaterasu, was born. As he washed his right eye, the moon god, Tsukiyomi, was born; and finally, as he washed his nose, Susano, the storm god, came to life. We should notice who is giving birth to these kami. It is Izanagi, the male.

It turns out that Susano was a troublemaker. He challenged Amaterasu to a contest to see who could have the most children, and he cheated with a fertility jewel. In the end he had more children, but Amaterasu had more sons, so she was the winner. Thoroughly displeased and angry, Susano stomped down the dykes between Amaterasu's rice paddies, defecated in the great hall, skinned the sacred pony from its tail to its head, and threw the carcass into the spinning room, causing Amaterasu to prick her finger on a spindle. Disgusted and angry, Amaterasu decided she had had enough, went into a cave, and slammed the door, saying that she was never going to come out. Of course, when the sun goddess goes into a cave and slams the door, the world gets dark, and the rice and other crops cannot grow. Thus the other kami realized that they had to entice her out, so they decided to hold a great party outside the cave. They hung a rope over the cave and put beautifully singing birds on it. They stomped on a bucket. Basically, they had a great time, and Amaterasu wondered how they could have so much fun without her.

As the party progressed, someone had an idea. The suggestion was made that they tell Amaterasu that they did not need her anymore because they had found someone more beautiful than she, and the suggestion was put into practice. Needless to say, this piqued Amaterasu's vanity, and she wanted to see this creature that was more beautiful than she was, so she carefully opened the cave door just a crack. Outside, someone held up a mirror which dazzled the sun goddess with her own beauty. Other kami pulled the door open and led Amaterasu from the cave. The sun, of course, came back up, the crops began to grow again, and harmony was reestablished. Susano was punished by having his beard clipped and was banished to the islands, and Amaterasu's sovereignty was confirmed.

Susano, however, redeemed himself. He found a beautiful maiden who was being threatened by a dragon with eight tails, which he killed, thereby saving the maiden. In one of the tails he found a jeweled sword, which he sent to Amaterasu as a peace offering. He married the maiden and became the father of a powerful dynasty of kami who ruled on earth in Japan. The most powerful of these offspring was Okuninushi (Great Lord of the Country).

After a time, Amaterasu decided that it was time to bring the Japanese islands under her full sovereignty. To that end she sent her grandson Ninigi to claim the islands for her, and as symbols of his authority, she sent with him the jeweled sword found in the dragon's tail, the fertility jewel with which Susano had cheated in their contest, and the sacred mirror used in enticing her from the cave. Ninigi must have been a consummate diplomat, for rather than confronting Okuninushi, he convinced him to assume the role of protector of the royal family, and Ninigi became the first ruler of Japan. His grandson, Jimmu Tenno, then became the first emperor of Japan, and the royal family still traces their lineage to Jimmu and through him to Amaterasu. It is no accident that the symbol on the Japanese flag is that of the rising sun.

The message of the myth. As we remember, a myth is intended to explain something. What do we learn about Japan and its people from this myth? First, the land of Japan is a unique creation of the gods, and the people are all descendants of these same deities. The royal family in particular is directly descended from the sun goddess. A nineteenth-century Japanese author details the historical significance of this story in the following words:

> People all over the world refer to Japan as the Land of the Gods and call us the descendants of the gods. Indeed, it is exactly as they say: our country, as a special mark of favor from the heavenly gods, was begotten by them, and there is thus so immense a difference between Japan and all the other countries of the world as to defy comparison. Ours is a splendid and blessed country, the Land of the Gods beyond any doubt, and we, down to the most humble man and woman, are the descendants of the gods. Nevertheless, there are unhappily many people who do not understand why Japan is the Land of the Gods and we their descendants. . . . Is this not a lamentable state of affairs? Japanese differ completely from and are superior to the peoples of China, India, Russia, Holland, Siam, Cambodia, and all other countries of the world, and for us to have called our country the Land of the Gods was not mere vainglory. It was the gods who formed all the lands of the world at the Creation, and these gods were without exception born in Japan. Japan is thus the homeland of the gods, and that is why we call it the Land of the Gods (Hirata Atsutane [1776–1843]).[2]

From Hirata Atsutane's words, it is clear that such a vision of Japan could lead to a theory of the divine right to rule the Asian basin. Precisely this occurred prior to and during the Second World War, and the myth, updated somewhat to appeal to modern ears, was used to underline loyalty to the emperor and the superiority of the Japanese people. Thus it was not an accident that General Douglas MacArthur required two things in the terms of surrender from the Japanese: (1) that the emperor deny his divinity and (2) that the shrines which had been nationalized and used as centers supporting the war effort be denationalized and returned to local control. It was MacArthur's intent to break the power of the myth. Did he succeed? Probably to some degree.

Emperor Hirohito reigned from 1926 until his death in 1989. He was succeeded by his son, Akihito. With a sixty-three-year hiatus between coronations, there was much debate whether Akihito would use the old enthronement ceremony, which traced the lineage of the emperor back to Amaterasu. Akihito chose to use the traditional ceremony. Do people still believe in the divine lineage of the emperor? That is a difficult question to answer, but within the last decade, a prominent mayor of a major Japanese city made a public statement that he did not believe in the divinity of the emperor. Within a month, someone tried to assassinate him.

The Japanese are still very loyal to the emperor, whose primary role is ceremonial. Much of the loyalty to the nation is now found in loyalty to companies and businesses. Such loyalty is leading Japan to a prominent place in the world economy.

The concept of a chosen land is not new to Latter-day Saints, for the new world was preserved so that in the end the fullness of the gospel could be preached to all the world from there. Rather than providing a reason for national dominance and a right to rule, the chosen land is the place from which missionaries will leave to preach the gospel in other lands, "conquering" them for God, not for a nation. Thus, being chosen for Latter-day Saints does not provide the basis for a divine right to rule, but the divine obligation to enrich human life wherever it is found.

— DOCTRINES

In Shinto there are no set doctrines, scriptures, or ethics. The primary emphasis is to be in harmony with the land and the kami. Doctrine and ethics come from Buddhism and Confucianism, both of which a person practicing Shinto may well hold. Essentially, Shinto deals with the here and now, and thus couples may be married by a Shinto priest. Ethics may come from both Confucianism and Buddhism, but the principles of social interaction are generally derived from Confucianism. Buddhism deals with the future life, so Buddhist priests may conduct the funeral of a family member. While the *Kojiki* and *Nihonshoki* contain the myth of Shinto, neither is considered scripture in the way Christians view their scriptures. They are not holy books or the words of God.

A combination of values and behaviors, derived from the above religions, is captured in what is known as the Bushido Code ("the Warrior Knight Way"), the medieval chivalric code of Japan. It was this code that defined the behavior and view of the samurai warriors of Japan. According to Noss and Noss, it has eight elements to it. The first was loyalty to the emperor and then to the immediate lord one served. Other virtues were gratitude; courage, by which life would be willingly given; justice; truthfulness, even if it were to lead to personal harm; politeness, even to enemies; reserve, in which no emotion should be shown; and finally honor, in which one willingly took his or her life to atone for failure or defeat.[3] It was the combination of these virtues that carried the kamikaze pilots of World War II into battle.

The word *kamikaze* means "divine wind" and refers to a time in 1281 when a large Mongol army was attempting to invade Japan. A huge typhoon, a divine wind, swept up the coast, utterly destroying the fleet and saving Japan from invasion. So when Japan was once again threatened by invasion by foreign powers during the Second World War, a new kamikaze was born, that of the suicide mission in defense of land and emperor. It was precisely these values that were enshrined in the Bushido Code. Today, as already suggested, these values find their manifestation in loyalty to companies as the Japanese enrich their country through the channels of legitimate business dealings.

WORSHIP AND RITUALS

THE SHRINE AND PRIESTS

There are two centers of worship in Shinto—the shrine and the home. We will first treat the shrine, of which there are more than 87,000 in Japan. A Shinto shrine is usually located near some natural object such as a beautiful waterfall, a mountain, a river, or a hill. It may also celebrate a family. The shrine houses the kami of that natural object or family, and thus, for example, we find shrines to the kami of Fujiyama or to the royal Meiji family. Anything awe-inspiring may be worthy of worship, and a temple will be built because of the self-existent spirit that is there. The author was told by a student that he and a companion had discovered a Shinto shrine on the top of a tall building in Tokyo dedicated to the kami of electricity, certainly a mysterious power that has affected all modern lives.

Torii gate at the entrance of the Ise Grand Shrine. Torii gates separate secular from sacred space.

As persons approach a Shinto shrine, they usually encounter a torii gate, which separates secular from sacred space, or more sacred from less sacred space. Thus, as persons enter the shrine area, they pass through a torii or perhaps a series of toriis. Entrance to the Meiji shrine in Tokyo, for example, occurs by passing through several gates. The torii has its roots in the myth reflecting the rope hung over the cave with the birds sitting on it.

Latter-day Saints certainly understand the concept of sacred space. Just walking onto the grounds of a temple is moving from secular to sacred space. Even non–Latter-day Saints feel the difference. As one enters the temple and proceeds beyond the recommend desk, one moves into progressively more sacred territory. This is accentuated particularly in the Salt Lake and Manti Temples as persons move progressively upward, ultimately entering the most sacred area, the celestial room. It is precisely for this reason that persons whose lives do not reach a certain level of sanctity are not admitted to the sacred precincts of the temple.

Just inside the entrance to a Shinto shrine is normally an ablution pavilion, where people may wash off their fingers and rinse out their mouths. This is part of purification, for the gravest sin is to come ritually impure into the presence of the kami. Priests must also be ritually pure, and should they have pollution that cannot be superficially removed, they may immerse themselves in a ritual bath. Better, however, is to avoid becoming impure before serving in the shrine.

Shinto shrines normally have a parish associated with them. This is a geographical area, and the people living within it are responsible to care for the kami and the shrine dedicated to that kami. This may include rebuilding the shrine every twenty to twenty-five years. In return, the kami is expected to watch over the people and their welfare. Shrines are managed by a lay committee. If the shrine is large enough, it may have one or more priests, and it is the responsibility of the lay committee to raise the funds to pay for the services of the priests. If the shrine is of insufficient size or prestige to be able to have priests, then the laity may fulfill the priestly functions.

In the past, the role of shrine priest was passed from father to son, but since the Second World War, priests attend schools to learn the rituals. From personal experience, the author has noticed that the motives seem to vary from priest to priest. I have met some who seem to have little belief in the kami but see themselves functioning more as museum curators preserving the traditions of Japan. On the other hand, I have met priests who are deeply immersed in the spiritual dimensions of Shinto and firmly believe in the worship and efficacy of the kami. An increasing number of priests are women; in the late 1990s there were 21,091 priests, 10 percent of whom were women.[4] The first function of the priests is to provide the daily offering of food to the kami, which is eaten spiritually, for without nourishment, a kami cannot function. They then ask the kami on behalf of worshipers to provide good health, prosperity, and success. They also remove impurities and even demons from people through the act of purification, which is carried out by waving a branch of the sacred sakaki tree (a low spreading, flowering evergreen) or a purification wand over the worshiper. Through purification, anything may be brought within the orbit of the kami, and thus Shinto can be quite open to new inventions and technologies. Priests may be asked to purify a new home, a car, a computer, a couple at a wedding, and any other number of things. Even demons may be exorcised.

Similarly, purification is very much a part of Latter-day Saint belief. Baptism under the hands of one having authority would be similar to a priest waving the cleansing wand over a person to bring about ritual purity. The purity that baptism or taking the sacrament brings is the purity of persons who have had their sins removed and who have taken upon themselves the purity of Jesus Christ. Latter-day Saint purity is much broader than that found in Shinto. Latter-day Saints also have ordinances of healing or other blessings to bring about quietness in persons who are afflicted with disease or who are troubled mentally or emotionally about something. Some of this Shinto priests can also do. Both Shinto and Latter-day Saints use priests to mediate cleansing power, each recognizing a divine channel from God through them. In the area of purity, then, there are some appropriate parallels.

SHRINE WORSHIP

The central shrine is divided into two areas—the honden and the haiden. The honden is the holy, sacred area of the shrine where the symbols or images of the kami are kept. This is the area that is solely for the priests. The other area, the haiden, is the place of offering and worship for the laity. The first act upon entering this area is to give an offering, which may be of money, material, or other valuable items. However, a symbolic offering is also appropriate and might just be a sprig from the sakaki tree or a paper streamer tied to a nearby tree. After the offering, worshipers ring a bell or clap their hands to gain the attention of the kami. Having done so, they may then offer prayers to the kami, and these are thoroughly personal prayers for the well-being of children, assistance in childbirth, good grades on an exam, and the many other things that we encounter as human beings. Near the main shrine at Meiji, the author saw a bulletin board with pegs on it where a person could hang prayers on three-by-five pieces of wood in the presence of the kami, and the topics of concern were those listed above. The bulletin board seemed to be very much like the prayer roll in the temples of Latter-day Saints. Following their prayers, worshipers clap to signal an end to their prayers and to show their thanksgiving. If their prayers are answered, they are expected to return to the shrine and thank the kami. The last act

Prayers hung on a prayer board at the shrine in Meiji.

is a communal meal in the presence of the kami, which is usually a symbolic drink of rice wine. Occasionally a family will rent a hall and have a meal in the presence of the kami.

HOME WORSHIP

Almost every Shinto home will have a *kamidana* (a "god shelf"). It is before the god shelf that daily offerings and worship take place. Just as in the shrine, food offerings are placed before the kami each morning to nourish them. These usually consist of rice, steamed vegetables, and sake. After they have been consumed spiritually by the kami, they may be used by the family materially. On the god shelf may be genealogical tablets for deceased relatives which are kami. There also may be symbols of other kami, particularly the kami of the local area. But if a family visited Ise, the shrine of Amaterasu, and brought home a small mirror symbolizing her, that might well be placed on the god shelf too. Thus various kami may be worshiped at the god shelf. Worship before the god shelf is very much like that in the shrine. Hands and mouth are rinsed off and out. The hands are clapped to attract the kami, and then prayers are offered. Hands are clapped to indicate the end of prayer, and many who practice Shinto would never dream of starting or ending a day without prayer. An interesting feature of home worship is that a Japanese family is likely also to have a butsudan either beside the kamidana or in the next room. This is a Buddhist altar and indicates the close relationship that has grown over the years between Shinto and Buddhism.

MATSURI

Matsuri are festivals that center on the shrine. Generally they are attended by the whole village, and even if persons never darken the door of the shrine at other times of the year, they turn out for matsuri, of which there is a variety. These are fun times.

O-Harai. The first festival is called O-Harai and is probably not technically a matsuri. This is a national act of purification that takes place twice a year, in June and December. In preparation for it, the priests go through a month of purification rituals in which they purify mind and body. They abstain from sex, strong drink, and foods that are not purified by a ritual fire.[5] At the ritual proper, which may be performed at many shrines, rituals of national cleansing are carried out. At a proper moment, the emperor, as the descendent of Amaterasu, grants the nation absolution.

Shogatsu Matsuri. Shogatsu Matsuri takes place from January 1 to 3. Houses are thoroughly cleaned, and gifts are given to superiors as tokens of appreciation for their work. Visits are made to the shrines, and after offerings are given to the kami, prayers are said for prosperity and health in the new year.

Obon. Obon occurs in mid-August and is actually a Buddhist celebration commemorating the annual return of the dead to the family homes. This is the time of year when the graves are cleaned and prayers are offered for the dead. Traditionally, reports are also made to the ancestors on the state of the family, as we have seen with Confucianism. What ties Shinto and Buddhism together in this festival is the Shinto practice of *bonodori*, a traditional dance, which honors those who have died and enables souls to become kami. Thus Obon includes both the Buddhist and Shinto elements.

Shadow Matsuri. Shadow Matsuri is an ordinary festival and does not directly involve the kami. It is still a festival that centers at the shrine and may be held at any time during the year. It climaxes with the carrying of the *mikoshi*, a very elaborate portable shrine, around the neighborhood for all to see. The author has seen one of these festivals parading down a main street in the heart of Tokyo.

Taisai. Taisai is a major festival and is often held at planting or harvest. It occurs in the area of the shrine, but the center is the mikoshi, which contains the symbols or images of the kami. The mikoshi is carried all through the neighborhood with the purpose of sanctifying the land and the people. All are exposed to the divine aura of the kami. Carrying the mikoshi sanctifies those who carry it, and thus both men and women will serve as bearers. This is a joyous event, since all are participating in the divine presence. Often a mikoshi from a neighboring village will be brought over, and there will be good-natured shoving and pushing to see which is the stronger kami. At the end of the day, after the people have felt the presence of the kami and the kami has surveyed his or her domain, the emblems are reenshrined and the festival ends.

BIRTH AND MARRIAGE

Apart from the above rituals, there are really only two others to mention. The first is the ritual at the birth of a child, which involves taking the infant to the shrine sometime after birth to be purified by the priests. The other ritual similarly involves purification of the bride and groom as a part of marriage.

— WOMEN

Some scholars believe that before Chinese influence came to Japan, women were equal with men. It is a woman, Amaterasu, who is the kami of the sun. It is she from whom the royal family is descended, and it is she who is essentially head of the kami pantheon. At the earthly level, in agrarian societies, some scholars argue, women worked with men and shared the burdens of life. With the coming of Chinese influence—Buddhism and Confucianism particularly—women were placed in a subordinate position to men, which is where a woman would be today in Shinto life. We must remember, however, that Shinto cannot be separated from the other two religions. We cannot tell where one stops and the other starts.

── Conclusion ──

Shinto is primarily about Japan and its people, and while there are shrines outside the country, the kami are truly Japanese. The religion is about living in harmony with the land, with nature, and with the kami. We in the West could learn something from those of the Shinto faith about reverence for the land and water and our responsibility for them.

── Notes ──

1. "Major Religions of the World Ranked by Number of Adherents," Adherents.com, last modified August 9, 2007, http://www.adherents.com/Religions_By_Adherents.html.
2. C. Scott Littleton, *Shinto* (New York: Oxford University Press, 2002), 34.
3. David S. Noss and John B. Noss, *A History of the World's Religions*, 9th ed. (New York: Macmillan, 1994), 375.
4. Littleton, *Shinto*, 98.
5. Noss and Noss, *History*, 373.

SOUTHWEST ASIA

The fire temple at Yazd, Iran, wherein is housed the most sacred of Zoroastrian fire, the Atash Behram.
Courtesy of Petr Adam Dohnálek.

CHAPTER 10

ZOROASTRIANISM

Zoroastrians and members of The Church of Jesus Christ of Latter-day Saints both believe in a strong sense of divine control which will end in victory over an evil personage.

Zoroastrianism is an ancient faith which arose in Persia (contemporary Iran). The number of Zoroastrians in the world today is not clear. It was held in the twentieth century that there were only 100,000 to 150,000, but recent studies have called that estimate into question, and the site we have been using for populations of the various religions now says the number of Zoroastrians may be around 2.6 million.[1] This number seems much too high, however. The Zoroastrian population is not the only thing difficult to assess. Zoroastrian history and theology are also obscure at times because sacred texts were destroyed by invading peoples such as the Greeks under Alexander the Great, and the Muslims. Thus, as we seek to understand Zoroastrian origins and history, our knowledge is limited by the loss of many of these sacred texts. Given that limitation, we will still be able to see the strength and power of this historic faith. Despite its small size, Zoroastrianism is important not only for its own beliefs but also because of its impact on Judaism, Christianity, and Islam, all of which were in contact with the faith at various points in their histories. Much of what follows is based on S. A. Nigosian's book *The Zoroastrian Faith: Tradition and Modern Research.*

— ORIGINS

SCRIPTURES

The scriptures of Zoroastrianism are the major source of knowledge for both the history and theology of the faith. Consequently, we will begin with them. Their overall name is the Avesta, which has two primary parts. The first part includes a portion known as the Gathas, which may date back to Zoroaster (or Zarathustra), the founder of the faith. In addition, there is much literature that is used in worship, as well as writings that deal with the major theological themes of the faith. The second part contains material for use in personal worship. The primary difficulty with the Avesta is that it arose over a period of more than a thousand years, thereby making it hard to determine what Zoroaster himself believed versus what later believers of the faith held. The existing texts, however, are our principal source for the content of the Zoroastrian faith.

FOUNDER

The founder of Zoroastrianism was a man named Zoroaster (Latin, Greek) or Zarathustra (Avestan). When he lived is debated. Nigosian states that there are various streams of thought. One is that he lived between 1500 and 1000 BCE. Another group of scholars places Zoroaster between 900 and 400 BCE. Clearly, there is no agreement as to when he lived, and Nigosian suggests that with all the conflicting opinions, the traditional dating of the sixth century BCE is as acceptable as any other.[2]

Nigosian stresses that very little is known with certainty about Zoroaster.[3] We do know that he was born into a religious environment that was similar to the Aryan religion we have already encountered in the Hindu chapter. Not only did the Aryans migrate into India, but they also moved into Persia and Greece and finally as far north as the Scandinavian countries. The Aryan religious environment was rich with a variety of gods, and consequently, so was that of the Persians. Apparently, Zoroaster prepared to become a priest, but around age thirty he began to have visions and to develop a deeply personal relationship with the god Ahura Mazda (Wise Lord). Out of those experiences he gained a desire to spread his faith but found this a very difficult task. He finally found a patron in King Vishtaspa, who accepted the faith, which then spread through his kingdom. Some authors suggest that Zoroaster participated in two wars to defend Zoroastrianism and died in the second while officiating at the fire altar, but this is difficult to confirm.[4] The above account marks the broad outlines of Zoroaster's life.

Latter-day Saints will see some interesting points of contact between Zoroaster and Joseph Smith. Both men began their work in an established religious environment, and both had visionary experiences that led them to challenge the existing religion. Zoroastrians see Zoroaster's death as a martyrdom, and certainly Latter-day Saints view Joseph's death in precisely that way. Both of these great religious leaders seem to have sealed their testimonies with the loss of their lives.

Zoroastrianism became the religion of Persia under the Achaemenid dynasty (559–330 BCE), with priests known as magi, and was practiced by such great rulers as Cyrus the Great, Xerxes, and others. Greek culture influenced Persia with the coming of Alexander the Great in 331 BCE, and this was followed by the influence of Parthians from eastern Persia, who ruled from 250 BCE to 226 CE. The Parthians were eventually defeated by the Sassanids of Old Persia, who reigned from 226 to 651 CE themselves, finally being defeated by Muslim armies. Zoroastrianism grew and was modified through these periods of political change.[5] Today the two largest communities of Zoroastrians are found in Iran, the land of its origins, and in India, where Zoroastrians are known as Parsis (Persians).

— ZOROASTRIAN PRINCIPLES

ZOROASTER'S THEOLOGY

On the basis of his visions and relationship with Ahura Mazda, Zoroaster condemned the Persian deities that were being worshiped, defining them as evil spirits and followers of the Lie. Followers of Ahura Mazda, the supreme God, were to follow Truth, of which Ahura Mazda was the father. It was Ahura Mazda who was the supreme being, the creator of all things, the bringer of all good and life. He was also the father of Good Mind and Right Mind. It is unclear whether Zoroaster viewed these as attributes of Ahura Mazda which could be conveyed to his followers or as beings like angels. Ritually, Zoroaster adopted fire as the representation of Ahura Mazda and Truth.

The heart of Zoroaster's thought focused on the freedom of choice that human beings must exercise. The soul was a battlefield between good, represented by Ahura Mazda, and evil, reflected in Angra Mainyu, who was coeternal with Ahura Mazda but not coequal. Humans were charged with the responsibility of making moral choices between good and evil, but they had a natural affinity for the good. At the end of this life, they would be judged at the "bridge of the judge," where the good would be sent to heaven and the evil to hell. In Zoroaster's mind, there was no doubt at the cosmic level about the outcome of the battle between good and evil. Good, Ahura Mazda, would be the winner over a much weaker foe. Ultimately, there would be two ages—the present age, in which the struggle between good and evil was played out in the human heart, and the future age, in which Ahura Mazda would reign alone.[6]

The above concepts resonate with Latter-day Saints. For them, free agency is an eternal principle which cannot be abrogated. Human beings use their free will to choose between right and wrong and to stand on the side of their Heavenly Father, his Son Jesus Christ, and the Holy Ghost, who represent that which is good. In addition, Latter-day Saints hold that human beings are pure upon entry into this earthly life. They are not contaminated with anything like original sin, and until they reach an age of accountability, they remain blameless before God. In contrast to Heavenly Father, Jesus, and the Holy Ghost stands Satan, who is constantly working to draw humans into the dark and evil side of life. He has, however, been defeated in Jesus' life, suffering, death, and Resurrection. So Satan's end is sure, but he is like a dragon which has been beheaded yet which continues to thrash about and still does great damage. In neither Zoroaster's nor Latter-day Saint thought is evil equal to God. Rather, it is something that exists because God permits it to exist for a time but is fully defeated in the end.

DEVELOPMENTS AFTER ZOROASTER

During Zoroaster's life, it seems that Ahura Mazda was clearly viewed as the supreme deity in the universe. Although he was opposed by the evil force, Angra Mainyu, there was no question of equality between them. However, with the rise of the Achaemenid dynasty mentioned above, there were changes injected into the religion, the most obvious being the reintegration of the old Aryan gods that Zoroaster had so clearly rejected. Thus, the magi, or priests, were serving other gods along with Ahura Mazda. This revised religion became that of the Sassanids. During their time, there were about forty-five angels or subdeities who also were being worshiped.

One of the principal developments was that the doctrine of evil was augmented. Angra Mainyu was no longer a relatively weak entity opposing Ahura Mazda but became the archenemy of humanity who was almost coequal with Ahura Mazda. He also became subordinate to another demonic figure who created all evil things.

Among Latter-day Saints, Satan is clearly an evil force opposed to the Father, the Son, and the Holy Ghost. In no way, however, is there any question of coequality, and Satan certainly did not participate in creation. Moses 4:23–25 makes it clear that even the thorns and thistles which make human life hard are part of God's creation, not Satan's work. The Father and the Son organize all life and nonlife.

ON THE GOOD SIDE

Ahura Mazda. According to Nigosian, Ahura Mazda "is self-created, omniscient, omnipresent, holy, invisible, and beyond human conceptualization."[7] He is the supreme ruler and is all-knowing, so nothing is hidden from him. He created both the heavenly and earthly realms and gives material and spiritual blessings to those who follow him. He guides humankind, and consequently, those who seek the good need to follow his guidance. He also forgives those who make mistakes, and in the end he will redeem even the wicked. It was these secrets of creation, life, and death that Ahura Mazda revealed to Zoroaster.[8] Everything that is good is a creation of Ahura Mazda. He creates nothing that is evil or disgusting. Ahura Mazda works in the universe through Good Spirit, which does not seem to have an existence apart from Ahura Mazda.

Holy Immortals. Besides the material realm, Ahura Mazda also created six spiritual powers or spiritual beings—Good Mind, Best Righteousness, Desirable Kingdom, Holy Devotion, Health, and Immortality. These are the Holy Immortals. Nigosian states, "Ahura Mazda created the [Holy Immortals] to aid him in his work. . . . Each has a specific character and an assigned sphere to act on behalf, or as agent, of Ahura Mazda. . . . Each [Holy Immortal] fulfills a twofold function: on the spiritual side each represents, or personifies, some specific virtue; and on the physical side each presides over some material object as its guardian spirit."[9]

Hence Good Thought, who is chief of the Immortals, personifies Ahura Mazda's thought and wisdom and will establish the kingdom of God when directed to do so by Ahura Mazda. Interestingly, married persons possess more of Good Thought than those who live a celibate life. In the physical realm, Good Thought guards the animals.

Best Righteousness personifies God's law and moral order while guarding fire. Desirable Kingdom personifies the royal powers of God, such as might, majesty, and sovereignty. In the physical realm, he guards the sky, protects warriors, and presides over metals. Holy Devotion is female and personifies immovable faith. She also guards the earth and protects herdsmen and farmers. Health and Immortality stand together, since both are the reward for a righteous life. Both are feminine. They are to bring help, pleasure, and joy to those who follow Ahura Mazda. At the physical level, Health guards water, and Immortality guards vegetation. In addition to the Immortals, there are lesser divine beings. All six of the Immortals and the lesser divinities are worshiped along with Ahura Mazda, thus removing any sense of pure monotheism from current Zoroastrianism.[10]

In Latter-day Saint thought, there is nothing equivalent to the Holy Immortals or the lesser divinities. The Father, the Son, and the Holy Ghost compose the Godhead, but there are no secondary deities. Messengers (angels) may be sent from heaven to earth, but these are either spirits waiting to assume an earthly existence or persons who have already lived on the earth. There is no sense in Latter-day Saint thought of beings created solely to serve in the heavenly court.

Fravashi and the human being. "[Fravashi] are the celestial originals of terrestrial duplicates—the double of every heavenly and earthly being or element."[11] They lived with Ahura Mazda well prior to the creation of anything. All persons, the natural world, and even the elements—that is, every entity created by Ahura Mazda—have their own Fravashi. The Fravashi provides guidance and help to persons. It functions much like a guardian angel. "This Fravashi is the higher double of the individual and acts as a divine voice, a guardian spirit, and a true guiding friend."[12] Even when a person sins, the Fravashi remains pure and unsullied, and though it warns a person, that individual alone is responsible for his or her actions. At a person's death, their Fravashi returns to the presence of Ahura Mazda and lives as the representative of the person or entity of which it is the archetype. It is not equivalent to the soul or the body which make up an earthly person.

ON THE EVIL SIDE

Ahriman. There is a dark side to the force in Zoroastrianism. Evil, or Ahriman, has an independent existence, is uncreated, stands against Ahura Mazda, and in later Zoroastrianism is almost equally powerful. For every good thing created by Ahura Mazda, Ahriman creates the opposite. Thus nothing evil arises from Ahura Mazda, and nothing good arises from Ahriman. Therefore, Ahura Mazda is wholly good and Ahriman is wholly evil. Consequently, "the phenomenal world consists of pairs of conflicting opposites: light/dark, truth/falsehood, health/sickness, rain/drought, pure/impure, good creatures/noxious creatures, life/death, heaven/hell."[13] Snakes, frogs, scorpions, lizards, and any other obnoxious creature are the products of Ahriman's work. He also creates the thistles and weeds that make human life miserable. His whole goal is to create pain and suffering and misery in the world. The one thing that Ahriman is not, however, is all knowing. Therefore, he does not know that he and his work are doomed and will be overcome by Ahura Mazda. There may be some parallel to this in Moses 4:6 regarding Satan, where we read, "And Satan put it into the heart of the serpent, (for he had drawn away many after him,) and he sought also to beguile Eve, *for he knew not the mind of God,* wherefore he sought to destroy the world" (emphasis added). Even though Latter-day Saints believe that Satan had once stood in the presence of God, this text would suggest that he never understood the Father's intent in creating the world and sending people into it.

Angra Mainyu. The opposite of Good Spirit, through which Ahura Mazda works, is now Angra Mainyu (Hostile Spirit or Evil Spirit), the demon of all demons, through which Ahriman works his evil in the world, be it in the moral realm or in the natural world.[14] He stands in absolute opposition to Good Spirit. He is the cause of all suffering and pain. He is surrounded by six "arch demons," which are opposites of the six good spirits. They drive away anything that is good, be it good thoughts, desires, hopes, or dreams. Their tools are lies and counterfeits of that which is good. They try to draw humans to make choices for evil rather than good, and they are assisted by a swarm of lesser demons at the earthly level. There is a cosmic combat between Ahura Mazda and Ahriman that works itself out at the level of the created world and in the heart of every human, since all have to make choices between good and evil. Humans will be judged in the end by how good their thoughts, words, and deeds were during their lives. In the end, all evil will be destroyed.

There is much here upon which Latter-day Saints may reflect. They certainly see Satan and his minions at work in every corner of this world, seeking to bring misery and suffering to the human family. As in Zoroastrianism, it is incumbent upon individuals to choose between good and evil and not to succumb to the enticings of these demonic forces. It also calls to mind 1 Nephi 13 and 14, which deal with the great and abominable church. In 1 Nephi 14, we see a cosmic conflict between the church of God and the church of Satan, there being only two "churches." This is comparable to the above noted cosmic combat between Ahura Mazda and Ahriman. Similarly, this cosmic conflict spills over onto the earth, where it manifests itself as the great and abominable church. The marks of this church are materialism, sensuality, and opposition to the church of God. These marks are to be found in all human organizations to one degree or another. They are even found among members of The Church of Jesus Christ of Latter-day Saints, where too many members are drawn to the materialism and sensuality of the world in their searches for monetary gain, approval of the world, and pornographic titillation. The difference between Zoroastrian and Latter-day Saint thought, however, is that in Latter-day Saint theology, for all the apparent power of evil, its source is not equal in power to God and his power. It exists in the world only by God's permission, and God uses it to shape and hone the Saints as they choose the right.

AFTER DEATH

When persons die, their souls stay near the body for three days, during which they contemplate all their thoughts, words, and deeds— both the good and the bad. Those who were good are comforted by angels, and those who were bad are assaulted by demons. On the fourth day, souls move to Chinvat Bridge (Bridge of Judgment), which spans hell and leads to paradise. There, souls are judged by three deities and then sentenced to either hell or paradise.[15] The souls that are good are met by a beautiful maiden who represents their good consciences, and they move easily across the Bridge of Judgment to paradise to await the general Resurrection. Those souls who were evil will be met by an ugly hag personifying their bad consciences, who leads them to the bridge, which rotates to present a knifelike edge from which they fall into hell, there to be tormented until the Resurrection. For those who have an exact balance between their good and evil deeds, there is an intermediate place for them until the Resurrection. There is no suffering here except that associated with seasonal temperature changes.[16]

For Latter-day Saints, life after death includes a variety of gradations immediately after death, as it does in Zoroastrianism. Those persons who attained the age of accountability and who followed Christ and received the saving ordinances of the gospel will enter paradise to await the Resurrection. From there they will be called to teach the gospel to persons in other areas of the spirit world who have not yet had the opportunity to know Jesus or receive saving ordinances under priesthood authority (D&C 138). This region of the spirit world seems to have a spectrum of people within it. There is a region of the spirit world known as hell, where those who die in their wickedness are sent, but they are not immune to the missionary efforts of those in paradise. Most of the spirit world might be comparable to the intermediate place in Zoroastrian thought or to purgatory in Roman Catholic theology.

THE LAST DAYS—THREE THOUSAND YEARS

Zoroastrians believe they are living in the final times of this world. The final three thousand years of the earth's existence began at the time of Zoroaster's birth. At the end of each successive thousand years, a savior figure will be born to progressively elevate the human population. Thus there are three savior figures, each being a son of Zoroaster, since some of his seed was preserved in a lake in Persia in which a maiden would bathe every millennium and become impregnated. At the end of the third thousand-year period, the human family will have overcome all evil, and those living at the time of the Resurrection will join those who are already resurrected.[17] Both heaven and hell have levels, or degrees. There are three degrees in the heavenly realm *prior* to the Resurrection in the regions of the stars, the moon, and the sun. The good soul passes successively through these until reaching the highest heaven.

At first blush, the immediate reaction of the Latter-day Saint to this last assertion concerning three levels in heaven is to see a close parallel to their own thought, especially with the tie to the stars, moon, and sun. But if we look more closely, we see that the correlation is not as close as it seems. While there are three levels of heaven in Zoroastrianism, they exist *before* the Resurrection, while Latter-day Saints talk about three degrees *following* the Resurrection and Final Judgment. Secondly, the good soul passes through all three levels in Zoroastrianism to arrive at the highest level, while among Latter-day Saints the basic assumption is that there is not progression between the degrees of glory.

We also see in Zoroastrianism a sense that they are now living in the "last days." This is now the third thousand-year period, running roughly from about 1500 CE to 2500 CE, if we assume that Zoroaster was born in the sixth century BCE. However, it seems that Zoroastrians believe that when the end does come, humanity will have progressed to a level approaching perfection, whereas for Latter-day Saints, humanity will have reached a state of warfare and degeneration prior to Christ's Second Coming and the Resurrection of the dead.

RESURRECTION

On the day of Resurrection, the earth, the fire, and the sea will all give up their dead, and bodies and souls will be reunited. For three days, evil persons will endure extreme punishment in hell, while the good individuals will spend three days in bliss. Those in the intermediate realm will continue in their neutral way. Then a river of burning liquid metal will engulf all the resurrected. To those who were righteous, it will feel like warm milk, but to the wicked it will be excruciatingly painful according to their sinfulness until all evil is burned out of them. Ahriman and his followers either will be thrown by resurrected beings into outer darkness to hide forever,[18] or there will be a huge final battle in which Ahura Mazda's followers will be triumphant and Ahriman and his followers destroyed.[19] After this, all people—the good and the newly refined ones with their evil now gone—will live in a newly created universe. Adults will remain forever forty years old, and children will be forever fifteen. In other words, Zoroastrians hold a doctrine of universal salvation.

For Latter-day Saints, the Resurrection is not a one-time event but a process. Some persons were raised at the time of Jesus' Resurrection, and others have been already raised, like John the Baptist, Peter, James, and Moroni, all of whom appeared to Joseph Smith. At the time of Jesus' Second Coming, the righteous will join Christ, and those dead who are either celestial or terrestrial in nature will be raised.[20] During the Millennium following Jesus' return, people will die and be instantly resurrected. At the end of the thousand years, the Resurrection of the unjust will take place, at which time the Final Judgment will occur and persons will be placed in one of the three degrees of glory. In one sense, salvation is almost universal, if by that we mean that few will go to outer darkness and not receive a degree of glory. If, on the other hand, we mean that salvation is exaltation in the celestial kingdom, then salvation will be far from universal.

— WORSHIP AND RITUALS

There are a variety of rituals and rites in Zoroastrianism, some of which are quite complex. Here we will deal with the most prominent.

INITIATION

The initiation ceremony of both boys and girls occurs between the ages of seven and eleven in India and between twelve and fifteen in Iran.[21] The boy or girl receives a white undershirt symbolizing purity, with a pocket in the front for symbolic good deeds. They also receive a sacred cord, which is worn around the waist and is composed of seventy-two threads, symbolizing the chapters in the Yasna, one of the sacred texts. Part of the ceremony is the reciting of a faith statement and committing oneself to the precepts encompassed therein. It states:

> I profess myself a Mazdean, a follower of Zarathustra, opposing the demons, accepting the doctrine of Ahura, one who praises the beneficent immortals, who worships the beneficent immortals. I accredit all good things, those that are indeed the best, to Ahura Mazda the good.[22]

Upon initiation, a boy or girl becomes an adult responsible for keeping the faith. The cord is tied and untied several times a day, each time reminding persons that they live before Ahura Mazda.

The obvious corollary to the Zoroastrian initiation is the baptism of boys and girls at the age of eight in The Church of Jesus Christ of Latter-day Saints. At this time, the young people become accountable for their actions insofar as they understand right and wrong, but they receive no symbols which they carry or wear. They are, of course, dressed in white at the time of their baptism as a symbol of purity, and they receive through the laying on of hands the gift of the Holy Ghost, which is invisible. They do receive these ordinances as a product of having covenanted (much as Zoroastrian young persons) with their Heavenly Father that they "are willing to bear one another's burdens . . . to mourn with those that mourn . . . and to stand as witnesses of God at all times and in all things, and in all places that [they] may be in, even until death, that [they] may be redeemed of God, and be numbered with those of the first resurrection, that [they] may have eternal life" (Mosiah 18:8–9). The physical symbols for Latter-day Saints come later in life, when they go to the temple. There they receive their temple garments, which are worn under their clothing. These have markings which remind the wearers of further covenants they have made and promises they have received in the context of temple worship. Clearly, the temple garments have some parallel to the sacred undershirt worn by Zoroastrians.

THE FIRE TEMPLE

Fire is the symbol of Ahura Mazda, and Zoroastrians worship before it, but they do not worship the fire itself. It is sacred because of what it represents. Great care is taken to keep it pure. John and David Noss give us a look into the fire temple:

> The worshipers come individually, at any time they wish. Inside the entrance each washes the uncovered parts of the body, recites the Kusti prayer in Avestan, and then, putting off shoes, proceeds bare-footed through the inner hall to the threshold—no further—of the fire chamber, where a priest accepts an offering of sandalwood and money and gives in return a ladleful of ashes from the sacred urn, which the worshiper rubs on the forehead and eyelids. Bowing towards the fire, the worshiper offers prayers (but not to the fire, for it is only a symbol), and then retreats slowly backward and with shoes replaced goes home.[23]

TOWERS OF SILENCE

To Zoroastrians, both the earth and fire are sacred and pure because, as creations of Ahura Mazda, they are good. They are not to be polluted, and a dead body is highly polluting. Thus, traditionally

Priests perform a sacred fire ceremony. Fire is the symbol of Ahura Mazda.
© Paul Gapper.

Tower of silence, Yazd, Iran. Dead bodies were once placed in these towers to avoid polluting either the earth or fire. Courtesy of Petr Adam Dohnálek.

a body would never be cremated, nor would it be buried. How then does one dispose of a dead body? The answer to this lies in the towers of silence.

After the body has been washed and dressed in clean clothes, the sacred cord is tied around the waist. There are a variety of rituals, but finally the body is carried from the house to a tower of silence. This is a round tower set on a hill made of stone, with a stone bottom, having three internal levels with niches in each level in which bodies can be laid. The upper level is for men, the middle level for women, and the lowest level for children. The whole tower is open to the sky. The corpse bearers bring the body from the house to the tower and lay it in a shallow depression. They then slit the clothing, thereby baring the body. They leave, and within thirty minutes all that is left are bones because vultures have stripped the body of all flesh. The bones are left to bleach in the sun and then finally are placed in a central pit to disintegrate. Since Iran has not permitted the use of the towers for forty years and in many other places Zoroastrian populations are small, there is another mode of disposal. In these cases, stone boxes shield the earth, and then the body is placed in a lead coffin inside the stone box. Both are then covered with earth, thereby protecting the ground from pollution.

From a Latter-day Saint perspective, God can reunite the body and spirit of a person at the time of the Resurrection, no matter what has happened to it (i.e., whether it is buried, consumed by fire, buried at sea, eaten by vultures, or lost in an explosion). However, given the option, and out of respect for the body which is created in the image of God, burial is the most common and approved means of dealing with the dead. The bodies are dressed in temple garments and temple robes and are buried following a funeral service. Some countries today require cremation, and in those instances, the bodies of Latter-day Saints are burned after being dressed in temple garments and robes.

— WOMEN

The basic stance within Zoroastrianism is that women have equality with men before Ahura Mazda, although women cannot function as priests. Women's positions have always been tied to cultural norms, and their primary role has been that of wife and mother, as in most other cultures. Laws of purity impact women with considerable force because both menstruation and childbirth make the women ritually impure, requiring periods of separation and purification before normal daily life can be resumed. With the coming of Western influence, Zoroastrian women are entering the job market and making their mark on a more equal basis with men.

Within the Latter-day Saint community, women are equal to men before God, and there is not such an emphasis on ritual purity. However, their most sacred role that no man can fill is that of wife and mother. They give birth to new lives and bring those children up in the nurture of a Christian family. No one can take their place. Like Zoroastrian women, Latter-day Saint women do not hold the priesthood, but they share in it with their husbands, which is a step beyond Zoroastrianism. Like their Zoroastrian sisters, many Latter-day Saint women hold positions of great responsibility in the secular world, but nothing replaces their natural role of wife and mother within the divine economy.

— CONCLUSION

There are commonalities between Zoroastrianism and The Church of Jesus Christ of Latter-day Saints. In both, there is a strong sense of divine control which will end in victory over an evil personage known as either Ahriman or Satan. It would appear that Ahriman, at least in later Zoroastrianism, has greater power than does Satan, but be that as it may, he and his followers will be cast out or destroyed. In Zoroastrianism, there are many nonhuman heavenly beings that function at various levels within the divine structure, thereby giving a multiplicity of gods, which is not found in Latter-day Saint thought. The Godhead in Latter-day Saint theology is composed of three individual persons, all of them divine, united in a social trinity that functions together as one. The Father, the Son, and the Holy Ghost together control all things with their creative and sustaining powers. As with Ahura Mazda in Zoroastrianism, they too will be victorious in the end over all that is evil, for nothing evil can dwell in their presence.

— NOTES

1. "Major Religions of the World Ranked by Number of Adherents," Adherents.com, last modified August 9, 2007, http://www.adherents .com/Religions_By_Adherents.html.
2. S. A. Nigosian, *The Zoroastrian Faith: Tradition and Modern Research* (Buffalo, NY: McGill-Queen's University Press, 1993), 16.
3. Nigosian, *Zoroastrian Faith*, 17–18.
4. David S. Noss and John B. Noss, *A History of the World's Religions*, 9th ed. (New York: Macmillan College, 1994), 391.
5. Noss and Noss, *History*, 396.
6. Nigosian, *Zoroastrian Faith*, 21–24.
7. Nigosian, *Zoroastrian Faith*, 71.
8. Nigosian, *Zoroastrian Faith*, 72–73.
9. Nigosian, *Zoroastrian Faith*, 75.
10. Nigosian, *Zoroastrian Faith*, 74–80.
11. Nigosian, *Zoroastrian Faith*, 82.
12. Nigosian, *Zoroastrian Faith*, 83.
13. Nigosian, *Zoroastrian Faith*, 85.
14. Nigosian, *Zoroastrian Faith*, 85.
15. Noss and Noss, *History*, 400.
16. Nigosian, *Zoroastrian Faith*, 92.
17. Nigosian, *Zoroastrian Faith*, 94.
18. Noss and Noss, *History*, 402.

19. Nigosian, *Zoroastrian Faith*, 95.
20. Douglas L. Callister, "Resurrection," in *Encyclopedia of Mormonism*, ed. Daniel H. Ludlow (New York: Macmillan, 1992) 3:1223.
21. Nigosian, *Zoroastrian Faith*, 99.
22. Nigosian, *Zoroastrian Faith*, 100.
23. Noss and Noss, *History*, 405–6.

Mount Sinai, Egypt. This is the traditional site where Moses received the oral and written Torah. Courtesy of Berthold Werner.

CHAPTER 11

JUDAISM

Judaism and Latter-day Saint Christianity are orthopraxic faiths, meaning that both focus more on how people practice their religion than on whether they know and understand all the theological intricacies.

Judaism is an ancient faith which shares strong ties with the other two great Abrahamic faiths—Christianity and Islam. There are fourteen million Jews in the world today,[1] with large concentrations in Israel and the United States. As we begin the study of Judaism, probably the most important thing to say to Christians is that they should forget most of what they think they know about Judaism, because their views are colored by reading the Jewish texts through the lens of Jesus' life, death, and Resurrection. No Jew reads his or her texts the way Christians do. The same needs to be said for Latter-day Saint Christians because not only do they view Jewish texts through the lens of Jesus Christ but they also add an additional lens of the Restoration, thereby wearing bifocals. Hence, it is important that we permit the Jewish people to speak for themselves about their history, faith, and practice and not try to make them proto-Christians.

— ORIGINS

ABRAHAM

The Jewish people trace their origins back to Abraham as the father of their faith. It was with Abraham, who probably lived around 1850 BCE, that God made a covenant in which he promised Abraham three things: that he would have numerous posterity, that this posterity would be a blessing to the nations, and that Abraham would receive a land:

> Now the Lord had said unto Abram, Get thee out of thy country, and from thy kindred, and from thy father's house, unto a land that I will shew thee:
> And I will make of thee a great nation, and I will bless thee, and make thy name great; and thou shalt be a blessing:
> And I will bless them that bless thee, and curse him that curseth thee: and in thee shall all families of the earth be blessed. (Genesis 12:1–3)

This covenant was the basis upon which Israel became God's chosen people, through whom these promises would be fulfilled. "Chosenness" for the Jewish people means not that they hold a special status before God because they are better than others, but rather that they have a special vocation or calling. That vocation is to bless the world with the understanding that there is one God who cares about and guides its people. No faith is more singularly monotheistic than is Judaism, and this commitment to the one God is captured in what is known as the *Shema*, which is the Hebrew word for "hear."

> Hear, O Israel: The Lord our God is one Lord: and thou shalt love the Lord thy God with all thine heart, and with all thy soul, and with all thy might. (Deuteronomy 6:4–5)

It is this message that the Jews are to carry to the world both in word and in action. As the Jewish people faced persecution across the centuries, they tended to turn inward, isolating themselves from other peoples and nations simply to survive. For many Jewish people, that very persecution, however, affirmed that they were chosen for God's service, because the evil in the world seemed to seek them out and try to destroy them. Where that much evil gathers, God's people have to be present.

In addition to believing that they are to become a great people and bless the nations with their knowledge of the one God, the Jewish people also believe that God gave Abraham the land which is roughly equivalent to modern-day Israel. Thus, many Jewish persons see their claim to the land of the modern state of Israel as going back almost four millennia. Interestingly, it was only Abraham's ancestors that finally claimed the land, for the only part that he owned was a cave in Hebron where he buried his wife Sarah and where he himself was finally buried. His primary role was to dedicate the land to God.

Part of the message of the one God was also that human beings were created in his image. No Jew believes that this means physical image, but the Latter-day Saint question would be, if not that, then what? In answer, there is more to the image of God than mere physical form, for with the attributes of deity, which is what Jews, Christians, and Muslims all understand to constitute the image, there does not need to be a form. A form, however, that does not have intelligence, rationality, relationality, compassion, mercy, and love is not created in the image of God. The Latter-day Saint understanding of the image of God is based on Joseph Smith's First Vision, in which he saw the Father and the Son standing before him and seeing that both entities had physical form, which Latter-day Saints rightly stress. They sometimes forget, however, that those who hold that the image must include the attributes of God are also correct and that the complete understanding of "image of God" must include both form and attributes.

MOSES

Abraham is the father of the Jewish people, but Moses is revered as the "Lawgiver." It is Moses who ascended Mount Sinai and received both the Oral and Written Torah from the hand of God. The giving of the law was a sign to Israel of the Jewish people's unique vocational standing before God, for the giving of the law was a sign of God's favor. It was never a burden, and one of the Psalmists makes this very clear.

> Blessed is the man that walketh not in the counsel of the ungodly, nor standeth in the way of sinners, nor sitteth in the seat of the scornful. But his *delight* is in the law of the Lord; and in his law doth he meditate day and night. (Psalm 1:1–2; emphasis added)

God gives the law to Israel, his chosen people, to keep them safe. When they walk within the boundaries God has set for them, nothing can threaten Israel.

Many Jews believe that God gave Moses two things on Sinai—the Written Law and the Oral Law. The first is what Latter-day Saints would call the books of Moses (i.e., Genesis, Exodus, Leviticus, Numbers, and Deuteronomy). They are also known as the Pentateuch. In addition to these, Moses was also given the Oral Law, which was passed down from generation to generation and needed to be unpacked over time.

> Moses received the Law from Sinai and committed it to Joshua, and Joshua to the elders, and the elders to the Prophets; and the prophets committed it to the men of the Great Synagogue (*Mishnah Aboth* [The Fathers] 1:1).[2]

This means that according to the rabbis, everything after the books of Moses is an unpacking of the Oral Law. According to this view, when Isaiah says, "Thus says the Lord," he does not mean that the Lord is speaking directly to him but rather that the Lord is inspiring him to say in his day and time what had been given to Moses on Sinai and

Sefer (handwritten) Torah raised during a bar mitzvah. The Torah is the most sacred part of the Tanak. Courtesy of Olivier Lévy.

210

passed down to him. Thus, a pronouncement today on cloning, for example, if accepted by the Jewish community, could be seen as liberating what was said at Sinai relevant to this issue.

SCRIPTURE

This is a good point to look at the Jewish conception of sacred writings, for they have several of them. The first collection of texts is the Jewish, or Hebrew, Bible. It has the same content, the same thirty-nine books, as the Latter-day Saint Old Testament but is in a slightly different order and is organized into three sections. Below are the sections arranged vertically, first with their Hebrew names and then the English translation of the names.

T	N	K	L	P	W
O	E	E	A	R	R
R	V	T	W	O	I
A	I	U		P	T
H	I	V		H	I
	M	I		E	N
		M		T	G
				S	S

The Hebrew Bible is known as the Tanak, a word created by taking the first letter of each of the three sections of the Hebrew Bible (TNK) and putting a vowel between them—TaNaK. The most sacred portion of this is the Torah, or Law, which was given directly to Moses. The Law is read completely through every year in the synagogue. The major and minor Prophets and the Writings, such as Job, Psalms, Proverbs, and Ruth, are an unpacking of the Oral Law received by Moses and passed on to future generations. They augment the reading of the Law during the year in the synagogue.

The largest problem faced by rabbis, as interpreters of the Law, was that the Torah gave directions for life without telling people how to fulfill what was commanded. As a case in point, what does it mean to keep the Sabbath day holy? The rabbis answered this by limiting, for example, the distance persons could walk on the Sabbath, and today Orthodox Jews still live within walking distance of a synagogue. The rabbis also banned thirty-nine categories of work, which limits significantly what a person can do on the Sabbath so that the Sabbath truly became a day of rest.

The rabbis tried to help the Jewish people live an obedient life before God by defining rules for daily life under six headings: (1) agricultural laws, (2) regulations for various festivals, (3) laws of marriage and divorce and related topics, (4) civil and criminal laws, (5) temple laws, and (6) laws of purity. The discussions were extensive and contained rabbinic arguments on both sides of an issue. Around 200 CE, these discussions were finally written down as the Mishnah. Up to this point, the discussions had been preserved by persons who had exceptional memories, but even for them, the burden of memorization was immense. The English version of the Mishnah cited here has 789 pages. Imagine holding all that in memory.

The rabbinic discussions did not stop with the completion of the Mishnah. They continued as commentary on the Mishnah and were collected in a second group of writings known as the Gemara. However, there were two Gemaras—a Palestinian Gemara and a Babylonian Gemara. With the fall of Jerusalem and the Roman destruction of the temple in 70 CE, many Jews fled Palestine to many areas, including the largest Jewish community in the world, which was in Babylon. After the Bar Kochba rebellion in Palestine, which took place from 132 to 135 CE, the Romans were tired of this troublesome people and banned all Jews from approaching Jerusalem. Therefore, many more Jewish people migrated to Babylon, but some stayed and settled in Galilee, which was still permissible. The rabbis in this latter group produced the Palestinian Gemara, while those rabbis who were in Babylon produced the Babylonian Gemara. These were written down around 450 CE. The Palestinian Gemara covered more subjects than did the Babylonian, but not in as great a depth as the latter.

If we add the Mishnah and the Gemara together, we have the Talmud, but two of them—a Babylonian Talmud and a Palestinian Talmud. It is the former which is most authoritative for the Jewish community today. It is on the basis of the Talmud that rabbis, who are judges in Israel, make their legal decisions, which is their primary responsibility. They were never "pastors" as we understand that word today. They were scholars of the Talmud, and it was upon their scholarship that judgments were made as they brought these ancient opinions into contact with human issues.

There is one additional writing that informs Jewish life, and this is the Midrash. While the Talmud deals with primarily legal material, the Midrash is based on the biblical text and contains sermon-like material and commentaries on the biblical texts. Often the material is very practical concerning how one should live a Jewish life and contains stories of people who have lived as they should. Probably the closest thing to the Midrash among Latter-day Saints would be the *Ensign*, by which they are inspired to live a Latter-day Saint life through stories of fellow Saints doing so. Thus, the Tanak, Talmud, and Midrash constitute the "standard works" for the Jewish people.

— THE PEOPLE

The Jewish people are defined not so much by what they believe as by how they practice their faith on a daily basis. There are two words between which we need to distinguish: orthodoxy and orthopraxy. Orthodoxy means that people believe the right things. Orthopraxy means that people do the right things. The reason that many Christian denominations claim that Latter-day Saints are not Christians is because they are not "orthodox"—they don't believe the right things. Within Judaism there is great latitude in what persons can believe. What is more important is whether Jewish people *do* the right things—"orthopraxy." Thus, the degree to which Jewish persons' lives adhere to "tradition" determines in large measure where they fall on the spectrum between "tradition" and "modernity." Thus, the diversity of Jewish groups within American Judaism looks like the following.

— TRADITION ———————————————— MODERNITY —

Ultra-Orthodox	Modern Orthodox	Conservative	Reform	Assimilated

Most Jewish persons live in the creative tension between tradition and modernity. Some, however, want nothing to do with the modern world. They have frozen time in response to the Enlightenment and thus still wear the clothing of seventeenth-century Eastern Europe. Their commitment is to keeping the traditions of Judaism while staying away from the enticements of the world. There is a tendency for Ultra-Orthodox Jewish people to live in enclaves where they can be separated from the broader community. They will live within walking distance of the synagogue, will keep a kosher kitchen (which we will explain later) and obey the kosher rules, separate men and women in the synagogue, have no women rabbis, and will not call a girl up to read from the Torah.

On the other end of the spectrum are people who have become so assimilated into the broader culture that they no longer see themselves as Jewish. They see themselves as British, American, or Canadian. Their identity lies outside Judaism, and they want no part in the traditions and practices.

Most Jewish people, however, live between the two poles of tradition and modernity. The Modern Orthodox Jews try to keep all the laws that are not related to the destroyed temple. Like the Ultra-Orthodox, they would live within walking distance of the synagogue, would separate men and women in synagogue, would keep a kosher kitchen and obey the kosher rules, would have no women rabbis, and would not invite girls up to read from the Torah.

Conservative Jews keep most of the traditional laws, but they see some of them as no longer relevant to the modern world. Conservative Jews would drive to synagogue, would probably not separate men and women in synagogue, and would keep the kosher laws and keep a kosher kitchen. Conservative Jews admitted women to the rabbinate in the mid-1980s, so both boys and girls may be called up to read from the Torah.

Reform Jews feel that the traditions were appropriate for the time in which they were instituted but that many traditions are no longer relevant to the modern world. For example, Reform Judaism has had female rabbis since the 1970s. Similarly, girls as well as boys are called up to read from the Torah when they reach the age of maturity. Families sit together in synagogue, and most Reform Jews would not keep a kosher kitchen and would not be fully bound by the dietary laws. Hence, there is wide diversity within American Judaism in the way Jewish people practice their faith.

— JEWISH THEOLOGY

As mentioned earlier, there is great diversity in Jewish thought. The one central belief is that there is one God in whose image human beings are created. Beyond this, most Jewish persons would hold that humans have two inclinations: a good inclination and an evil one.

Having been endowed with free will, or agency, the Jewish people are to make decisions between good and evil as defined by God in the Law. Because of the inclinations within them, they can be drawn toward good or evil, and the environment in which they live has much to do with this. The Law is to help them create a positive environment and make appropriate choices—they are to be obedient to God's commands. Because God has delivered the Jewish people from bondage in Egypt and continues to work in their midst, Jews should stand before him in awe and love. These are the motivating factors that lead to obedience. Beyond these basic principles, there is great variation in what Jews may believe because they are not defined by their beliefs (orthodoxy) but by their practice (orthopraxy).

Latter-day Saints will find much in these thoughts familiar. They understand agency or free will to be an eternal principle that cannot be abrogated. Even though human beings live in a fallen world, they still have their agency and can respond to God as he approaches them. Yes, there is an internal tension between what Latter-day Saints call the "natural man" and their better selves that know what God would have them do. They desire to do God's will because they know he first loved them in Jesus Christ. As John states, "For God so loved the world, that he gave his only begotten Son, that whosoever believeth in him should not perish, but have everlasting life" (John 3:16). To that love Latter-day Saints respond in love. Out of that love Latter-day Saints act, and if their obedience is not rooted in their love for God, then their obedience is slavery.

— JEWISH PRACTICES

FESTIVALS

In the Jewish, Christian, and Islamic faiths, God works in history. He is not an absent deity but involves himself in the very fabric of human life. Therefore, most of the Jewish festivals remember God's workings in particular events in Israel's history. It is around these events that Jewish life revolves, creating a spiritual rhythm throughout the year. Below we will exam some of the principal festivals of the Jewish calendar.

Sabbath. Sabbath is the weekly festival that held Judaism together through its many difficult times across the centuries. Life revolves around the Sabbath, for beginning about the middle of the week, persons look forward to it and draw strength from it in expectation. In the first part of the week they look back on it, drawing strength from it in retrospect. The Sabbath celebrates two acts of God's creative work: (1) the creation of the world and its people and (2) the creation of Israel through God's deliverance of the people from Egypt.

Sabbath celebrations begin in the home just before sundown on Friday and extend through Saturday until three stars are visible in the evening sky. Just prior to Friday sundown, the woman of the house lights two candles and says a blessing over them. This ritual must be done prior to the actual Sabbath because one of the forbidden categories of work is lighting a fire. Following this, hands are laid on the children's heads, and they are given a blessing. Sabbath begins with a synagogue service following which the family returns for the Sabbath meal at which there are two loaves of Sabbath bread and wine in addition to the meal. A Jew may be on the low end of the social structure during the week, but on Sabbath he or she is a king or a queen before God. Sabbath is a day of joy, and this is underlined by the double portion of light (two candles) and bread (two loaves) and the presence of wine.

Just as God rested on the seventh day, so also are the Jewish people to rest, and not only they but anyone else in the house. Thus, visitors, hired help, slaves, and animals all are to rest. According to early rabbis there were thirty-nine categories of work which were not to be done. Worshiping, reading, praying, napping, walking a limited distance outside, and spending time with the family are all approved activities. However, in the modern world, cooking, telephoning, playing an instrument, driving (for Orthodox Jews), sewing, writing letters, text messaging, and using a computer are all forbidden. For them, the Sabbath is truly a day of rest. Perhaps Latter-day Saints could learn from this worshipful attitude. Even God rested on the seventh day, according to Genesis. "Can his children do less?" would be the Jewish question.

Rosh Hashanah. The Hebrew words *Rosh Hashanah* mean "head of the year." In other words, this is a New Year's Day which occurs in late September or early October, but it has far different connotations for the Jewish people than it does for most other peoples. When most people think of New Year's Day, they think of celebrations and noisemakers and parties. However, Rosh Hashanah ushers in the Ten

Days of Awe, which culminate in Yom Kippur, the Day of Atonement. These are the most sacred days of the Jewish calendar. The symbol of Rosh Hashanah is the shofar, or ram's horn, which is blown one hundred times during the day. The shofar has always been a horn of warning, in this case warning the Jewish people that in ten days God will sit down on his throne and determine what will happen in the next year. Thus, the Ten Days of Awe are a time of introspection during which people examine their lives, ask God for forgiveness for the things they have done against him, and ask their family and friends to forgive them for things they have done to harm them, since God cannot forgive these sins. They were not done against him.

Yom Kippur. As noted above, Yom Kippur, the Day of Atonement, is the culmination of the Days of Awe. The people fast for twenty-five hours, dress in white as a symbol of purity, and focus on repentance for sins committed in the past year. All work is prohibited. At the end of the day, there is a service in the synagogue which ends on a note of hope, since all things now lie in God's hands. Following the service people go home and break the fast as a family and begin the New Year.

Succoth. The Festival of Succoth, or Tabernacles, occurs five days after Yom Kippur. Originally a harvest festival, Succoth also recalls the forty years of wandering in the wilderness following the Exodus from Egypt. Dependent upon which part of the Hebrew Bible one reads, the wandering had one of two meanings. The first, found in the book of Numbers, was punishment for Israel's complaining and disobedience in the wilderness. Israel wandered for forty years until the entire generation that had come out of Egypt died. Even Moses and Aaron did not enter the promised land. The only exceptions were Joshua and Caleb, who believed God could have led them to victory in Canaan shortly after the Exodus. Because others did not have this degree of faith, they wandered until they were extinct.

The second view of the wanderings is found in Hosea. Here the period of wandering is viewed as the honeymoon between God and Israel. During these years, Israel was wholly dependent upon God for everything, and anyone who has ever been in the Sinai desert knows that Israel's survival could have occurred only with God's care. It is this view that Succoth underlines. It celebrates God's providential care of his people.

The central symbol of Succoth is the Sukkah (the booth, or tabernacle). In the desert, people did not need shelter from rain but rather from the sun, so they built shelters. These are replicated during Succoth by building a booth on one's balcony or in the backyard. The booth must have three sides and a roof through which one can see the stars. Thus, the roof is often made from palm leaves. Since Jewish festivals involve families and are tailored to interest children, the children get to decorate the Sukkah. Hence, their artwork and other things are put on the walls. The family is expected to take their meals in the Sukkah, and if the parents can be convinced to do so, they will all sleep in it, weather permitting. If a family has no place to build a booth, the synagogue builds one, and the family may go there to take their meals. Thus, Succoth is a time to remember God's providential care of Israel, not just in the wilderness but always.

Passover and unleavened bread. Passover and the Festival of Unleavened Bread are the most sacred holidays in the Jewish calendar

A two-story Sukkah made with palm leaves and a roof
through which one can see the stars. Courtesy of Ori229.

after the Days of Awe. Passover is a spring festival that occurs in March or April. The very name defines the festival, for it celebrates the angel of death passing over the homes of the Israelites in Egypt (Exodus 12:21–30). As the Jewish people celebrate the Passover, they "remember" what the Lord has done for them, but remembering in the Jewish context is not merely a mental exercise. Rather, it is participation in the event remembered. We see this in Deuteronomy 26:5–6. As the Israelites were on the verge of entering the land of Canaan, they were commanded to bring offerings to the Lord once they entered the land. The reason is articulated in the Deuteronomic passage as cited below.

> And you shall make response before the Lord your God, "A wandering Aramean was my father; and he went down into Egypt and sojourned there, few in number; and there he became a nation, great, mighty, and populous. And the Egyptians treated us harshly, and afflicted us, and laid upon us hard bondage." (RSV)

At the beginning of this passage, the people of Israel are recalling their history. The wandering Aramean was Jacob, or Israel. He went down into Egypt to escape the famine in his day, and then years later, his descendants were enslaved by the Egyptians. In this first part of the passage, the Israelites are in a sense standing outside the story. But suddenly things change! The Egyptians treat "us" harshly. No longer is this a remembered event. Now "we" are in the story. It is "we" that are in Egypt and suffering! So it is with the Passover festival. The Israelites are once again coming out of Egypt and being delivered by the Lord as they participate in the Passover meal. Once again, "we" are in Egypt. This is what true remembrance is. So also, as Latter-day Saints "remember" Christ in the sacrament, it should be more than a mere historical backward look. They take upon themselves Jesus' life, suffering, death, and Resurrection. They are there with him, and because they reparticipate in his atoning work, they leave the sacrament table as clean and pure as they were on the day of their baptism.

The Passover meal centers on four questions,[3] each asked by a child. As with most Jewish festivals, the next generation, the children, is always involved so that Jewish historical events become their events, too. The four questions are as follows, and each gives an opportunity to explain what God did for Israel at the time of the Exodus from Egypt.

1. Why is it that on all other nights during the year we eat either bread or matzoh, but on this night we eat only matzoh?

This festival is known as Passover and the Feast of Unleavened Bread (matzoh, also pronounced matzah). Passover lasts seven or eight days. The Israelites had to leave Egypt in such haste that the bread did not have time to rise, and so unleavened bread is a reminder of the pressure of exiting Egypt. Matzoh is like a cracker without a great deal of taste. Before Passover, every bit of leaven has to be removed from homes. Parents will plant rolls or other leavened items around the house for the children to find so that it can be removed. Matzoh is eaten all through the eight-day period. A serious event becomes an opportunity for children to participate and to begin to "remember."

2. Why is it that on all other nights we eat all kinds of herbs, but on this night we eat only bitter herbs?

As should be evident most of the Passover ritual (Seder) is symbolic. Here the bitter herbs signify the bitterness of bondage and slavery. The bitter herbs are normally carrot stick–like pieces of horseradish. As one eats one of these, tears stream down the face, sinuses burn, and one definitely remembers the pain of forced labor. It gives a wonderful opportunity to explain what slavery meant for the Jewish people in Egypt and invites all participants, including children, into the events of Jewish enslavement in Egypt.

3. Why is it that on all other nights we do not dip our herbs even once, but on this night we dip them twice?

Before the meal, there is an appetizer usually consisting of lettuce leaves or celery stalks. The lettuce or celery is dipped into salt water, clearly a symbol of the tears of the enslaved. There is also a mixture of fruits and wine that is smeared on a piece of unleavened bread. On this are placed a couple of pieces of the bitter herbs, and then it is topped off with another piece of unleavened bread. This "sandwich" is then eaten. The fruit mixture recalls the mortar that the Israelites had to make to construct bricks while under the lash of their Egyptian taskmasters. Again, this is an opportunity to expand on the Exodus story, not only for the children but also for all gathered around the table.

4. Why is it that on all other nights we eat either sitting or reclining, but on this night we eat in a reclining position?

Most all the pictures of Jesus and his disciples show them seated at a traditional table on chairs while eating. One has to wonder how at Bethany Mary was able to anoint Jesus' feet if this were the case (John 12:1–8). Did she just crawl under the table? Hardly, because Jesus and his disciples were *reclining* at the table at the Last Supper and undoubtedly at other meals. Many people of Jesus' day ate at a table called a *triclinium*. This was a table in a U shape, but it was only about a foot high. Servants could work in the U while the participants lay on their left sides on cushions around the outside of the table. Thus, Jesus' feet were extended out from the table where Mary could have easy access to them. Likewise, we read in John that when Jesus announced that one of the disciples would betray him, Peter indicated to John to find out who it was. John tells us that the beloved disciple "then lying on Jesus' breast saith unto him, Lord, who is it?" (John 13:25). John was reclining on the right of the Savior and simply leaned back and asked his question.

Clearly, this is not the usual table arrangement today. Thus, Jewish people, each time they drink one of the four cups of wine that are part of the Passover meal, lean to the left as they drink, simulating reclining at a table as in days of old. This entire festival represents their chosenness, their vocational position before God, and their ultimate victory over slavery and the powers of evil. Hence, Passover and the Festival of Unleavened Bread are celebrations of God's liberating power.

The obvious parallels to Passover and Succoth among Latter-day Saints are the various persecutions and "exoduses" that they experienced as part of the church's early history. Latter-day Saints had to flee from persecution in Missouri and Nauvoo, Illinois. The flight in 1846 and 1847 which led the Saints across the western plains to the promised land of the Great Basin is annually commemorated with Pioneer Day celebrations on July 24. For the most part, these are more like a Fourth of July event than a religious worship service. But there is an underlying thankfulness to God for his providential care during the great trek. This element is best captured in the great hymn "Come, Come, Ye Saints." The third verse is the Latter-day Saint hymn of the exodus.

We'll find the place which God for us prepared,
Far away in the West,
Where none shall come to hurt or make afraid;
There the Saints will be blessed.
We'll make the air with music ring,
Shout praises to our God and King;
Above the rest these words we'll tell—
All is well! All is well![4]

Once the Saints arrived in the Salt Lake Valley, the significance of the geography was not lost on them. There was a freshwater lake which drained into a salt lake after flowing through a forty-mile-long river which they named the River Jordan. The only real surprise is that they did not name Utah Lake the Lake of Galilee. Just as Passover and Succoth recognize God's preservation of the Israelite people from the plagues of Egypt and terrors of the desert, so Pioneer Day recognizes God's providential preservation of the Saints as they found their promised land in the West of the United States.

Purim. A popular festival is Purim, which remembers the story of Esther. King Xerxes ruled Persia from 486 to 465 BCE (he is presumed to be the King Ahasuerus mentioned in the book of Esther). At a banquet given for his nobles, Xerxes called for his wife, Queen Vashti, to come and let all his guests see how beautiful she was. Vashti, however, refused to come apparently because by this time, most everyone was quite drunk. As a result, Xerxes banished her from his presence because of the precedent that would be set for the wives of his nobility if the queen could refuse the order of the king without consequence. This, of course, meant that a new queen had to be found to fill her place, and ultimately the beautiful Esther was enthroned. Nobody, however, knew that she was Jewish.

Because of the animosity that existed between Esther's uncle, Mordecai, and Haman, the king's second in command, an edict was issued by the king at Haman's instigation that all the Jews in the kingdom were to be destroyed in eleven months. Mordecai went to Esther and asked her to intercede with the king on behalf of the Jews. Because anyone entering the presence of the king without invitation would be killed on the spot unless the king extended his scepter toward that person, Esther asked Mordecai and the whole Jewish community to fast with her and her maidservants for three days. At the end of the fast, she entered the throne room, and Xerxes extended his scepter toward her and asked what she wanted. In response, she invited the king and Haman to dinner that night. When asked again what she desired, she invited the two to return to dinner the next evening, at which time she would lay her request before the king. That night, however, the king could not sleep, and so he read some of the recent chronicles of the kingdom, only to discover that Mordecai had saved the king's life and had never been rewarded. Haman happened to be in the next room, and the king asked him how a person should be rewarded who had done a great service for the king but had never been recognized. Thinking that the king was referring to him, Haman suggested that the person should be clothed in robes the king had worn, placed on a horse the king had ridden, and then led through the streets by a high noble so that the people could all honor this person. The king told Haman to do for Mordecai what he had just suggested. That night, the king and Haman returned to dine with Esther. She disclosed Haman's plot to destroy Mordecai and all the Jews for personal vengeance. The king had Haman hanged on the very gallows that Haman had built for Mordecai and issued an edict permitting the Jewish people to defend themselves when people sought to fulfill the first edict the king had issued, which could not be rescinded.

It is this story upon which the festival of Purim is based. Purim is a regular work day, but in the evening, all the children dress up as Xerxes, Esther, or Mordecai and go to the synagogue. They take with them noisemakers, and then the story of Esther is read. Each time the name Haman is pronounced, the room explodes in whistles, catcalls, and other noise. The person reading pretends to be upset, since he cannot read until the noise diminishes. As one approaches the end of the book of Esther, the name Haman is mentioned more and more frequently, and thus the decibel level rises progressively. It is an evening of good fun with a very serious message to proclaim about Jewish persecution and the way God protects his people.

Hanukkah. Hanukkah, like Purim, is a minor festival. Life continues as usual during it, but, Hanukkah resembles Purim in that it too remembers the persecution of the Jewish people and their deliverance. In this case, the persecutor was Antiochus IV of Syria, who had become enamored of Hellenistic (Greek) life. According to 1 Maccabees, he issued an edict in 167 BCE that all practices not in harmony with Greek ways were to be abandoned. What this meant for the Jewish people was that their Torah scrolls were to be destroyed, circumcision no longer practiced, the kosher laws ignored, and so on. In addition, the Syrians offered a pig on the altar of the temple, thereby polluting it. When one of Antiochus's officials went to Modin, the hometown of the Maccabees, to gain compliance with the edict, he was unceremoniously killed by a Jewish priest named Mattathias. Mattathias and his five sons fled into the hills, where they gathered followers to oppose the Syrian forces. Judas, son of Mattathias, became the first leader of the Jewish forces. His additional name Maccabeus, which probably means "hammer," was later applied to his whole family. Three years after Antiochus's decree, the Jews took control of Jerusalem, enabling the cleansing and rededication of the temple. This became the basis for the eight-day long holiday of Hanukkah ("dedication"). According to a later Talmudic claim, part of that rededication was the relighting of the temple lamp, the menorah, but there was only enough pure oil to burn for one day. The miracle of Hanukkah, sometimes called the Feast of Lights, is that this limited supply of oil lasted for eight days until a new supply could be prepared. Thus, the central symbol of Hanukkah is a nine-branched menorah (distinct from the temple menorah with its seven lamps). Eight of the candles sit in a row, and a ninth candle sits above or behind the others. This last is known as the helper candle and is lit each night and then used to light the candles for that day (one on the first day, two on the second day, and so on). Once again, we have a festival remembering a persecution lifted by God's hand.

RITES OF PASSAGE

There are two principal rites of passage in Judaism—circumcision and bar or bat mitzvah. Circumcision is performed on a male child on the eighth day following birth and is the ritual practice of removing the foreskin on the penis as a mark of the covenant between God and Israel. Today, virtually all males born in the United States are circumcised, but that is not the case in Europe. Thus, during the Nazi persecutions of the Jewish people, it was a relatively simple matter to identify Jewish men.

Bar mitzvah is performed in every form of Judaism. At the age of thirteen, a boy is called up to read the Torah lesson for the day, having studied Hebrew after school since first grade. He becomes a "son of the commandment," which is what *bar mitzvah* means. He is now responsible for keeping the whole law. He has reached the age of accountability. Bat mitzvah commits a girl to the same standard of keeping the law, since *bat mitzvah* means "daughter of the commandment." A girl who is a Conservative or Reform Jew studies Hebrew just like the boys and is called up at age twelve to read from the Torah. It is this reading that is the actual bar or bat mitzvah. The party afterward is completely secondary and unnecessary to the religious aspect of the rite.

Bar and bat mitzvah play a role similar to the baptism of boys and girls at age eight in the Latter-day Saint community. Baptism and confirmation recognize that at this age, young persons can now tell the difference between right and wrong and can be held accountable for their decisions. Latter-day Saints are now to lead a life reflective of their life in Christ in the same way that a Jewish young person is to lead a Jewish life by following the commandments of God.

Bar Mitzvah at the Western Wall in Jerusalem. It is during this rite of passage that a young man becomes a "son of the commandment." Courtesy of Alwyn Loh.

225

PURITY

The center of ritual purity has always been the mikveh throughout Jewish history. In the excavated remains under the Wohl Museum in Jerusalem are the houses of priestly families. In every house there is a mikveh, which was a bath of living water, with water running in and out of the bath. Before serving in the temple, the priests would immerse themselves in the mikveh, thereby removing ritual impurities which can be produced by any emission from the body. Today the mikveh is used primarily by Ultra-Orthodox and Modern Orthodox women.

At the beginning of a Jewish Orthodox woman's menstrual period, sexual relations between husband and wife cease for fourteen days. At the end of those fourteen days, the woman dips herself in the mikveh at the synagogue and becomes ritually pure once again. Therefore, she and her husband can once again resume sexual relations. This timing also guaranteed larger families, as the fourteenth day of a woman's menstrual cycle is usually near the day of ovulation. Rabbi Rosen, who taught in the Brigham Young University Jerusalem Center for Near Eastern Studies, felt that this ebb and flow of sexual relations between husband and wife kept a vitality in the Jewish marriage that was sometimes missing from the marriages in other traditions.

PRAYER

Prayer is an important part of Jewish life and is usually considered a group process. Historically, ten men (a quorum) were required to hold these group prayers and are still required in Orthodox Judaism. However, Conservative Judaism allows women to be counted in the quorum if the rabbi of the synagogue permits them to be counted. Reform Judaism believes in complete egalitarianism between men and women, so women may always be part of the quorum.

During prayer, a prayer shawl is worn and a leather box is tied to the forehead and another to the left or right arm, depending on whether a person is left- or right-handed. A right-handed person, for example, would wear the small box on the left arm so that he or she could wind the strap with the right hand. During prayer, the head is covered with the prayer shawl, symbolizing that the wearer is wrapped in the responsibility of keeping God's commandments. The leather boxes, known as *tefillin* or phylacteries, contain sections of scripture from Deuteronomy 6:4–9; 11:13–20; Exodus 13:1–10; and 13:11–16, all of which command that God's word should be kept near one's head and hand.[5] Both the boxes and the prayer shawl are physical reminders of the Jewish people's obligations before God.

KOSHER

The word *kosher* means "fit," particularly fit to eat, as discussed in Leviticus 11:2–3, 9, and 13ff. This passage says:

> These are the beasts which ye shall eat among all the beasts that are on the earth. Whatsoever parteth the hoof, and is clovenfooted, and cheweth the cud, among the beasts, that shall ye eat. . . . These shall ye eat of all that are in the waters: whatsoever hath fins and scales in the waters, in the seas, and in the rivers, them shall ye eat. . . . And these are they which they shall have in abomination among the fowls; they shall not be eaten, they are an abomination.

What this means for the Jewish diet is that they may eat cattle, sheep, and goats, all of which have a split hoof and chew their cud. They may not, however, eat camels, which do chew their cud but do not have split hooves. Likewise, the pig is off the menu, for although it has a split hoof, it does not chew cud. As far as life from fresh- or saltwater, only those life forms that have fins and scales may be eaten, so this would mean most fish like salmon, trout, blue gills, and cod are permitted. However, eels, lobsters, shrimp, and oysters would all be forbidden. Most birds are not kosher because they live off carrion, which is unclean. Chickens and turkeys are, however, permitted.

Jewish people are always to live before God in constant awareness of his sovereignty over them. Every time Jewish people sit down to eat, they are reminded of the commandments of God because of the kosher rules. The author is convinced that a large reason for the kosher regulations is to bring discipline into the Jewish life, and discipline in one area—food—spills over into discipline in other areas.

There is another passage in the Hebrew Bible that has had a significant effect on Jewish kosher practice, and that is Exodus 23:19. The last part of the verse, almost in passing, states, "Thou shalt not seethe a kid in his mother's milk." Apparently, this was originally a pagan cultic practice, but as one thinks about it, it also seems to add insult to injury. A person takes a young goat from its mother, prepares it for cooking, and then milks the mother so that the young goat can be cooked in its mother's milk. Something is wrong with this scenario! Be that as it may, what these verses have come to mean to Judaism is that milk and meat products should not be mixed. Thus, if persons go to a Jewish restaurant, they will be asked whether they wish to sit on the meat or milk side. Common things that most non-Jewish people eat which would be banned are cheeseburgers or pizza with pepperoni and cheese, for example. The ban of mixing meat and milk extends to the contents of a kitchen. A truly kosher kitchen would have two sets of plates, two sets of silverware, two sets of pots and pans, and perhaps even two sinks or two dishwashers. Each set would be fully dedicated to either meat or milk. Orthodox and Conservative Jewish people will generally keep kosher kitchens, while Reform Jews probably would not. Once again, we see the discipline in daily life that is required of practicing Jewish persons. Such discipline is a constant reminder that we always live before God.

Latter-day Saints also have their dietary rules, but they are not as all-encompassing as are the Jewish ones. The Word of Wisdom, found in D&C 89, addresses diet, and we have already examined these rules when we talked about vegetarianism in Jainism.

— WOMEN

Jewish and Latter-day Saint women have much in common. The focus for traditional women in both religions is the home and the children. Thus, their roles are different from those of men, but this does not mean that they are not equal to men, for they are. Both male and female are created in the image of God. Interestingly, Jews believe that God endows women with greater "intuition" than men, and most Latter-day Saints would probably affirm that this is true. In traditional Judaism, women could be involved in commercial activities including buying and selling property. Seven of the fifty-five prophets mentioned in the Hebrew Bible were women (i.e., Sarah, Miriam, Deborah, Hannah, Abigail, Hulda, and Esther).[6] It is true that men and women are separated in traditional synagogues for prayer, but this is so that both will focus on their reason for being there, although women are considered to have the greater power of concentration. This is very similar to the

Latter-day Saint practice of separating men and women in the temple so that both focus on the endowment ceremony. In Conservative and Reform Judaism, women's roles have been enhanced, with women serving as rabbis and leading congregations. Latter-day Saint women also lead at virtually all levels of the church but lead in relation to women and children, while men hold roles that require priesthood authority and thus serve as bishops, stake presidents, Seventies, Apostles, and members of the First Presidency. Having served in congregations outside the Latter-day Saint context, the author believes that these unique roles give men in the Latter-day Saint communion an identity and a function that they do not have in Protestant Christianity. For example, in the congregations where the author has served, women were often the stalwarts of the church, and the men were often unclear about the role they played. Priesthood clarifies this uncertainty.

— CONCLUSION

There is much that is shared between Judaism and Latter-day Saint Christianity. Both are orthopraxic faiths, meaning that both focus more on how people practice their religion than on whether they know and understand all the theological intricacies. They are ways of life, with one faith group looking forward to the coming of the Messiah and the other looking back and claiming that he has come.

— NOTES

1. "Major Religions of the World Ranked by Number of Adherents," Adherents.com, last modified August 9, 2007, http://www.adherents .com/Religions_By_Adherents.html. In this chapter we refer to biblical Israelites as Jews. Also, general statements about Jews refer to practicing Jews.

2. *The Mishnah*, translated from Hebrew with introduction and notes by Herbert Danby (London: Lowe & Brydone, 1967), 446.

3. "Kosher4Passover," Factor, LLC., http://kosher4passover.com/4questions .htm.

4. William Clayton, "Come, Come, Ye Saints," *Hymns* (Salt Lake City: The Church of Jesus Christ of Latter-day Saints, 1985), no. 30.

5. Leo Trepp, *Judaism: Development and Life*, 3rd ed. (Belmont, CA: Wadsworth, 1982), 273–75.

6. Tracey R. Rich, "Prophets and Prophecy," Judaism 101, http://www.jewfaq .org/prophet.htm#Who.

Canterbury Cathedral, Canterbury, England, one of the most famous Christian structures and the cathedral of the archbishop of Canterbury, leader of the Church of England. © Val Brinkerhoff.

CHAPTER 12

CHRISTIANITY

As diverse as Christianity is, its central focus is always on Jesus Christ. Every tradition, be it Eastern Orthodox, Roman Catholic, Protestant, or Latter-day Saint, is seeking to explain what it has heard God saying to it through his revelation of himself in Jesus of Nazareth.

Because the aim of this chapter it to deal with certain aspects of the Christian faith that have perhaps not been fully understood by Latter-day Saints, it is a bit different in character from the other chapters. Issues of worship, symbols, and practices are woven throughout the doctrinal sections. There is no section on women because the role of women differs so much within various Christian traditions that there is no way to deal with it in short compass. Given these constraints, I hope that all will better appreciate and understand their Christian neighbors of whatever denomination.

Christianity is the largest religion on the face of the earth, with 2.1 billion adherents, meaning that slightly over one-quarter of all the peoples of the world are Christians.[1] Christianity is very diverse in practice and even in theology. There are common theological threads, however, that run through most Christian denominations, including Latter-day Saints, and it is these that we will explore in this chapter. As we do so, we will hold a dialogue between Latter-day

Saint Christians and Christians of the other denominations within the Christian family. As we carry out this enterprise, we will discover a vast arena of commonality as well as points of difference that exist between Restoration Christianity and the traditional Eastern Orthodox, Roman Catholic, and Protestant forms of Christian belief and practice. Protestants come from various roots, but they are represented by various adherents like Methodists, Presbyterians, Baptists, and Lutherans. The important issue is that all parties to this dialogue be represented properly.

— ORIGINS

Christianity is rooted deeply in Judaism. Its founder, Jesus, was a Jew and was a teacher within that context. Some Jews began to see Jesus as the long-awaited Messiah, but they did not fully understand what that meant. For most Jews, the Messiah was to be a king like David who would deliver Israel from her enemies, and in Jesus' day, the enemy was Rome. Only gradually did Jesus' followers, or disciples, discover that he was not at all what they had expected. He was the Messiah, who would give his life for the sins of the world, a truth they understood only after his Crucifixion and Resurrection. That knowledge so altered them that they went out and turned the world upside down with their message that God had come down among human beings in the man Jesus of Nazareth, who was now known as the "Christ," the Greek word for Messiah. For the current audience, there is no need to explore the particulars of Jesus' life and ministry, for they are well known. The Christian community continues to this day to try to understand more fully him and his work, and it is to this struggle for understanding that we now turn.

For Christians of the traditional denominations, the source book for their theology is the Bible, which contains the Hebrew scriptures, or what Christians call the Old Testament. In addition, there is the New Testament, which contains the four Gospel accounts of Jesus' ministry along with the book of Acts, which tells the story of how the early Christian Church spread through the Mediterranean world. Furthermore, there are letters from Paul the Apostle to the Gentiles, as well as other pastoral letters from leaders of the early Christian Church. All this culminates with the book of Revelation, which

Image of Christ from Hagia Sophia, Istanbul, Turkey.

assures the early Christians that God will conquer all opposition in the end. Catholic Christians, both Roman and Orthodox, include as canonical the Apocrypha, which contains writings from the period between the Old and New Testaments. Latter-day Saint Christians add three other volumes of scripture to their canon (the Book of Mormon, the Doctrine and Covenants, and the Pearl of Great Price).

—— CHRISTIAN THOUGHT ——

JESUS AND REVELATION

I have had both Catholic and Protestant friends tell me that they do not believe in continuing revelation. My usual response is to ask them if they pray, for I am convinced that anyone who prays expects an answer. For Latter-day Saints, that answer is part of what they would call continuing revelation, and when put in those terms, my friends of other Christian traditions readily agree that they too believe God continues to speak to them personally, not only through prayer but also through the Spirit and through the scriptures. They add, however, a caveat that Jesus is *THE* revelation of God; and if God stood in our midst in the person of the man Jesus of Nazareth, and if scripture bears witness to that one revelation, then there is no more that needs to be said. Nothing can be added to that revelation, for it is complete in and of itself.

Latter-days Saints too hold that *THE* revelation of God occurred in Jesus Christ, who said that whoever sees him also sees the Father. He is that one glorious revelation of God. Latter-day Saints also say, however, that God continues to tell the human family *things* about himself, his world, and his church that are not clear or even present either in the self-revelation of God in Christ or in the scriptural witness about him. This too is continuing revelation, but revelation that comes through prophets and apostles, not merely individuals. Thus, Latter-day Saints hold that God has more to say to his church than is contained in any of the canonical texts, and this "more" comes through his living prophet and apostles of the modern church.

SCRIPTURE, TRADITION, AND CREEDS

The term *Magisterium* refers to an authoritative place to which persons can turn for definitive answers on faith and morals. Catholics have this in the pope and the cardinals, who reside in Rome. Latter-day Saints have it in the prophet and apostles. Protestants claim it exists within the pages of the Bible. Because people choose to follow the pope or the prophet, their statements become normative for most Roman Catholics and Latter-day Saints. However, when scripture becomes the only norm, differences exist in how the texts are interpreted, and this has led to a wide variety of denominations in the Protestant world. These denominations often arise from differing interpretations of biblical texts. Given that, there can be no doubt within the Protestant world that "scripture alone" as read with the aid of the Holy Spirit is the source of doctrine and practice.

Roman Catholics, however, add another dimension to their source of theology. It is "tradition." In John 21:25 it says, "And there are also many other things which Jesus did, the which, if they should be written every one, I suppose that even the world itself could not contain the books that should be written." Canonical scripture is not the only source of knowledge about Jesus' works and words. What Jesus said and did was passed to the Apostles, who then passed it on to the church fathers, who passed it to the church. This is "tradition."

Therefore, the Roman Church guided by tradition, not the individual, becomes the authoritative interpreter of the scriptures. The Roman Catholic Church tells its members what they should see in the scriptural witness. Latter-day Saints do something similar. While scripture may be read for personal edification, in the end it is LDS Church leaders, meaning the prophet and apostles, who ultimately tell Latter-day Saints what they should be seeing in the canonical texts.

Creeds also play a major role in Protestant, Roman Catholic, and Eastern Orthodox Christianity. These arise as the result of questions that surface in a church over issues of doctrine. One of the earliest of these was the Apostles' Creed, which states the following:

> I believe in God the Father Almighty, Maker of heaven and earth;
>
> And in Jesus Christ His only Son our Lord; Who was conceived by the Holy Ghost; Born of the Virgin Mary; Suffered under Pontius Pilate; Was crucified, dead, and buried; The third day He rose again from the dead; He ascended into heaven; And sitteth on the right hand of God the Father Almighty; From thence He shall come to judge the quick and the dead.
>
> I believe in the Holy Ghost; The Holy catholic church; The communion of Saints; The Forgiveness of sins; The Resurrection of the body; and the Life everlasting. Amen.[2]

This is a good general summary of the Christian gospel. A couple of items should perhaps be clarified for Latter-day Saint readers. Firstly, the Holy Ghost is not the parent of Jesus, but rather the agent of conception. Secondly, the word *Catholic* means universal and does not mean "Roman Catholic Church." Thirdly, the "communion of saints" is the Christian Church both visible on earth and invisible on the other side of the veil. After this came other creeds, some of which contain propositions that Latter-day Saints might question from their particular faith perspective. However, the main point is that creeds attempt to answer issues and problems that have arisen in a church by calling councils and having them resolve the problems.

Creeds have often been looked at rather negatively by Latter-day Saints because of what Jesus told Joseph Smith in the First Vision. After he asked his question concerning which church he should join,

Joseph says, "I was answered that I must join none of them, for they were all wrong; and the Personage who addressed me said that all their creeds were an abomination in his sight; that those professors were all corrupt; that: 'they draw near to me with their lips, but their hearts are far from me, they teach for doctrines the commandments of men, having a form of godliness, but they deny the power thereof'" (Joseph Smith—History 1:19).

Clearly the Lord did not want Joseph to be in doubt about the churches of his day. There were concerns not only with certain doctrinal issues but especially with the religious climate of Joseph's day. Their members professed to love the Lord, but when they started going off to different denominations, Joseph reports, "It was seen that the seemingly good feelings of both the priests and the converts were more pretended than real; for a scene of great confusion and bad feeling ensued—priest contending against priest, and convert against convert; so that all their good feelings one for another, if they ever had any, were entirely lost in a strife of words and a contest about opinions" (Joseph Smith—History 1:6). People could not claim to love Jesus and denigrate their denominationally different neighbor. If we love the Lord, we will love our neighbor. Otherwise our "creeds" or professions of faith are a lie.

D&C 10:52–55 (emphasis is added) explains the value that the Lord places on churches outside the Latter-day Saint sphere:

> And now, behold, according to their [Book of Mormon prophets' and disciples'] faith in their prayers will I bring this part of my gospel to the knowledge of my people. Behold, I do not bring it to destroy that which they have received, but to build it up.
>
> And for this cause have I said: If this generation harden not their hearts, I will establish my church among them.
>
> Now I do not say this to destroy *my church*, but I say this to build up *my church*;
>
> Therefore, whosoever belongeth to *my church* need not fear, for such shall inherit the kingdom of heaven.

The question here is, what church is he not going to destroy but rather build up? This revelation was given in the summer of 1828, almost two years before the establishment of The Church of Jesus Christ of Latter-day Saints. In the author's opinion, the church referred to here was the Christian churches that paved the way for the Restoration and still do. These other Christians are our fellow travelers on our way back to our Heavenly Father. Joseph Smith put this in proper perspective when he said, "[I]f I esteem mankind to be in error shall I bear them down? No! I will lift them up. & [*each*] *in his own way if I cannot persuade him my way is better*! & I will ask no man to believe as I do. Do you believe in Jesus Christ &c? So do I. Christians should cultivate the friendship with others & will do it."[3]

God works in many ways and through many channels. If persons find God in different ways than we do, we should, according to Joseph, support them in that faith and help them grow spiritually in their own way—be that through the Latter-day Saint way, the Presbyterian way, or the Baptist way.

THE TRINITY

As we approach the doctrine of the Trinity, we should be aware that any competent Catholic or Protestant theologian will say that this is *THE* mystery of God and cannot be fully understood. It can only be accepted, because it is ultimately beyond human understanding. Having said this, part of the definition of the Trinity is very straightforward. It simply says that there are three simultaneously coexisting persons in the Godhead, a statement with which Latter-day Saints should have no trouble. The most obvious difference between the traditional Christian view and that of Latter-day Saint Christians is that in Restoration doctrine, the Father is embodied. There is full equality between the three members of the Godhead in traditional Christian thought while there is a slight subordination of the Son and the Holy Ghost before the Father in Latter-day Saint thought. Eastern Orthodoxy also has a sense of this subordination with which Latter-day Saints would feel at home.

When the Son becomes incarnate in Trinitarian thought, the Godhead merely stretches. All three members are still fully God, but the Son is embodied, having taken on human life. The same holds true for Latter-day Saints, but for them, there are two embodied beings in the Godhead.

Latter-day Saints often like to ask persons who believe in the doctrine of the Trinity who the Son was praying to in the Garden. For a person who understands the Trinitarian doctrine, that is a nonsensical question, for they know well the passage at the beginning of Matthew which states that Jesus was in the water, the Father's voice spoke from heaven, and the Spirit descended as a dove. The Son was praying to his Father in Gethsemane regardless of whether one is a Trinitarian or a Latter-day Saint.

There are, however, people known as "modalists," who hold that there is one God who wears different masks. Sometimes he wears the mask of the Father, but when he does, the Son and the Holy Spirit do not exist. Likewise, when he wears the mask of the Son, the Father and the Holy Ghost do not exist. Thus, the question "Who was the Son praying to in the Garden?" makes perfect sense for modalists because for them, the answer is no one. Nobody is out there. All too often many Christians hold the modalist view when they think they are articulating the doctrine of the Trinity, but that view was declared a heresy in the third or fourth century CE.

What happens when the Son ascends to the presence of the Father? The Son is a fully embodied resurrected person who is wholly God and wholly human in both traditional and Latter-day Saint Christianity.

Whether before, during, or after the incarnation, there are always three simultaneously coexisting persons in the Godhead, whether one is a traditional Christian or a Latter-day Saint Christian. So the issue is not whether there are three persons in the Godhead. There are. This is the doctrine not of the "One-nity" but of the "Tri-nity." Rather, the real issue between traditional Christians and Latter-day Saint Christians is the question "How are they one?"

For traditional Christians, they are one in "essence" or "nature," and as we have already seen competent theologians say, this is ultimately inexplicable and is the mystery of God. They just accept the doctrine. Latter-day Saint Christians, however, see the oneness as a unity of love, will, purpose, and action. Interestingly, the New Testament talks only about what the three members of the Godhead do. It is not until the Christian message moves out into the Greek-influenced world that the question switches to "What is the Godhead like?" It is at that point that the philosophical answer of the "one essence" is put forward and accepted at the Council of Nicaea in 325 CE.

But how did we get to the point of viewing the Godhead through the "one essence" lens? It was because the early Christian Church was trying to hold two things together that did not necessarily have to be held together. The Old Testament tells us there is one God. In the New Testament, we find three persons—the Father, Son, and Holy Ghost—who are recognized as divine. How can both be true? The traditional answer was and is that the *one* God had three persons within him who are composed of *one* divine essence.

Is there a possibility, however, that in the New Testament one might learn something new? Regardless of whether persons are traditional Christians or Latter-day Saint Christians, in the incarnation of the second person of the Godhead, we learn something we did not know before. Traditional Christians learn that the God of the Old Testament, whom they know as Jehovah, has a Son—Jesus. Latter-day Saint Christians learn that when Jehovah, the God of the Old Testament, becomes incarnate as Jesus, he reveals that he has a Father. In either case, we know something that we did not know before. We learn that there are actually three members of the Godhead—Father and Son and Holy Ghost.

Latter-day Saint Christianity has additional information beyond that supplied in the Old and New Testaments. They root their knowledge of the nature of God in Joseph Smith's First Vision, in which the Father and the Son together appeared to Joseph, thereby negating in the minds of Latter-day Saints the doctrine of God being one inexplicable mystical essence of three persons. There are simply three distinct persons bound together in love, will, and purpose.

THE FALL

The doctrine of the Fall is pivotal theologically for both traditional Christians and Latter-day Saint Christians, but both understand it in quite different terms. Therefore, we will contrast the approaches. In traditional Christian thought, God places Adam and Eve in the Garden of Eden, where they are mortal, fully able to procreate, and have agency, and where they are to live until they die, to be immediately resurrected. The garden is viewed much as Latter-day Saints view the Millennium, in which people will be born, live to a certain age, die, and in the twinkling of an eye be resurrected. In traditional thought, Eve chose to try to become like God, therefore causing her and Adam to be ejected from the garden to the earth where they were still mortal, could still procreate, and may or may not have agency, dependent upon the particular denomination which one consults. Some persons would hold that Adam and Eve, and thus we, are so fallen that we have no ability to respond to God, and therefore God does everything, if we are to be redeemed (Calvinist traditions). Others hold that we have contracted original sin (usually pride) from Adam and Eve, which must be removed before we can make choices (Roman Catholic). Others would say that although fallen, people still have their agency, and Eastern Orthodox, Methodists, and Latter-day Saints would fall into this category. We can schematize the traditional view of the Fall as follows:

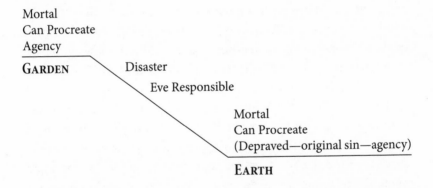

In this scenario, the Fall is a disaster, and Eve is the one who caused it. Granted, Adam followed along, but Eve was the real culprit.

As for Latter-day Saint thought, in Moses 2:27–28 we see that God in the premortal existence created male and female in his image and then commanded them to "be fruitful, and multiply, and replenish the earth." Immediately there is a tension between the coming garden and earth, for we know that Adam and Eve are not intended to live in the garden but rather on the earth, which they are to replenish. God, however, places them in the garden, where they are immortal and cannot procreate but do have agency. Then he gives them a command that too often is considered to be a contradictory command to the first. That command is "And I, the Lord God, commanded the man, saying: Of every tree of the garden thou mayest freely eat, but of the tree of the knowledge of good and evil, thou shalt not eat of it, nevertheless, *thou mayest choose for thyself,* for it is given unto thee; but, remember that I forbid it, for in the day thou eatest thereof thou shalt surely die" (Moses 3:16–17; emphasis added).

The problem with considering this a contradictory command is that God does not give contradictory commands, so something else must be happening here. In law, there is moral law and statutory law. The first implies that something is inherently wrong, while the second establishes a standard for a particular place and time. For example, a statutory law is one that a city might institute, like defining a speed limit on a main street. If persons violate this, they have broken not a moral law but simply a law established by a particular municipality for that particular street. This is the kind of law given to Adam and Eve in the garden when they are told not to eat of the tree of knowledge.[4] In reality, God is giving them information and notes that they may choose for themselves. There are definitely consequences if they choose to partake of the fruit, but still they may choose. To put this in colloquial language, God is saying to them something like, "If you want to stay comfortable and unchallenged here in the garden, don't eat of that tree over there. But if you want to grow, you are going to have to do what I told you in the premortal life and go out and replenish the earth. It is up to you." At this point, Satan appears on the scene. In reality, he is the tragic/comic character. He believes he is disrupting God's plan when in reality he is doing exactly what God wants him to do. While Satan is tempting Eve in the garden, we and the hosts of heaven were probably cheering Eve on. "Come on! Eat the fruit! We want a future!" Happily, Eve lived by the Spirit and understood to some degree what was required of her. She chose to eat and give all humanity their future. Adam understood and joined her.

[Adam said,] Blessed be the name of God, for because of my transgression my eyes are opened, and in this life I shall have joy, and again in the flesh I shall see God.

> And Eve, his wife, heard all these things and was glad, saying: Were it not for *our* transgression we never should have had seed, and never should have known good and evil, and the joy of our redemption, and the eternal life which God giveth unto all the obedient. (Moses 5:10–11; emphasis added)

Both rejoiced in the choice they had made to leave the garden, but Eve subtly reminded Adam, by saying "our" transgression, that he would have remained in the garden had it not been for her insight. Thus, by their choice, Adam and Eve opened the future for the entire human family. For Latter-day Saints, the Fall is a fortunate fall, and Eve is the heroine of the story. Schematically, the Fall looks like the this:

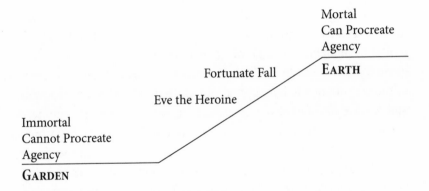

Here the tension between the garden and the earth is clear. The garden is a temporary stopping point for Adam and Eve which enables them to make their own choices concerning their willingness to confront the trials of earth life and ultimately death. In this case, the Fall is upward—a fortunate fall—and Eve is the heroine. She opens the door to eternal progression for the human family by her *choice!*

The Atonement of Jesus Christ

For all Christians, the Atonement is the antidote God provides for the effects of the Fall. Not all agree on how it works because in truth, that is a mystery. However, no active Christian doubts that the Atonement has rebuilt the bridge to God that was broken in the Fall.

There is a debate among Christians, however, whether the Atonement is "unconditional," meaning that one gets the effects of it whether or not one wants them; or whether it is "conditional," meaning that one has to do something for the effects to take place. As we will see below, Latter-day Saints believe that both concepts hold, and so we will examine this doctrine by looking at the Latter-day Saint perspective and comparing that to the traditional models of the Atonement.

Unconditional effects. According to Latter-day Saint thought, the Atonement covers unconditionally the effects of the Fall brought about by Adam and Eve's choice to leave the garden. By this choice, Adam and Eve blessed the human race unconditionally with two things—temporal death and spiritual death. The latter means that from the time of the Fall, the human family has been separated from the Father and has experienced God's workings through the Son (Jehovah) and the Holy Ghost. The question is whether either of these effects is broken unconditionally by the Atonement; of course, the answer is yes. Christ's Resurrection ensures that the entire human race will be resurrected due to his victory over death. But what about our separation from God? Will we all unconditionally return to his presence? I often get a mixed answer to that question when I ask it in class, but there are two things to be considered here. The first is the second article of faith (emphasis added): "We believe that men will be punished *for their own sins*, and not for Adam's transgression." If all the human family is not returned to God's presence, then at least some persons are suffering for something they did not do themselves. This runs contrary to the second article of faith. Secondly, we need to consider Alma 11:44:

> Now, this restoration shall come to all, both old and young, both bond and free, both male and female, both the wicked and the righteous; and even there shall not so much as a hair of their heads be lost; but every thing shall be restored to its perfect frame, as it is now, or in the body, and shall be brought and be arraigned before the bar of Christ the Son, and God the Father, and the Holy Spirit, which is one Eternal God, to be judged according to their works, whether they be good or whether they be evil.

The scriptures teach that because of the unconditional effects of the Atonement, all people return to the presence of the resurrected Lord to be judged. This author believes, based on Alma 11:44, that all members of the Godhead will be at the judgment bar, with the Son judging on behalf of them all. The unconditional effects of the Atonement may be diagrammed as follows.

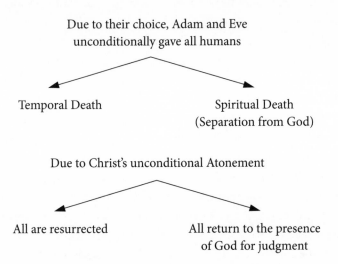

Due to their choice, Adam and Eve
unconditionally gave all humans

Temporal Death   Spiritual Death
                            (Separation from God)

Due to Christ's unconditional Atonement

All are resurrected   All return to the presence
                            of God for judgment

The question now is whether, once in the presence of God, persons get to stay there. That will depend on their relationship with Christ, because what is not covered in the unconditional effects of the Atonement are persons' individual sins. These have nothing to do with Adam and Eve but are the sins we have committed ourselves. These sins are removed by the conditional aspects of the Atonement: the "if . . ." ! And what is the "if"? It refers to whether we have let Christ have our sins or whether we are still carrying them.

Conditional effects arising from humility. The only thing that can save us from our sins is the Atonement of Jesus Christ, meaning his suffering, death, and Resurrection. Nothing in this world or any other world can do this for us. Hence, the question becomes, how do we access the power of the Atonement? The simple answer is that we do things God's way, which requires that we stand in humility before him. If we do, we will permit Jesus Christ to encounter or meet us. This is what faith is all about. Faith is a relationship—a relationship or encounter with Jesus—just like marriage is a relationship between a man and a woman. When we meet Christ, he holds up a mirror to us, and we see ourselves as we truly are (sinners in need of repentance and a Savior). Isaiah realized this when he encountered Jehovah in the temple in Isaiah 6. His first reaction was not, "Wow, I've seen God," but rather, "Woe is me! for I am undone; because I am a man of unclean lips, and I dwell in the midst of a people of unclean lips: for mine eyes have seen the King, the Lord of hosts" (Isaiah 6:5). Even the great Isaiah saw himself for what he was when confronted with his Lord and God. So it was with Peter, who met the same person, but in his case, it was the incarnate Jehovah—Jesus. In Luke 5 we read about a great catch of fish that had occurred at Jesus' direction. "When Simon Peter saw it, he fell down at Jesus' knees, saying, Depart from me; for I am a sinful man, O Lord" (Luke 5:8). In the cases of both Isaiah and Peter, the relationship or encounter with the Lord led to a realization of how far they were from being what he would have them be. That is why faith is the first principle of the gospel. Without an encounter with Jesus, we do not know who we are, and we do not know that we need to change. We can open ourselves to such an encounter by reading the four Gospels, the Book of Mormon, and other scriptures prayerfully and by attending the temple, thereby letting the Spirit direct us to Jesus.

Meeting Jesus leads to the second principle of the gospel—repentance. We realize our need to change. This is the experience of all Christians, be they traditional Christians or Latter-day Saint Christians. At this point, most traditional Christians would say that they have done what God has asked of them to make use of the Atonement of Jesus Christ. They have faith, have repented of their sins, and now intend to lead a disciple's life. Latter-day Saints, however, believe that God has given them additional ways to access the Atonement, and this is what separates them from Christians of all other traditions. Latter-day Saints hold that there are required sacramental acts or ordinances *administered by the Latter-day Saint priesthood* which God asks of them if they are serious about coming fully to Christ. Following faith and repentance, Latter-day Saints understand baptism to be a required saving ordinance that opens the way for return to the presence of God. It must be by full immersion and administered by an authorized person holding the priesthood of God. It is viewed as so essential that it is done in the temples of the church by proxy for those who are dead and who had not been baptized by priesthood authority.

There is a passage in the Book of Mormon that says, "For we know that it is by grace that we are saved, after all we can do" (2 Nephi 25:23). The problem with this statement is that too many Latter-day Saints wonder what they have to do or how many laws they have to keep before grace begins. Latter-day Saints believe, as do Eastern Orthodox Christians, that human beings are expected to make a contribution toward their salvation, since the Fall never destroyed their agency. But contribute what and how much? The answer is that humans are asked to contribute the first three principles of the gospel: faith in Jesus Christ, repentance, and submission to baptism. If they do that, they are in the kingdom of God, as Stephen E. Robinson says.[5] To prove this, God gives each person a gift—the gift of the Holy Ghost through the laying on of hands by priesthood holders. This does not mean that one has reached perfection or that the Holy Ghost will not push us to grow, but it does mean that if the Spirit is in our lives, we can be assured that we stand approved before God, for we stand before him, clothed in Christ. Below is a diagram showing the relationship between our human responsibility, the gift of the Holy Ghost, and the Atonement.

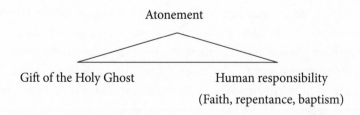

Atonement

Gift of the Holy Ghost   Human responsibility
                                          (Faith, repentance, baptism)

Many Christians hold that humans are so warped by the Fall that they are incapable of responding to God, and therefore God has to do everything. There can be no human responsibility or cooperation with God. Some Latter-day Saints, on the other hand, believe they have to do it all. From this author's perspective, both of these positions are wrong. Latter-day Saints are expected by God to contribute their faith in Christ and repent and submit to baptism. That is their contribution. God then gives them the gift of the Holy Ghost, which makes the Atonement present every day of their lives, for we all need it daily because we still sin. In addition to being a witness of God's approval of us, the Holy Ghost is also the power pack that enables us to live the life of a disciple that God asks of us. Our works flow out of our relationship with Jesus. Works do not create a relationship with Jesus because Jesus comes to us first.

In addition to the ordinances of baptism and the gift of the Holy Ghost, Latter-day Saints believe they have access to other saving ordinances in the temple, such as the washings and anointings, the endowment, and the sealing ordinances. All of these—faith in Christ, repentance, baptism (renewed weekly by the sacrament, or "Lord's Supper"), the gift of the Holy Ghost, and temple ordinances—are *channels of grace* which attach persons to the Atonement of Jesus Christ.

In all these things, Latter-day Saints are admonished to "endure to the end," a phrase found often in the Book of Mormon. But endure in what? In four places in the Doctrine and Covenants, this question is answered.[6] We are to "endure in faith" to the end, and this drives us daily back to the first principles and ordinances of the gospel: *faith in Christ*, repentance, baptism (or sacrament), and the gift of the Holy Ghost. We are not just to "hang in there" but rather are to "hang on to Christ in faith."

What about Christians who are not Latter-day Saints? Can they, as a response to their faith and repentance, have the Holy Ghost in their lives? Most assuredly, for the Holy Ghost that my wife and I knew before we were Latter-day Saints is the same Holy Ghost that we know as Latter-day Saints. There is a spectrum of divine power that influences the human family beginning with the Light of Christ, which is then followed by manifestations of the Holy Ghost, which are available to persons of any faith, and then culminates in the gift of the Holy Ghost, which is available to Latter-day Saints.[7]

The Light of Christ is something that everyone brings into the world with him or her, and it gives each individual a basic moral guideline for which each is accountable. Many have called it the "conscience." There is little real doctrinal content in the Light of Christ. If that is desired, then persons have to let the Holy Ghost into their lives, and when they do, they receive manifestations of the Holy Ghost, which may be sporadic or virtually constant, depending on their spiritual maturity. However, to have the *gift* of the Holy Ghost, which leads to all that God has in store for his family, one must receive it from authorized priesthood holders. As a convert, I know that the experiences of manifestations of the Holy Ghost and the gift of the Holy Ghost feel the same because the source is the same Holy Ghost. But the meaning is radically different, for manifestations are available to anyone of any faith who seeks God's will for them. The gift of the Holy Ghost, however, comes only in response to the prior priesthood ordinance of baptism, thus being available, from a Latter-day Saint perspective, only to those who have submitted themselves to the priesthood of The Church of Jesus Christ of Latter-day Saints. We might draw the divine influence as follows:

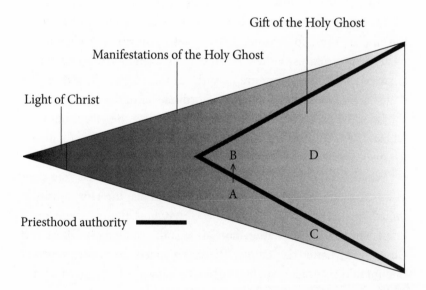

Note that when one crosses the priesthood line from manifestations to gifts (A to B), persons do not get more of the Holy Ghost. Rather, they move into a realm where they can receive the saving ordinances of the gospel, and it is the issue of priesthood authority that separates Latter-day Saint Christians from Christians of other traditions. Similarly, persons like John Wesley, Mother Teresa, or Mahatma Gandhi may have lived so closely to God that they may have had manifestations of the Holy Ghost virtually constantly (C), similar to the Holy Ghost's influence on the most spiritually advanced Latter-day Saints (D). The latter, however, have access to the saving ordinances of the gospel, which may not be accessible to the others until they pass through the veil. There is little doubt, however, that great souls like the ones mentioned above will accept the ordinances done for them by proxy.

Turning back a bit and remembering that the only things that save us from our sins are Jesus' Atonement, what are the roles of faith in Christ, repentance, baptism, the gift of the Holy Ghost, and the ordinances of the temple? Once again, they are the *channels of grace* that tie us into Christ's Atonement. These are the places where God has assured us that we can meet him in Jesus Christ and the Holy Ghost and where we can find the cleansing power of Jesus that sets us free from our sins.

The question now is whether justice is happy, for mercy cannot rob justice. But justice does not care who pays for our sins. It just must be paid because God's commandments cannot be broken without payment. If Jesus pays for my sins, that is fine, just as it is fine if I wish to pay for them. Since Jesus pays the price, mercy has not robbed justice, and justice is happy with the payment. This enables persons who have walked God's path to receive the fullness of joy, or what Latter-day Saints term "the celestial kingdom."

Conditional effects arising from pride. The alternative to standing before God in humility is to stand in pride. We will do things our way instead of God's way. What would the consequences of this decision be? First, even though persons may have faith in Jesus Christ and have repented of their sins, they will limit the number of channels of grace that are operative to acquire the full benefits of the Atonement. They will turn away from the need for saving ordinances, thereby requiring that they pay at least part of the price for their sins. As long as they refuse the saving ordinances, they will continue to separate themselves from God's path. Justice will be happy because those who refuse the saving ordinances will be paying the price for their decisions. The fullness of joy, however, will not be open to them. Instead, they will receive a lesser joy defined by Latter-day Saints as terrestrial or telestial glory. The effects of standing before God with either humility or pride can be diagrammed as below:

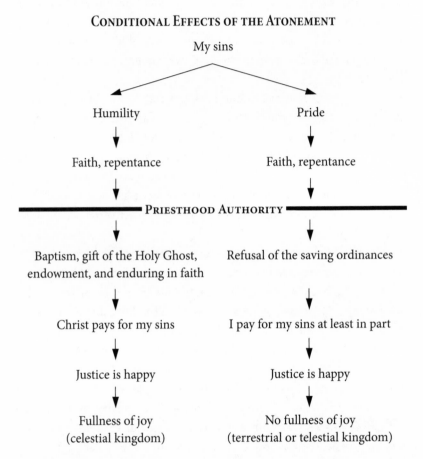

CONDITIONAL EFFECTS OF THE ATONEMENT

My sins

Humility

Pride

Faith, repentance

Faith, repentance

PRIESTHOOD AUTHORITY

Baptism, gift of the Holy Ghost, endowment, and enduring in faith

Refusal of the saving ordinances

Christ pays for my sins

I pay for my sins at least in part

Justice is happy

Justice is happy

Fullness of joy
(celestial kingdom)

No fullness of joy
(terrestrial or telestial kingdom)

Note that the horizontal line is priesthood authority. Most Christians hold that faith and repentance are all that God asks of us, but Latter-day Saint Christians affirm that saving ordinances administered by the priesthood are required to demonstrate to God that we will do things his way.

—SACRAMENTS—

Sacraments are events within a church where people encounter God through Jesus Christ and the Holy Ghost. Both the Roman Catholic Church and the Eastern Orthodox Church have seven

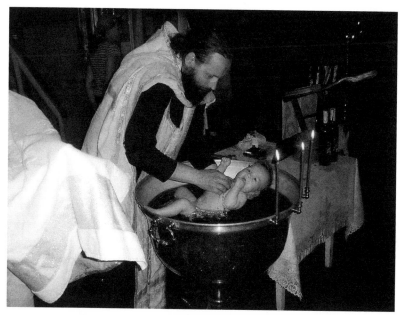

Orthodox infant baptism by immersion. Courtesy of Shustov.

sacraments. As we discuss these, we will note where these two traditions differ from one another.

SACRAMENTS OF INITIATION

Baptism. Baptism is the sacrament of initiation into a Christian church. In Roman Catholicism, baptism removes original sin, enabling persons to begin with a clean slate and to be responsible for the decisions they make. According to Timothy Ware, "Most Orthodox theologians reject the idea of 'original guilt' [or sin]. . . . Humans (Orthodox usually teach) automatically inherit Adam's corruption and mortality, but not his guilt."[8] So there is nothing of which a person needs to be cleansed except the sins they themselves have committed. In both Roman Catholicism and Eastern Orthodoxy, infants are baptized, but the Orthodox practice signifies God's claim on the child before the infant is aware of God and has nothing to do with original sin, although there is a concept of "emergency baptism" which seems to create a middle position. In Orthodoxy, infant baptism would be similar to the Latter-day Saint practice of blessing an infant shortly after birth. Roman Catholic baptism is usually done by pouring water on an infant's head three times, while in Orthodox traditions, the child is fully immersed three times, symbolizing a mystical burial and resurrection with Christ. Both baptisms are done in the name of the Father, the Son, and the Holy Ghost. Because baptism marks the soul, it is a nonrepeatable sacrament in both traditions.

Among Protestants, baptism is one of the two sacraments they celebrate. It may be done in a variety of ways from full immersion of a believing adult to sprinkling an infant. Latter-day Saint baptism is a "believer baptism" normally done at the age of eight by complete immersion under the hands of a priesthood holder.

Confirmation or chrismation. In the Roman Catholic Church, confirmation is when young persons confirm their faith for themselves and become full, active members of that church. They are confirmed by a bishop through the laying on of hands for the gift of the Holy Ghost. Since Catholics normally baptize infants, confirmation occurs quite a bit later, usually when a young person is between the ages of twelve and fifteen. Like baptism, this sacrament marks the soul, so it is nonrepeatable.

Among Orthodox Christians, baptism and chrismation (their word for confirmation) are done one right after the other. This is the time when a person, even an infant, receives the gift of the Holy Ghost, becomes a full member of the people of God, becomes a prophet, and receives a share in Christ's royal priesthood. The ritual is carried out with an oil called *chrism*, which is administered to various parts of the body with the sign of the cross (to the forehead, eyes, nostrils, mouth, ears, breast, hands, and feet) while the priest says, "The Seal of the gift of the Holy Spirit." Endowed members of the Latter-day Saint community will recognize that there are similarities between the Orthodox chrismation and the washings and anointings which take place in the Latter-day Saint temples. Chrismation is the sacrament of reconciliation for Eastern Orthodox Christians when a member has left the church or been excommunicated.

Among Latter-day Saints, baptism and confirmation take place in close proximity to one another, often on the same day. The confirmation is done by a holder of the Melchizedek Priesthood who lays his hands on the head of the newly baptized member and commands him or her to receive the Holy Ghost and then gives a blessing.

Should a Latter-day Saint be excommunicated, he or she would need to be rebaptized and reconfirmed.

Eucharist. In the Roman Catholic Church, the normal order of initiatory sacraments for new adult members would be baptism, then confirmation, followed by the Eucharist, which is what Latter-day Saints call "the sacrament." It is the celebration of the Lord's Supper. Because there is, however, such a gap in time between baptism and confirmation in the Roman Catholic Church, young people born in the church will first take communion when they are seven or eight. In Eastern Orthodoxy, the Eucharist is received even by infants. Among Latter-day Saints, quite young children, at the discretion of parents, receive the bread and water of the sacrament. In all traditions, this is a repeatable sacrament, and the one through which people most often encounter Christ. The Eucharist, or Holy Communion, is also the second sacrament accepted by Protestants. For Protestants, a sacrament must have been either administered to Jesus (baptism) or initiated by him (the Lord's Supper, or communion). Thus, there are only two sacraments in Protestantism.

SACRAMENTS OF HEALING

Penance and reconciliation. This sacrament in Roman Catholicism is often known as "confession," but that is only a part of penance. Penance begins with a deep self-examination both spiritually and behaviorally. One then goes to the confessional, which traditionally has permitted the penitent to be anonymous, although recently confession has been face to face with the priest. This can lead to follow-up and pastoral care, which has always been the practice in Eastern Orthodoxy. Once in the confessional, penitents tell the priest how long it has been since their last confession and whether it was a "good confession," meaning, did they say what they should have said, and did they mean it? Too often people view Catholic confession as an act that just wipes away sins without any real need for change. This is absolutely not true, any more than Latter-day Saint youths can "sow their wild oats," confess to the bishop, and automatically go on their missions. Following the confession, the priest will give the person penance to perform and then pronounce an absolution for their sins. The latter is effective only if the penance is performed with faithfulness and true repentance. For example, if a person were to confess to theft, the penance might be to make restitution and to turn himself or herself in to the authorities. However, if the penitent is an eight-year-old who confesses to bullying his sister, the priest might tell him to stop the practice and to say two "Our Fathers" (the Lord's Prayer) or three "Hail Marys." Since Mary is the mother of Jesus, many Catholics ask her to intercede for them with her son, and the Hail Mary expresses that wish.

> Hail Mary,
> Full of Grace,
> The Lord is with thee.
> Blessed art thou among women,
> and blessed is the fruit
> of thy womb, Jesus.
> Holy Mary,
> Mother of God,
> pray for us sinners now,
> and at the hour of death.
> Amen.

It should be noted here that confession is the sacrament of reconciliation in the Roman Catholic Church if a person has been excommunicated. Confession in the Eastern Orthodox tradition has always been face-to-face with the priest, as stated above. The confession is actually given to God with the priest as a witness. At the end of it, the Orthodox priest will give a penance and absolution, but he also has always had the ability to give pastoral care and follow-up with his parishioners because he knows their struggles.

Anointing. Anointing is the second sacrament of healing and deals with both the physical and spiritual dimensions of human life. In past years, anointing in Roman Catholicism was used primarily at the time of death. Since the Second Vatican Council (1962–65), it has been used much as Latter-day Saints use the ordinance of anointing. It is a sacrament to bring about healing and is carried out by anointing with consecrated oil, usually once per illness. But as Eastern Orthodoxy stresses, it may have two faces—one toward health and healing and the other toward release and death.

SACRAMENTS IN THE SERVICE OF THE COMMUNITY

Holy Orders. Taking Holy Orders means that a man or woman has taken the religious life as a full-time vocation. Women can become nuns, and men can become brothers (lay members of a religious order) or priests or both. Taking Holy Orders involves vows of celibacy, obedience, and possibly poverty. Like baptism and confirmation, assumption of these roles marks the soul, and a person wishing to be freed from Holy Orders usually has to be released by Rome. Clearly, those assuming Holy Orders serve the Roman Catholic Church by being able, as unmarried persons, to go where they are needed and to do what they are asked to do by their superiors.

Major orders are bishops, priests, and deacons in both Roman Catholicism and Eastern Orthodoxy. Bishops ordain people to all of the above offices. The primary difference between Roman Catholicism and Orthodoxy is that in the latter tradition, priests may be either married or unmarried and celibate. If one chooses to be married clergy, the choice and the marriage must take place before ordination. If a spouse dies, the priest is not permitted to remarry. Bishops are celibate and must be drawn from the unmarried clergy. Vatican II in the Roman Catholic Church (1962–65) declared Holy Orders and marriage to be equally valid vocations, and since that time, the recruitment of priests and nuns has been more difficult.

Marriage. Marriage serves the Catholic community by providing new members raised in strong Catholic families. The soul is also marked by marriage, and this is one of the reasons that divorce is not permitted in the Roman Catholic Church, in addition to Jesus' statement that what God has joined together, no one should put asunder.

Eastern Orthodoxy holds marriage in high esteem. Human beings are meant to live in relationships unless God gives someone the special grace of living a celibate life. However, divorce is permitted, and Eastern Orthodoxy recognizes that sometimes, though sad, it is healthier for a couple to separate than to stay together. In Roman Catholicism, in Eastern Orthodoxy, and among Latter-day Saints, sexual relations should exist only within marriage. In Roman Catholicism, use of contraception is banned, since sexual relations are for bringing children into the world. Eastern Orthodoxy, however, permits the use of artificial birth control methods, as do Latter-day Saints, since sexual relations also bind couples together in a special, intimate way. All traditions condemn abortions.

Having looked at the seven sacraments of the Catholic communion and the two sacraments of the Protestant churches, it is clear that Latter-day Saints are far more like the Catholics sacramentally than they are like Protestants, as the following chart shows.

— CATHOLICS —	— LATTER-DAY SAINTS —
SACRAMENTS	ORDINANCES
Baptism	Baptism
Confirmation or chrismation	Confirmation
Eucharist	"The sacrament"
Penance	(Not an ordinance)
Anointing	Anointing
Holy Orders	Ordination to the priesthood
Marriage	Marriage

Latter-day Saints are a very ordinance-oriented people. In the ordinances, people meet Christ in special ways, and this becomes true also with the ordinances of the temple. In actuality, Latter-day Saints have more ordinances than Catholics do sacraments.

THE MASS

To many who are not Catholic, the Mass is a bit of a mystery because they do not know what is transpiring, even though the service is now in the language of the people rather than in Latin. Sadly, this lack of understanding prevents non-Catholics from appreciating the beauty and spiritual power of the Mass. Yet, anyone who has sung in a high school or university choir more than likely has sung portions of the Mass, if not a full mass. Here we will look at the portions of the Mass that are used every Sunday in the Roman Catholic Church and which are the clothesline on which other elements of the worship service are hung, such as hymns, prayers, scripture readings, and sermons. The Greek and Latin words will be used for their titles, and then these will be translated, since most people have probably sung the Mass in its original languages.

KYRIE (LORD)

Lord, have mercy.
Christ, have mercy.
Lord, have mercy.

The Kyrie is the beginning of the mass. The worshipers come as sinners in need of forgiveness, and they come calling on the one, Christ, who can forgive.

GLORIA (GLORY)

Glory to God in the highest,
and peace to his people on earth.
Lord God, heavenly King,
almighty God and Father,
we worship you, we give you thanks,
we praise you for your glory.

Lord Jesus Christ, only Son of the Father,
Lord God, Lamb of God,
you take away the sin of the world:
have mercy on us;
you are seated at the right hand of the Father:
receive our prayer.
For you alone are the Holy One,
you alone are the Lord,
you alone are the Most High,
Jesus Christ,
with the Holy spirit,
in the glory of God the Father. Amen.

This next element of the mass is an act of praise. It begins with the words the angels sang at the time of Jesus' birth and then continues with acts of praise to all three members of the Godhead. The central figure, however, is Jesus Christ, the Lamb of God, the one who can have mercy, the one who takes away the sins of the world and thus the sins of the worshipers.

CREDO (WE BELIEVE)

We believe in one God,
the Father, the almighty,
maker of heaven and earth,
of all that is seen and unseen.

We believe in one Lord, Jesus Christ,
The only Son of God, eternally begotten of the Father,
God from God, Light from Light,
true God from true God,
begotten, not made, one in Being with the Father.
Through him all things were made.
For us men and for our salvation
he came down from heaven:
by the power of the Holy Spirit
he was born of the Virgin Mary, and became man.
For our sake he was crucified under Pontius Pilate;
he suffered, died, and was buried.
On the third day he rose again
in the fulfillment of the Scriptures;
he ascended into heaven
and is seated at the right hand of the Father.
He will come again in glory to judge the living and the dead,
and his kingdom will have no end.

We believe in the Holy Spirit, the Lord, the giver of life,
who proceeds from the Father and the Son.
With the Father and the Son he is worshiped and glorified.
He has spoken through the Prophets.
We believe in one holy catholic and apostolic Church.
We acknowledge one baptism for the forgiveness of sins.
We look for the resurrection of the dead,
and the life of the world to come. Amen.

This is the Nicene Creed, which is used in worship services around
the world in both Catholic and Protestant churches. This third element

of the mass is a statement of the worshipers' beliefs and sketches the broad outlines of Christian doctrine. Note that it is divided into three sections, the first dealing with the Father and his work, the second with Jesus' work, and the last with the work of the Holy Spirit, or Holy Ghost. Most of the creed could be said by Latter-day Saint Christians, but with reservations concerning certain statements about the Son, particularly the phrase "one in Being with the Father." There might also be some question about the word "catholic," but we should remember that it simply means "universal." Further, Latter-day Saints would be concerned about how the apostolic authority is passed from one generation to the next, as would a Roman Catholic, an Eastern Orthodox, an Anglican, a Presbyterian, or a Methodist. Thus, having come as sinners in need of help, having praised the members of the Godhead who can and do help, the worshipers through the creed now say what they believe.

SANCTUS (HOLY)

Holy, Holy, Holy Lord, God of power and might,
heaven and earth are full of your glory.
Hosanna in the highest.
Blessed is he who comes in the name of the Lord.
Hosanna in the highest.

The fourth element of the Mass is again an act of praise with Christ at its center. The first part of the Sanctus comes from Isaiah 6 as Isaiah encounters Jehovah in the temple and the seraphim say the first two lines to one another. The Hosanna portion of this is taken from Psalm 118:25–26 and are the words the crowds shouted as Jesus entered Jerusalem on the Sunday before his crucifixion. Thus, we have two Old Testament passages used in praise of Jesus.

At this point, the Mass transitions into the portion focused on the Eucharist. There are several prayers, all of which stress Christ's victory over death and his future coming in glory. Just prior to the taking of the Eucharist, the final piece of the Mass is said or sung.

AGNUS DEI (LAMB OF GOD)

Lamb of God, you take away the sins of the world:
have mercy on us.

> Lamb of God, you take away the sins of the world:
> have mercy on us.
> Lamb of God, you take away the sins of the world:
> grant us peace.

Essentially, the Agnus Dei is a prayer directed to Jesus Christ, who does in fact remove sin and thereby grants peace to those who come to him.

Eucharist. The Eucharist, or Holy Communion, is the culminating act of the Mass. Catholics believe that the bread and the wine literally become the body and blood of Christ, based on Christ's statements at the Last Supper that "this is my body" and "this is my blood." Thus, when Catholics take the bread and the wine, they have truly come into the presence of Christ and participate in the sacrifice that removes their sins. For Latter-day Saints, Christ is also present in the elements of the sacrament, but he is present spiritually. When Latter-day Saints take the bread and water, they take Christ upon themselves and thereby are momentarily as clean and pure as they were on the day of their baptism. Very quickly this cleanliness is marred by sinful thoughts, words, or actions, but the communicant was clean momentarily because of Christ's presence.

Looking back, let us see the path we have traveled in the Mass. The participants begin with a statement of their need for Christ because of their sin (Kyrie). Next, they praise the members of the Godhead, but with special reference to Christ, who removes sin (Gloria). They then together profess their faith in the work of the members of the Godhead, once again with special emphasis on the work of Jesus (Credo). Another act of praise occurs (Sanctus) with Christ as the focal point. Just prior to taking the Eucharist, Christ is petitioned to remove the sins of the worshipers and to give them peace (Agnus Dei). The worshipers then enter the presence of Christ as they partake of the Eucharist. Theologically, this sequence makes great sense and is beautifully augmented with the other changeable elements of the Mass. In reality, the Mass shares a parallel with the endowment ceremony, in which persons move progressively toward the presence of God, which is finally realized in the celestial room of the temple.

Items used during the Eucharist. ©Jorge Royan, http://www.royan.com.ar/.

MARY

Mary holds a very high place in Roman Catholicism, and there are four doctrines that are useful to understand. Because Mary is Jesus' mother, Roman Catholics believe that she can intercede in a special way with her son on their behalf. Thus, she is chief of the saints, and the following doctrines have risen around her as the Roman Catholic Church has contemplated her place in God's work. Latter-day Saints have one doctrine comparable to these.

Immaculate conception. This is a doctrine about Mary, not about Jesus. Roman Catholics believe that all human beings inherit original sin from Adam, and that would include Mary. If, however, Mary is to be a pure vessel that would not pass such sin on to Jesus, thereby making him unfit to be the perfect sacrifice that he had to be, her original sin had to be removed. According to this doctrine, that is precisely what happened. At the moment of Mary's conception in the womb of her mother, Anna, Jesus applied the Atonement to her, thereby enabling her to be born without sin. She was, therefore, a pure vessel into which Jesus could enter.

Virgin birth. The doctrine of the virgin birth states that Mary conceived through the power of the Holy Ghost. This does not make the Spirit the parent of Jesus, but rather it is just the agent of conception

261

while the Father is the parent. This is the doctrine that Latter-day Saints share in common with Roman Catholics, for this is what both Luke 1 and Alma 7 affirm.

Perpetual virginity. Not only do Catholics believe that Mary was a virgin when she conceived, but they also believe that she remained a virgin for the rest of her life. Persons with different views point out that the scriptures speak of Jesus' brothers and sisters and "James the Lord's brother." Catholics respond that these may be children of Joseph before he married Mary or that the terms could include cousins in Jesus' day. This doctrine underlines the absolute purity of Mary as the mother of God.

Bodily assumption. The doctrine of Mary's bodily assumption into heaven at the time of her death is the most recent of the above doctrines and was canonized in 1950. The Roman Catholic Church determined that it did not make sense for Jesus to let his mother deteriorate in a grave, so logically, he must have taken her immediately to himself. As the author, I have little problem with this doctrine, for the God I know can do things like send a flaming chariot to pick up Elijah. Such an act would certainly be within the realm of God's love and his power.

THE CROSS

The cross is a universal symbol of Christianity which Latter-day Saints have chosen not to adopt in order to distinguish Restoration Christianity from historical Christianity. Having said that, it is important that Latter-day Saints understand what the cross symbolizes for most Christians. There are actually three basic crosses among Christians (the Roman Catholic crucifix, the empty cross of Protestantism, and the crucifix of Eastern Orthodoxy). Each is a profound symbol defining Christ's atoning work.

The Roman Catholic crucifix shows Christ hanging on the cross, head down in death. Some have suggested that Roman Catholics worship a dead Christ, but this is utterly wrong, as one would know by attending a mass and observing the emphasis on the risen Christ. But what the dead Christ does show is the price that Jesus paid for our sins. He gave himself so fully to us that he was willing to die for us while we were still sinners. Thus, this crucifix shows the extent to which God is willing to go to save us.

The Protestant cross is an empty cross. As a cross, it proclaims the Atonement and, like the Roman Catholic crucifix, the extent to which God was willing to go to free us from sin. It is, however, an empty cross, and in its emptiness, it proclaims that Christ is no longer dead but is risen. So the Protestant cross stresses both Christ's sacrificial death and his Resurrection.

The Eastern Orthodox crucifix is perhaps the most complete symbol of them all. This symbol shows Christ crucified on the cross, but often his head is raised in triumph. What the Orthodox cross has done is combine Jesus' suffering and death, by showing Christ crucified, with his Resurrection, by displaying the risen Christ on the cross. Of all the symbols, it best reflects the Gospel of John's emphasis on "Christ's hour," which is both his death and Resurrection.

There is nothing in any of these symbols that contradicts Latter-day Saint thought, and it is important that Latter-day Saints respect these sacred symbols and understand them for what they are—profound portrayals of what Jesus has done for the human family in his triumphant overcoming of all that separates humanity from God.

THE REFORMATION

Protestant Christianity has many of its roots in the Reformation, which is normally dated from October 31, 1517, when Martin Luther (1482–1546) nailed his Ninety-Five Theses to the church door in Wittenberg, Germany. In the theses, he challenged the Catholic practice of selling indulgences to release persons from purgatory to raise money for the renovation of churches in Rome. Luther never intended to start

Martin Luther

a new denomination. He simply wanted to discuss in an academic setting a practice that he felt was at variance with the scriptures. He ultimately defended himself before the Holy Roman Emperor,

Charles V, and was excommunicated, forcing his followers to
kidnap him and hide him away
for two years. Out of his activity grew the Lutheran Church,
which is especially prominent
in Germany, Denmark, Norway,
Sweden, and Finland.

Another Reformer named
John Calvin (1509–64) was a
French Catholic who had been
studying law and became converted to the Reformation way
of thought. He went to Geneva,

John Calvin

Switzerland, where he was given full authority to run the city by
his theological principles. Both he and Luther wrote biblical commentaries on virtually every book of the Bible, but Calvin was also
very systematic in his thought, so he became the theologian of the
Reformation. His major work is *The Institutes of the Christian Religion*,
which any Protestant writing theology today still has to take into consideration. The Calvinist tradition gave rise to the Dutch Reformed
Church and to the Presbyterian Church which arose in Scotland
under the guidance of John Knox (1514–72).

The Reformation currents affected England just at the time that
Henry VIII (1491–1547) wanted to divorce Catherine of Aragon and
marry Anne Boleyn. When the pope refused to grant the divorce,
Henry returned to an ecclesiastical model that diminished Rome's
influence on England. Before 600 CE, the English church traced its
apostolic lineage to St. Andrew. At that time, the king was head of
the church and approved the appointment of bishops and other high
ecclesiastical authorities, so this became Henry's model. He denied
Rome's authority and was excommunicated from the Roman Catholic
Church. In response, he became head of the Church of England; con-
fiscated all Catholic monasteries and estates, thereby increasing the
Crown's wealth; and organized clergy under his direction, once again
approving bishops. He changed almost nothing, however, in the worship practices of the Mass. Later persons arose who challenged the

formalism of the Church of England, some wanting to "purify" the church and others wanting to separate from it and create their own Calvinist tradition. Some of this latter group came to the New World on the *Mayflower* and established Plymouth Colony in 1620, and some of the former group sailed to the New World in 1630 and established Massachusetts Bay Colony. Essentially, the two colonies held the same theological views, and out of them came the Congregational Church.

On the continent of Europe, a group arose espousing "believer baptism," and they became known as Anabaptists, meaning "to baptize again." Virtually all children were baptized in Europe as infants. Thus, when the Anabaptists rebaptized people as adult believers, they were saying that the Catholic and the general Protestant baptisms were not effective. This led to persecution from both Catholics and Protestants. Probably the best-known Anabaptist was the Dutch Menno Simons (1496–1561), who founded the Mennonites, out of which grew the Amish. One of the English separatists who was influenced by the practice of believer baptism was John Smythe (1570–1661). He became recognized as the father of the Baptist tradition, which Roger Williams (c. 1603–83) followed when he was exiled to Providence, Rhode Island.

In eighteenth-century England, a group of students gathered regularly at Oxford to study the scriptures and to live a disciplined Christian life. Their lives were so methodical that they became known as "Methodists." The best-known of this group is John Wesley (1703–91). Once ordained in the Church of England, he came to the colony of Georgia in the New World to convert the Native Americans and the frontiersmen to Christianity as he understood it. He was so rigid, however, that he ended up leaving the colony, having failed in his endeavor. Upon returning to England, he was one night attending a meeting in a hall on Aldersgate Street in London. A person was reading from the Preface of Luther's commentary on the book of Romans, and Wesley reported that he "felt his heart strangely warmed." This was the beginning of the experiential Christianity which became known as the Methodist Church. Wesley traveled all over England, preaching wherever he could, often outside because he was banned from preaching in

Church of England buildings. In 1784, even though he was not a bishop, Wesley ordained Thomas Coke to be the superintendent of the Methodist Church in America. It and the Baptist Church soon became the churches of the frontier because neither required trained clergy as did the Presbyterian or Congregational Churches.

The roots of all Protestant denominations in the United States reach back to these early beginnings. Their theologies are informed by the theological principles we have examined throughout this chapter, although there are different emphases that mark them.

— CONCLUSION

As diverse as Christianity is, its central focus is always on Jesus Christ. Every tradition, be it Eastern Orthodox, Roman Catholic, Protestant, or Latter-day Saint, is seeking to explain what it has heard God saying to it through his revelation of himself in Jesus of Nazareth. Undoubtedly, the differences between the faiths occur because the work of God is far too magnificent and grand for our small human minds to fully comprehend it. If we return to the idea in Jainism that each of us sees truth from different perspectives, then the true God, who reveals himself in Jesus Christ, may best be seen as a composite of all of our insights into who and what Jesus is and does. Perhaps instead of drawing artificial lines in the sand between one another, we should be willing to listen to what each has heard of the Emmanuel, the God with us in Jesus Christ. Perhaps we should see if others' insights may not highlight something in our own traditions that we would have otherwise missed. It would be wise to remember that God is infinitely greater than we are. Thus, he must "babble like a baby" for us to understand him. He even speaks our language so fully that he, Jehovah, was willing to enter our world as a mere mortal, laying aside his glory, that he might suffer, die, and be raised on behalf of sinful and imperfect human beings like ourselves.

— NOTES

1. "Major Religions of the World Ranked by Number of Adherents," Adherents.com, last modified August 9, 2007, http://www.adherents .com/Religions_By_Adherents.html.

2. Front inside cover of Henry Van Dyke, *The Book of Common Worship* (Philadelphia: General Division of the Publication of the Board of Christian Education of the United Presbyterian Church in the United States of America, 1964).

3. Andrew F. Ehat and Lyndon W. Cook, eds., *The Words of Joseph Smith* (Provo, UT: Religious Studies Center, Brigham Young University, 1980), 229; emphasis added.

4. See Dallin H. Oaks, in Conference Report, October 1993, 98.

5. Stephen E. Robinson, *Believing Christ* (Salt Lake City: Deseret Book, 1992), 25–26.

6. Doctrine and Covenants 20:25, 29; 63:20; 101:35.

7. Dallin H. Oaks, "Always Have His Spirit," *Ensign*, November 1996, 78–82.

8. Timothy Ware, *The Orthodox Church*, new ed. (New York: Penguin Books, 1997), 224.

Mosque of Muhammad Ali Pashan, Cairo, Egypt. Mosque means "place of prostration." © Val Brinkerhoff.

CHAPTER 13

ISLAM

Both Islam and Mormonism are highly ethical and moral faiths. For each, prayer is central to understanding God's will. Each has a historically rooted tradition that takes persons into God's presence and allows them to covenant with God that they will change their lives.

Given all the inaccurate media attention Islam has received since 9/11, this chapter becomes important to set the record straight about this great and attractive faith. There are 1.5 billion Muslims,[1] and Islam is one of the fastest-growing religions in the world. Islam is absolutely monotheistic. The religion is highly ethical in its teachings, and the Qur'an (its sacred book) addresses primarily how persons should live before God. As we have seen in recent years, there are definitely different views among Muslims of how Islam should be lived, which has led to some of the misunderstandings about what the religion stands for. Hopefully, this chapter will clarify what the Prophet Muhammad actually taught, what is in the Qur'an, and what are some of the inappropriate teachings of some who claim to be Muslim.

— ORIGINS

ISLAM AND MUSLIM

As we begin, we should clarify two terms: *Islam* and *Muslim*. *Islam* means "submission," in this case submission to God. A Muslim is "one who submits." Thus, Islam is the name of the faith, and Muslims are those who practice the faith. There are no "Islams," only Muslims, although one may speak of the "Islamic faith" or of "Islamic institutions."

PRE-ISLAMIC ARABIA

The origins of Islam lie in what is today Saudi Arabia. The heart of pre-Islamic Arabia was the oasis of Mecca, which held prominence for two reasons. First, it was a major caravan stopping point on the trade route which ran from present-day Syria in the north to Yemen in the south. It was therefore quite cosmopolitan, since persons of various nationalities and religions passed through it. Its inhabitants were also caravanners, so they too traveled and came into contact with Byzantines and Persians from the two dominant empires to the north.

Mecca's second claim to fame was that it was a religious pilgrimage center, for there was a shrine in the midst of it called the Ka'aba, a cube-shaped structure around and in which were statues of the multiplicity of gods that were worshiped on the Arabian peninsula. There was the high God known as Allah, which simply means "the God" in Arabic, but he was distant. Hence, his three daughters and other, nearer figures known as *jinn*—which were fairylike beings made from fire—were worshiped.[2] We meet one of these in the story of Aladdin and his lamp, for the English word for *jinn* is *genie*. These could be friendly or hostile. There were also ghouls, which were evil. Consequently, the world was filled with beings that needed to be appeased, and Mecca offered a center for the worship and control of all these beings. It was into this environment that Muhammad was born.

MUHAMMAD

The Meccan years. Muhammad was born in 570 CE and died in 632 CE. His father died before he was born, and his mother died when he was six, leaving him an orphan. He lived briefly with his grandfather, but his primary caregiver was his uncle Abu Talib, who

was respected but not particularly well-off financially. He was a cara-
vanner, so Muhammad was able to travel with him as far north as
Syria. In his travels, Muhammad met Christians and Jews. There is
no evidence that he read their holy books, and Muslims make the
point that Muhammad was illiterate and could not have created the
Qur'an. Latter-day Saints often stress the marginal formal learning
that Joseph Smith had to emphasize that he could not have created
the Book of Mormon.

Muhammad had some concerns as he grew to adulthood. The
polytheism and idolatry around him troubled him. He believed
that there was one God. Also, the religious festivals in Mecca were
often excuses for immoral behavior on the part of the participants.
In addition, he was deeply troubled by the female infanticide that
was too often practiced in his culture. The dowry laws required that
the family of the bride pay a large dowry to the family of the groom.
Many families of girls found this difficult, if not impossible, to do, so
upon the birth of a daughter, they would simply take her out and bury
her alive in the sand.

Muhammad followed the trade of his uncle and was hired to
manage the caravans of a wealthy widow named Khadija. She became
so impressed with Muhammad's integrity and honesty that she proposed marriage to him when he was twenty-five and she was forty.
They had six children, four daughters and two sons. Both of the sons
died young, and only one daughter outlived Muhammad. It was a
very happy marriage. Khadija was Muhammad's friend and confidant
as well as his wife.

Once married to Khadija, Muhammad had space in his life to
pursue his religious interests. Annually he would go on a retreat to
Mount Hira north of Mecca and there join other individuals seeking
the one God. On one of these retreats when he was forty (610 CE),
he received his call to be a prophet of God. While the Qur'an is not a
biography of Muhammad, there are a few chapters which reflect some
aspects of this early period. For example, in Sura 53 (chapter 53) of
the Qur'an we read:

By the Star when it goes down,—your companion is neither astray nor
being misled, nor does he say (aught) of (his own) desire. It is no less

than inspiration sent down to him: he was taught by one mighty in power. Endued with wisdom: for he appeared (in stately form) while he was in the highest part of the horizon: then he approached and came closer, and was at a distance of but two bow-lengths or (even) nearer; so did (Allah) convey the inspiration to his servant—(conveyed) what he (meant) to convey. The (prophet's) (mind and) heart in no way falsified that which he saw. (Sura 53:1–11)[3]

This sura reflects Muhammad's call on the Night of Power. Just before dawn the angel Gabriel appeared on the horizon and drew within two bow shots (Possibly two hundred yards) of Muhammad. He then called him to read or recite: "Proclaim! (or Read!) In the name of thy Lord and cherisher, who created—created man, out of a leech-like clot; Proclaim! And thy Lord is most bountiful,—he who taught (the use of) the Pen,—taught man that which he knew not" (Sura 96:1–5). Muhammad had no idea what he was supposed to proclaim or read and was terrified, so he fled down the mountain to Khadija. It was Khadija who assured Muhammad that this experience was from God. Once Muhammad accepted his call, he would receive revelations from God or Gabriel by either hearing them or receiving them in his mind.[4] Once he had memorized the message, he would repeat it to family and close friends and occasionally at the Ka'aba, the cubic shrine.

Muhammad's message challenged idolatry, thereby endangering one of Mecca's primary sources of income. In addition, his revelations called for social justice, including duties to the poor and the elevation of women in society. All this had the potential to undercut the social fabric of Mecca, so the ruling tribe, the Quraysh, aligned themselves against Muhammad and the handful of followers that had gathered around him. Even though he was supported by several influential persons in the community—Khadija, his uncle Abu Talib, and his future father-in-law, Abu Bakr—Muhammad was progressively marginalized, and his followers were persecuted. Problems became so great that Muhammad sent some Muslims to Abyssinia (current-day Ethiopia) to find religious freedom. They were followed by representatives of Mecca to try to convince the king of Abyssinia to send them back, but after a debate between representatives of the two groups, the king decided to permit the Muslims to stay and ejected the Meccans.

In 619 Khadija died, and shortly thereafter, Abu Talib, never a Muslim, died, removing two of Muhammad's primary supporters. In addition, the persecution deepened as Muslims were not allowed to participate in Meccan trade, thereby removing their livelihood and bringing them down into poverty. Even Abu Bakr was shoved to the edges of the community. In 620, as Muhammad was mourning at the Ka'aba, Gabriel and other angels appeared to him, placed him on the back of a winged horse named Buraq, and flew him to Jerusalem. After leading prior prophets—Adam, Moses, Abraham, and Jesus, to name a few—in prayer, Muhammad ascended through the heavens into God's presence, where he was commissioned as the seal of the prophets, meaning that he confirmed their messages and that he was the last prophet.

The persecutions in Mecca continued, and in 622, six men from the community of Yathrib, about two hundred miles to the north of Mecca, arrived for pilgrimage in Mecca. They had another objective, however, and that was to find a person to lead their community. They had heard of the Prophet, so they interviewed him and then offered him leadership of the community without conditions. Muhammad accepted and began to send his followers in small groups to Yathrib. Word spread that the Prophet was planning to leave, but the last thing the Meccans wanted was for him to be two hundred miles to the north, where he could cause real trouble. Consequently, a pact was made that one person from each clan would participate in the assassination of Muhammad, thereby preventing reprisal by one clan upon another. Word of the plot reached Muhammad, and he and Abu Bakr fled Mecca, arriving in Yathrib after eight days of travel. The trip to Yathrib is known as the Night Migration (Hijra) and marks a turning point in Muslim history, for from this point on, Muhammad could establish his own institutions within the faith. The year 622 CE is also the beginning of the Muslim calendar, which is lunar and therefore has a slightly shorter year than the solar year. Thus, 2011 is 1432 H, or 1432 lunar years after the Hijra.

The Medina years. Once Muhammad arrived in Yathrib, the name of the town was changed to Medina, meaning "city of the Prophet," and it truly was that. Here he laid the foundation for the practices of Islam. He erected the first mosque in Medina. *Mosque* means "place of prostration," which can be anywhere, but the first building used as a place of prostration or prayer was constructed in Medina. Prostration during prayer was begun with worshipers facing Jerusalem, the place from which Muhammad ascended to the presence of God. However, because many of the Jewish population in Medina were working with the Meccans behind the Prophet's back, the direction of prayer was changed when a revelation came directing the worshipers to face Mecca. Weekly services were established on Friday, and the call to prayer was first given prior to those services. Shortly, the call was given before each prayer time. Finally, the taking up of alms for the poor and in support of the cause was instituted.

The Medina years for the most part were not years of peace. The Muslims understood themselves to be in a state of war with Mecca because they had been unjustly evicted solely because of their faith. Sura 22:39–40 states, "To those against whom war is made, permission is given (to fight), because they are wronged;—and verily, Allah is Most Powerful for their aid;—(They are) those who have been expelled from their homes in defiance of the right,—(for no cause) except that they say, 'Our Lord is Allah.'"

As those who had been unjustly driven from Mecca, the Muslims had no compunction about raiding the Meccan caravans. This led to several battles with mixed results for both sides. In 628 CE, Muhammad and his unarmed followers went on pilgrimage to Mecca, placing the Meccans in a very difficult position because as guardians of the Ka'aba, they had to allow all pilgrims access to it. This forced the Meccans to negotiate with the Muslims on an equal footing. The result was a ten-year peace treaty in which the Muslims agreed not to enter Mecca that year, but every year hence they could go for three days, and the Meccans would allow them access to the shrine. In 630 CE, a tribe allied with the Meccans attacked a tribe allied with the Muslims, and the Muslims saw this as breaking the treaty. When the Muslims appeared ten thousand strong on the hilltop above Mecca, the Meccans capitulated. Many expected there to be a bloodbath because the Muslims had been so badly treated by the Meccans. The Prophet, however, simply issued a general amnesty except for anyone who attacked the Muslims. This amnesty should tell us a good deal about the character of the Prophet Muhammad as well as the nature of Islam.

After delivering the Qur'an and the foundational principles and practices of Islam, Muhammad died in 632 CE after a brief illness.

Without going into detail, Latter-day Saint Christians will see many parallels between Muhammad and Joseph Smith. Both received their call through a divine vision or encounter. Each was to deliver the final message from God. Each faced persecution and opposition, and each established his own city and center for the faith. The Muslims ultimately won over their enemies, partly through a show of power. The Prophet of the Latter-day Saints, however, was assassinated, and the Saints then had to flee Nauvoo, the city of Joseph, into the wilderness. There they were still followed and hounded even to the degree that they stood ready to burn their homes and move on once again if the government chose to try to force them to live differently than they believed God called them to live.

Successors to the Prophet. Upon Muhammad's death, there was no clarity concerning his successor. Most Muslims thought the senior companion, Abu Bakr, should be the successor, or Caliph. A small portion believed that the successor should be Ali, Muhammad's cousin and son-in-law, since they thought succession should follow family lines. This discussion should be familiar to Latter-day Saints, since upon the death of Joseph Smith his successor was not clear. Most followed Brigham Young, the President of the Quorum of Twelve, while some believed that Joseph Smith III should succeed his father. In both religious traditions the majority prevailed, but a small minority group continued. In Islam the majority are known as Sunnis, while the minority are known as Shi'ites, or the "party of Ali." Among Latter-day Saints, the majority is The Church of Jesus Christ of Latter-day Saints, while the minority was known as the Reorganized Church of Jesus Christ of Latter Day Saints and is known today as the Community of Christ.

The first three successors to the prophet were Sunnis—Abu Bakr, Omar, and Uthman. Finally, Ali became the fourth successor, but he was unable to heal the rift between the two groups, finally being assassinated. He was succeeded by his son, Hussan, who abdicated after a year, and then by another son, Husayn. Husayn and a small group of Shi'ites were massacred by a large group of Sunnis in 680 CE, and the Caliphate passed back to the Sunnis. However, the Shi'ites never believed that the first three Caliphs were legitimate and believed that only with Ali and his sons had the leadership passed into legitimate hands, with leaders known as *Imams*. The difference between a Caliph and an Imam is that the Caliph was primarily a political leader but not a religious leader of the community as Muhammad was. The office of the Caliph ended with the fall of the Ottoman Empire in 1918. The Imam, on the other hand, had both a political and religious aura about him. He was not a prophet but was more than a political leader and carried religious authority. Hence, in Iran today, it is the religious head of the country, not its president, who is the true leader.

THE SUNNIS AND THE SHI'ITES

Islam has numerous groups within it. It is not at all homogeneous, but the discussion above requires us to look further at the Sunnis and the Shi'ites. As we have seen, they arose out of the debate over who should succeed the Prophet. Eighty-five percent of the Muslim world is Sunni, and 15 percent is Shi'ite. Most of the Shi'ite population live in Iran (95 percent Shi'ite) and Iraq (60 percent Shi'ite). Sunnis are widely dispersed around the world, with the largest Muslim country being Indonesia. Both groups claim to follow the traditions of the prophet and, therefore, practice much the same way. Shi'ism, however, has always seen itself as the true preserver of Islam but has felt marginalized in the Islamic world.

The uniqueness of the Shi'ites is that they do not believe that the succession of Imams ended with the death of the third Imam, Husayn. Most believe that the succession continued until the Twelfth Imam, who rather than dying went into hiding in 873 CE. He continued to communicate with the community through persons known as "gates," or "Babs." At a future date, he would return as the "restorer" to prepare the way for the return of Jesus, who Muslims believe did not die on the cross (someone else did), rather asserting that he was taken up to heaven and will return as he promised. When he returns, he will usher in a short period of peace, die, and be buried next to the Prophet Muhammad. At the time of the Resurrection, the two will rise together. Before the Resurrection, the righteous and the wicked dwell in their graves. The graves of the righteous are spacious and light, and these people receive daily visions of the place awaiting them in heaven. The wicked are also in their graves, which are small and crush in on them. They too receive daily visions, but of their place in hell. At the time of the Resurrection, the wicked and the righteous will rise and enter their final destiny—the joys of heaven or the pains of hell.

Sunnis also believe in a future restorer, but he is an unknown figure. He too will come to prepare the way for Jesus' return, who when he comes will usher in the age of peace, die, be buried next to the Prophet, and then rise alongside him. Hence, the major difference between the two groups is over the identity of the future restorer. Is he unknown, or is he the Twelfth Imam who will return?

MUSLIM THOUGHT AND PRACTICE

THE FIVE PILLARS OF ISLAM

Statement of faith. Islam's fundamental theology is captured in the faith statement, "There is no God but Allah, and Muhammad is his messenger," and when persons say this with faith before two witnesses, they become Muslims. The first thing to notice about the confession is that God (Allah) is before all things. He is uncreated, all-knowing, and all-powerful. Nothing exists outside of him that he has not made. No greater sin exists than to try to put something in his place. It is this God who communicates with and gives commandments and guidance to the human race, whom he created. He sends his messages in three ways.

First, he sends prophets, and Muslims would agree whole-heartedly with the statement in Amos 3:7: "Surely the Lord God will do nothing, but he revealeth his secret unto his servants the prophets." The first prophet was Adam, and later came Noah and Abraham. At Abraham there is a split in the tree of prophets, with Isaac being the forerunner of the Jewish and Christian side, which culminates in Jesus, and Ishmael being the precursor of the side that concludes with Muhammad. Through all the Jewish, Christian, and Islamic prophets, God has spoken to the human family. Some of them, like Jesus and Muhammad, have left texts and are known not only as prophets but also as "messengers," while others have simply spoken God's word in their day and time and are prophets. Given this, it is most proper to speak of Muhammad as a messenger.

Secondly, God communicates through angels who were created to live in the heavens and serve God. We have already met one of these in the person of Gabriel. It is probably wise to realize that there is a "dark side to the force." When God created Adam, he required all the angels and jinn to bow down to him, but one jinn, Iblis, refused to do so, saying that he was a being of fire, while Adam was just a piece of dirt. He is the satanic figure in Islam. As in Christianity, he has no power of his own but can do only that which God permits.

Thirdly, God communicates fully and finally through the Qur'an, and if we are to understand Islam, we need to stop and consider the Qur'an more fully. The best way to understand its importance is to compare its place in Islam with the place of the Word of God in Christianity. In both Christianity and Islam, the Word of God exists with God. If we think of the incarnate Word in Christianity, it is Jesus Christ, and the Bible is what delivers him to us. Thus, to attack Jesus in any way is to attack the very heart of the Christian faith. In Islam, the Word of God becomes incarnate in a book, the Qur'an, and to be perceived as attacking it is to attack the heart of Islam. The Qur'an is delivered by Muhammad the messenger. Thus, what at a cursory glance seems like an equation of Jesus/Muhammad and Bible/Qur'an is really the equation Jesus/Qur'an and Bible/Muhammad. If we do not understand this absolute centrality of the Qur'an to Islamic life, we will never understand Islam. Islam draws its lifeblood from the Qur'an in the same way Christianity finds its life in Jesus.

With the coming of the Qur'an, many reforms took place in Arabian life. The Qur'an prohibited the use of alcohol. It forbade gambling. It elevated women, which we will discuss later. It banned aggression while permitting defensive warfare. Thus, it changed the ethical climate of Arabia.

Prayer. Prayer is at the heart of the Muslim life. Perhaps another word for it might be "praise," for Sunni Muslims stop five times each day to praise God and pray to him (Shi'ites pray three times). The call to prayer is given from mosques before each prayer time: before sunrise, midday, midafternoon, sundown, and nightfall. The prayer call gives a sense of the character of Muslim prayer, and the elements are generally repeated at least twice.

God is most great.

I witness that there is no God but Allah.

I witness that Muhammad is the messenger of Allah.

Come to prayer.

Come to salvation and prosperity.

God is most great.

There is no God but Allah.

There is a definite pattern of rituals that goes with these prayer times. The first rite is to wash the hands, mouth, nose, right arm, and left arm. The worshiper then wipes his or her hand over the head and then washes the right foot and then the left foot. Most of the

Prayer tower (minaret), Abu Dhabi, UAE, from which the calls to prayer are announced. Prayers are at the heart of Muslim life and are led by an Imam or prayer leader. Public domain.

washings are done three times as ritual purification prior to prayer. The prayers are led by the Imam or by a prayer leader, who may be any knowledgeable male. Later we will look at women's piety. Women are not excluded from the mosque but are generally at the sides, at the back, or in a balcony. There are various postures assumed during the prayers, from standing to kneeling to prostration, and it is the latter position that is central to prayer, for it is a graphic demonstration of "submission." Many Muslims, after a lifetime of prayer, will have the "mark of prostration" on their foreheads—a bruise from pressing their foreheads to the floor. Practicing Muslims stop five times a day for about twenty minutes to remember and praise God. What a wonderful way to establish a continuing religious presence in one's life, for every act becomes informed by these regular prayer times. At the end of the prayers, the worshipers shake hands with those on either side of them to signify inclusion in the community.

Friday's midday prayers are special services during which all men are expected to attend the mosque. Women, because of their family responsibilities, are excused from them but may come if they wish. The primary difference between the Friday midday prayer and those on other days is that there is a sermon delivered. The sermon can touch on many things, but it can at times be very highly political. In 2011 we saw the Friday prayers spill out into the streets of Algeria, Egypt, Syria, and other Middle Eastern countries as people voiced their desire for political freedom.

Almsgiving. Muslims are expected to give to charitable causes, and when they give alms, they purify their remaining resources for their own use. This is much like Latter-day Saints, who give 10 percent of their income and by doing so consecrate the other 90 percent for personal use. In Islam, the amount varies depending upon the kind of property that is involved. For example, persons give one-tenth of the produce of the land. However, from cash assets that have been held for over a year, people are to give 2.5 percent. Houses, furniture, personal possessions, and the things which a person uses to make a living are not assessed. But this is really only the base. Most Muslim countries do not have the social safety nets that Western countries do, so the care of the poor falls on the community. After Friday prayers, there will always be persons standing outside the mosques with their hands out for contributions. These are the poor, and this is the community's way of caring for them, so almsgiving is an ongoing process.

The fast. During the month of Ramadan, the month in which Muhammad was called, Muslims are required to fast. Since Islam is on a lunar calendar that is not periodically corrected, it is impossible to tie Ramadan to the Western calendar. Ramadan moves through the entire calendar approximately every thirty-three Islamic years. The month is a time of personal self-examination, and usually Muslims read the Qur'an completely through. The fast lasts for thirty days. Fasting means that no one may eat, drink, smoke, or have sexual relations during the daylight hours. Fasting begins each morning when it becomes light enough to tell the difference between a black and a white thread and ends when that difference can no longer be distinguished. After sunset, the fast is traditionally broken with a few dates and some juice. Later in the evening, families gather for large meals, but they are to invite the poor to join them or provide food for the poor. Before early morning prayers, a meal is eaten, and then the fast begins again for the day as people remember the miracle of Muhammad's call and his bringing of the Qur'an.

Pilgrimage (Hajj). The pilgrimage to Mecca is expected once in the lifetime of each person who is physically and financially able to go. It has parallels with the endowment ceremony in that it is centered on scriptural characters and ultimately leads to a place that is considered to be in God's presence. After completing their own pilgrimages, persons may then go on behalf of others who are unable to go, or they may go even for the dead, much as Latter-day Saints do vicarious work for the dead in the temples. The pilgrimage is held in the last month of the Islamic calendar year and, like the fast, moves over time through the year. The pilgrimage lasts for six days, beginning on the eighth day of the month. Persons can go to Mecca at other times of the year and do some of the rituals of the pilgrimage, but those visits do not count as a pilgrimage. It must be done with others at the defined time. Only Muslims are allowed in Mecca and Medina because these are sacred space to Muslims in the same way that temples are sacred space to Latter-day Saints. Nothing secret goes on in either case, but persons who are not Muslims or Latter-day Saints cannot attend the pilgrimage or the temple.

Persons arrive in Mecca ahead of the pilgrimage, and as they approach a line outside Mecca, males put on the ihram and take upon themselves the state of Ihram. The ihram as a garment is two pieces of white cloth, one which is wrapped around the waist and the another which is worn over the left shoulder. All men must wear this and remove all signs of rank or wealth. Women may wear a white garment but are not required to do so. Instead, they may wear their native dress. Thus, those persons dressed in white show the unity of Islam, while those women dressed in their native clothing highlight the diversity of Islam. The state of Ihram is a state of purity in which no sexual contact is permitted and nails and hair are not cut. Also, green trees may not be harmed or animals killed, except dangerous ones such as scorpions. As we examine the pilgrimage, we will highlight the major events, leaving out some of the lesser rituals.

Day one—the eighth day of the month. The first act of the pilgrimage is to walk around the Ka'aba, which Muslims believe Abraham and his son Ishmael built on a site where Adam had built an altar. This introduces the narrative that will be followed through the pilgrimage, which focuses on Abraham, Hagar, and Ishmael. When Sarah, Abraham's wife, was unable to have a child, she offered her servant, Hagar, as a wife to Abraham, according to Islamic tradition. When Hagar had Ishmael, a jealous Sarah required Abraham to drive out Hagar and Ishmael, who eventually found themselves near the present site of Mecca. Hagar saw that Ishmael was rapidly dehydrating and so began a frantic search for water, running back and forth between two low hills. While she was doing this, Ishmael was lying under a bush kicking his heels in the sand. Suddenly, water appeared under his feet, and through God's goodness they were both saved.

Thus, after circling the Ka'aba, the next major act is to walk rapidly back and forth between the two low hills, imitating Hagar's search for water. Following this, the pilgrims drink from the well Zamzam, which is believed to have appeared in response to Ishmael's and Hagar's needs and which reminds the pilgrims that God will also meet their needs. Following these rituals, people begin to move out of Mecca toward the town of Mina, which is about four and a half miles away. There they perform the evening prayers and spend the night.

Ka'aba, Mecca, Saudi Arabia. The first act of pilgrimage is to walk around the Ka'aba.
Courtesy of Aiman Titi.

Day two—the ninth day of the month. The morning prayer is done in Mina, and then the pilgrims move another four and a half miles toward Arafat, where they must be by noon. Arafat is a broad plain with a volcanic cone in its center. It is at Arafat that the "standing ceremony" takes place, for this is where the worshipers are closest to God and where he is most ready to forgive. Worshipers may read the Qur'an, recite prayers, ask forgiveness, repent of their sins, or listen to impromptu sermons. Each Muslim stands alone before his or her God in the midst of two million other people. If one does not participate in the standing ceremony at Arafat, one has not done the pilgrimage. This is the celestial room of the pilgrimage. At sundown people leave Arafat quickly and return about a quarter of the way to Mecca, stopping at Muzdalifah for the night prayers.

Day three—the tenth day of the month. The morning prayer is said in Muzdalifah, and then the pilgrims move once again toward Mina. As they go, they pick up either 49 or 70 pebbles. Upon reaching Mina, the largest of the three pillars of Satan is stoned with seven stones. These pillars represent the three times that Satan appeared to Abraham and Ishmael as they were going to sacrifice Ishmael at God's command. Each time Satan appeared and tried to dissuade them from performing the sacrifice, they drove him away by throwing stones at him. As the pilgrims stone the great pillar, they are stoning their own Satans and temptations and recommitting themselves to following God's ways.

Notice that it is Ishmael who is to be sacrificed in Muslim thought, not Isaac as in Christian and Jewish belief. Muslims point out that even the Old Testament says that it was Abraham's *only* son (Genesis 22:2) who was to be sacrificed, even though the text identifies that son as Isaac. However, according to Muslim thought, the son of Abraham, who was truly "the only son," was Ishmael, and Isaac was never Abraham's only son. He was his second son.

Following the stoning of the pillar of Satan, Muslims may offer a sheep, a goat, a cow, or a camel. In the past, pilgrims slaughtered the animal, but today one may buy a voucher which guarantees that an animal will be sacrificed in the pilgrim's name and its meat packed and sent to the poor. This sacrifice recalls that God provided a substitute for Ishmael through the ram caught in the bush, and as the animal is sacrificed, persons should recall God's providential care of them also.

After the sacrifice, the state of Ihram ends, and men have their heads shaved and women have a lock of their hair cut. Essentially, the constraints of the state of purity are lifted except the one banning sexual contact. Pilgrims return to Mecca to circumambulate the Ka'aba seven times as before, and then they return to Mina for a three-day festival. On each of the three following days, seven stones are thrown at each of the three pillars of Satan. People can leave after the twelfth or thirteenth day of the month. Whichever day they leave, they return to Mecca, walk around the Ka'aba seven times, and ask permission from God to end the pilgrimage. Some then go on to Medina, only two hundred miles to the north, and some even go on to Jerusalem, the third holiest city to Muslims. Trips to Medina and Jerusalem are not a part of the pilgrimage.

JIHAD—A SIXTH PILLAR?

Some Muslims claim that jihad is the sixth pillar of Islam, but much hangs on how one translates the word. The literal meaning is "struggle" or "striving," and so any struggle for the faith, such as reading the Qur'an, saying prayers, or participating in the fast or the pilgrimage could be jihad. The Prophet Muhammad, upon returning from a battle, once made the comment that they had completed the little jihad and now needed to continue with the great jihad. When asked what the latter was, he responded that it was the war against evil within oneself. Struggle for the faith may include its defense when threatened, and then jihad can be "holy war," much as Captain Moroni's war in defense of his family, faith, and nation was a holy war. In Islam, if one were to die in a true holy war, that person would go immediately to paradise to await the Resurrection. Unfortunately, the term *jihad* has been hijacked by Islamic extremists, who have used it as an excuse to entice many into suicide bombings and other acts of violence for political reasons, often killing their own people. In the Hadith, a collection of sayings originating with the Prophet, it is recorded, "It is related from Abdullah bin Omar, 'The Apostle of God forbade the killing of women and children.'"[5] Unfortunately, it is women and children and other noncombatants that have suffered the most from supposed acts of jihad by Islamic radicals, which places the radicals far beyond the realm of true Islam. It is wrong to paint all of Islam with their brush.

WOMEN

The treatment of women varies across the Islamic world not because the Qur'an is unclear about the place of women but because cultures are hard to change. The Qur'an makes it very clear that men and women are equal before God. Granted, they have their different roles, with the man being the provider and the woman being the one who manages the home and the children, but this does not make them unequal. The roles of the Muslim woman are very much like those of the Latter-day Saint woman. It has been said that Muslim women in the seventh century CE had more rights than did an English woman until late in the nineteenth century. Islam was far ahead of its time. Under the Qur'an, women could own and inherit property, they were to receive the dowry from their husband as an insurance policy against divorce or death, and they could run businesses.

Islam has spread rapidly across the world. Over a billion people accept its message, but sometimes cultures change slowly, and this is especially true of relationships between men and women in cultures that are male-dominated. Women have different roles and privileges dependent upon the country where they live. In Egypt and Jordan, women seem to choose to wear traditional Islamic dress or Western clothing, and sisters may choose differently. In Indonesia, women and men sit in the same college classes, but the women wear the long robe and the traditional head covering. In Saudi Arabia, women are required to wear the traditional robe and head covering and are generally separated from men, but they can become doctors. In Afghanistan, under the Taliban, girls were not permitted to get an education. Turkey is a secular society, and women are not permitted to wear the robes or the head coverings. The treatment of women by men varies just as widely from country to country and often depends on the cultural norms men have learned. In some countries, women are definitely demeaned, but that is not what Islam teaches about their place before God and all others.

Women also play a critical role in religious education. It is the women who teach the children the prayers and Islamic life at home. As noted, women may go to the mosque, and there are certain places in the mosque for them to pray. This is not because they are inferior but because of the positions people take during prayer. A woman in the position of prostration could well be a distraction to a man behind her, so the sexes are separated, much as men and women are separated in the Latter-day Saint temples. The separation prevents distractions. In Islam, female piety is usually expressed and practiced in the home, but women may also visit shrines, where they find socialization with other women as well as a quiet place to express their faith and prayers.

— CONCLUSION

There is much that is common between Islam and The Church of Jesus Christ of Latter-day Saints. Both believe in a succession of prophets beginning with Adam; but for Islam, Muhammad is the seal, and therefore the last, of the prophets. Latter-day Saints believe that there is a series of living prophets today, beginning with Joseph Smith and the Restoration. Both are highly ethical and moral faiths. For each, prayer is central to understanding God's will. Each has a historically rooted tradition that takes persons into God's presence and allows them to covenant with God that they will change their lives. Both ban alcohol and gambling. Both await Jesus' return, although Muslims see him as a prophet and Latter-day Saints see him as the Son of God. Both believe in a general Resurrection of the dead, although they differ in whether the end is heaven or hell or whether there are various degrees of glory.

Unfortunately, because of some of the extremists within Islam, the Western press has tended to focus on the negative actions of some Muslims to the almost total exclusion of seeing the enormous good that Islam brings into the lives of average people. Hopefully, some of that good is reflected here.

— NOTES

1. "Major Religions of the World Ranked by Number of Adherents," Adherents.com, last modified August 9, 2007, http://www.adherents .com/Religions_By_Adherents.html#Islam.
2. Daniel C. Peterson, *Muhammad: Prophet of God* (Grand Rapids, MI: Eerdmans, 2007), 21.
3. *The Holy Qur'an: English Translation of the Meanings and Commentary*, rev. and ed. the Presidency of Islamic Researches, IFTA, Call and Guidance (Medinah, Saudi Arabia: The Custodian of The Two Holy Mosques King Fahd Complex for The Printing of The Holy Qur'an).
4. Peterson, *Muhammad*, 51.
5. Robert E. Van Voorst, *Anthology of World Scriptures*, 6th ed. (Mason, OH: Cengage Learning, 2008), 324.

Shrine to the Bab, Mount Carmel, Haifa, Israel. Here the remains of the Bab are enshrined. Courtesy of Tom Habibi.

CHAPTER 14

BAHÁ'Í

Within the Bahá'í Faith is a concept of continuing revelation through which God addresses the human family. There is profound compassion for the human condition and a desire to better humankind.

The Bahá'í Faith (Bahá'í meaning "Follower of Splendor") is the newest of the religions we will examine, arising almost at the same time as The Church of Jesus Christ of Latter-day Saints. The Bahá'í Faith has around seven million members, located in virtually every country of the world.[1] Bahá'ís have a strong sense of worldwide unity, not just among themselves but in their view of all races, religions, and peoples. They are inclusive of all persons and see God constantly working in this world through the various religious communities from the time of creation to the present and into the distant future. Theirs is a powerful message to a badly fragmented world which moves toward isolationism, not the direction that God would have the human family go. Bahá'ís have been and continue to be persecuted, primarily in the land of their birth—Iran.[2] Today their worldwide headquarters is in Haifa, Israel, located on a beautifully landscaped property on the slopes of Mount Carmel.

— ORIGINS

THE BAB

The roots of the Bahá'í Faith lie in Shi'ite Islam, but the faith should never be considered a sect of Islam. It is its own religion. As stated in the Islam chapter, the Shi'ites believe that the Twelfth Imam went into hiding in 873 CE and that he was contacted thereafter through "gates," or "Babs." In the Bahá'í Faith, the concepts of the Hidden Imam and the Bab are brought together, for on May 23, 1844, Siyyid Ali-Muhammad (b. 1819) announced to one person that he was the one for whom people waited, meaning that he was the Twelfth Imam returned. On December 20, 1844, he made the same pronouncement to a group at the Ka'aba in Mecca. He became known as the Bab, and he saw himself preparing the way for one greater than he. He was a kind of John the Baptist.

His claim to be the returned Hidden Imam immediately met opposition from the Shi'ite clerics in Persia (today Iran). Clearly, such a claim threatened their position, and the persecution of the Babi community was launched with brutality so extreme that it almost defies description. The Bab proposed an entirely new society, much as did Muhammad or Joseph Smith, which would have challenged the existing views on economics, marriage, divorce, inheritance, and other issues. This idea of a new society challenged the status quo which kept the powerful in charge. The Bab was imprisoned, and then on July 9, 1850, he and a companion were brought out for execution by a firing squad made up of 750 Armenian Christian soldiers who did not want to execute him. They fired, and when the smoke had cleared, the Bab had disappeared, and his companion stood unhurt. A search for the Bab ensued, and he was found back in his cell completing a letter. He was brought out again, and a regiment of Muslim soldiers was marched out to perform the execution. This time both men were killed, but Bahá'ís see the first event as proof of God's continuing involvement in human history by honoring the wishes of the Armenian Christians.

BAHA'U'LLAH

One of the Bab's earliest followers, declaring his faith in 1844, was a nobleman by the name of Mirza Husayn Ali (b. 1817). He carried on a constant correspondence with the Bab and became recognized in the Babi community as the best interpreter of the faith. As his stature and role increased within the community, he gave various sacred names to its members, taking upon himself the name Baha'u'llah, meaning "Glory to God." His social standing kept him free of the persecution through which other members of the community were passing, but finally in 1852, he too was arrested. He was put in a dungeon in Tehran that had been a water cistern, and thus there was

Baha'u'llah. Public domain.

no outlet for sewage, making it a horrible place to be imprisoned. While there, he recounts the following experience:

> One night, in a dream, these exalted words were heard on every side: "Verily, We shall render Thee victorious by Thyself and by Thy pen. Grieve Thou not for that which hath befallen Thee, neither be Thou afraid, for Thou art in safety. Ere long will God raise up the treasures of the earth—men who will aid Thee through Thyself and through Thy Name, wherewith God hath revived the hearts of such as have recognized Him." . . . During the days I lay in the prison of Tihrán [Tehran], though the galling weight of the chain and the stench-filled air allowed Me but little sleep, still in those infrequent moments of slumber I felt as if something flowed from the crown of My head over My breast, even as a mighty torrent that precipitateth itself upon the earth from the summit of a lofty mountain. Every limb of My body would, as a result, be set afire. At such moments My tongue recited what no man could bear to hear.[3]

Latter-day Saints reading this account cannot help but recall the Lord's words to Joseph Smith as he languished in Liberty Jail in March of 1839.

> My son, peace be unto thy soul; thine adversity and thine afflictions shall be but a small moment;

291

And then, if thou endure it well, God shall exalt thee on high; thou shalt triumph over all thy foes. . . .

And thy people shall never be turned against thee by the testimony of traitors.

And although their influence shall cast thee into trouble, and into bars and walls, thou shall be had in honor; and but for a small moment and thy voice shall be more terrible in the midst of thine enemies than the fierce lion, because of thy righteousness; and thy God shall stand by thee forever and ever. (D&C 121:7–8; 122:3–4)

Baha'u'llah's experience in the dungeon confirmed to him that he was the one for whom the Bab was waiting, and there are indications that the Bab believed this before his death. After four months of imprisonment, Baha'u'llah, again in part because of his social standing, was released on the condition that he go into exile. He chose to go to Baghdad in present-day Iraq. His half brother, Mirza Yahya, challenged him for the leadership of the Babi community, and Baha'u'llah willingly gave up the leadership and retreated into the mountains. In 1856, the community begged him to return and assume leadership.

Mansion of Bahjí, Acre, Israel, where Baha'u'llah spent the last years of his life under house arrest. Courtesy of Arash Hashemi.

Even though Baha'u'llah was in exile, people constantly sought him out. His popularity began to trouble his enemies in Persia and, by extension, the Ottoman rulers of the area. In 1863, he was moved to Constantinople, but just before he left Baghdad, while he stood on an island named Ridvan (Paradise) in the middle of the Tigris river, he announced to a few of his closest associates that he was the one for whom they were waiting.

Even in Constantinople people flocked to see him, and the guards, impressed by his holiness and graciousness, continued to admit people into his presence. In December of 1863, he was moved again, this time to Adrianople, Turkey. As a result, Mirza Yahya tried again to take over leadership of the community, trying twice to have Baha'u'llah assassinated, but by 1864 the entire Baha'í community had aligned itself with Baha'u'llah. In 1867, Baha'u'llah wrote a series of letters to the "kings of the earth" calling upon them to sublimate national interests to the well-being of all humankind. An excerpt reads as follows:

> The time must come when the imperative necessity for the holding of a vast, an all-embracing assemblage of men will be universally realized. The rulers and kings of the earth must needs attend it, and, participating in its deliberations, must consider such ways and means as will lay the foundations of the world's Great Peace amongst men. . . . It is not for him to pride himself who loveth his country, but rather for him who loveth the whole world. The earth is but one country, and mankind its citizens.[4]

His opponents used these letters as a sign of an international conspiracy, leading the Ottoman authorities to move Baha'u'llah in 1868 to one of the worst prisons in their empire—Acre, across the bay from Haifa, Israel—where they assumed he would die from the terrible conditions. It was said that if a bird flew over the prison, it would die in flight from the stench. Once again, the people were not to be denied, for they flocked to see this holy man, and once again, the guards let them in. Finally, in 1877, Baha'u'llah was moved to a country estate where he spent the remainder of his life under house arrest, but he at least had access to the people who wanted to see him. He died May 29, 1892.

The Successors

Baha'u'llah was succeeded by his eldest son, Abdu'l-Baha, who was recognized as the authoritative interpreter of the Baha'i Faith and the perfect human example of how to live the faith. Abdu'l-Baha was responsible for spreading the faith to Europe and North America and bringing the Bab's remains to the slopes of Mount Carmel in Haifa, Israel, where they now lie enshrined. He died in 1921.

Abdu'l-Baha was succeeded by his eldest grandson, Shoghi Effendi Rabbani, who went to university at Oxford in England. He was known as the Guardian of the Faith and its interpreter and guide. Under his leadership, the faith expanded worldwide, and it was he who made it possible for the Universal House of Justice to succeed him upon his unexpected death in 1957. Today the Baha'is are governed by the Universal House of Justice, which is composed of nine men elected for five-year terms. The decisions they make through prayer, study, and consultation are viewed as binding on the community.

The writings of the Bab and Baha'u'llah are foundational to the faith. Probably one of the most important writings is Baha'u'llah's Kitab-I-Aqdas, which covers virtually every area of life. In addition to the writings of the two founders, the works of Abdu'l-Baha and Shoghi Effendi are also considered authoritative guides for the faithful.

— Baha'i Teachings

God

God in the Baha'i Faith is much like God in the Muslim faith. There is only one God, who has created all things from nothing. He is the Unknowable Essence, but humans can know him through his works and his Manifestations.

The Greater and Lesser Covenants

God has made the Greater Covenant with the entire human family. He covenanted to send, approximately every one thousand years, a Manifestation to lead the human family to a higher plane. A Manifestation is a different kind of being than normal humans. He had a spiritual premortal life and is morally perfect. There is a very real sense of spiritual evolution within the Baha'i Faith, with each Manifestation building on the work and teachings of the prior Manifestation. Thus, there is only one religion of God, and all the Manifestations teach it, but they give to the human family new aspects of that religion when they come. For example, Abraham taught the human family that there is one God. Moses taught the law of the one God. The Buddha taught that humans should be detached from themselves and the things of the world which will never bring them to God. Jesus taught that we are to love God and our fellow human beings because God loves us. Muhammad taught that we are not to be fragmented into clans and tribes but that we should be transcending these narrow boundaries and binding people together in nations. And now Baha'u'llah comes to teach us that even that is too narrow and that we should learn to see that humanity is all one family. He teaches that all our destinies are interlaced with one another and that there must be a unified government. No Manifestation is wrong; rather, each Manifestation stands on the shoulders of the predecessors and adds to what they have given the human family. Bahá'ís now look forward another thousand years to another Manifestation who will help humanity grow further, and they believe this succession will continue on forever. There is no concept of the end of time or history in Bahá'í thought.

The Lesser Covenant is that which is made between a Manifestation and his followers. Thus, Jewish people follow the Lesser Covenant between themselves and Moses. Christians follow the Lesser Covenant between themselves and Jesus, and Muslims follow the Lesser Covenant between themselves and Muhammad. If persons truly understand the Bahá'í message, they will know that with the arrival of a new Manifestation, they should add to the Lesser Covenant with the Manifestation they are currently following and establish a new covenant with the new Manifestation. Thus, the Bahá'í Faith invites Buddhists, Jews, Christians, and Muslims to participate in the new covenant that has been revealed, but should they choose not to do so, they are still part of the one religion. If persons attend a Bahá'í meeting, no matter what their faith tradition, they may well be invited to pray in their accustomed way or to share a passage from their sacred scriptures, for we are all of one human family and of one religion.

BELIEFS

Bahá'ís believe firmly that persons should be open to all truth wherever it is found. Humans should be open-minded and lay aside prejudice and superstition. Thus, science and religion are not antithetical to one another but rather are two ways of accessing knowledge that is complementary. Religion, for example, tells us who created, but not how. That is the province of science. Hence, there is no necessary conflict between science and religion, and when there is an apparent conflict it is usually because persons have limited knowledge in both fields. People should be humble before the two disciplines.

Men and women are completely equal in the Bahá'í Faith and may serve in all capacities in the faith, although it is an anachronism that only men twenty-one years or older may be elected to the Universal House of Justice. Bahá'ís feel that there needs to be more of a feminine influence in the world, with the ideals of relationality and love overriding the more confrontational male model. In line with this idea, members of the Bahá'í Faith believe in universal education, but if that is not possible, they believe that women should be educated because they raise the next generation. Brigham Young of the Latter-day Saint faith made a similar assertion.

Bahá'ís feel that the extremes of wealth and poverty which exist in our modern world are wrong. They assert that a voluntary limit should be placed on what any one person makes and that persons should distribute their excess to the broader community, though they do believe in private ownership. Mutual assistance and helpfulness are the real watchwords of their economic policies. This sounds very much like the law of consecration found in The Church of Jesus Christ of Latter-day Saints. Its aim was to see that everyone had the necessities of life, but where there was excess, it was shared with those in need. Similar to the Bahá'ís, the church practiced private ownership under the law of consecration, but the goal was to limit inequities in economics.

Bahá'ís also believe that our international problems exist in part because we cannot communicate with one another. Thus, Bahá'ís believe that there should be a universal auxiliary language. Children would learn their native language from birth, but around the age of five or six, they would begin to learn the auxiliary language so that people around the world could communicate directly with one another. There is no language specified at this time, but English, Arabic, and Chinese could be contenders.

Bahá'ís abstain from the use of alcohol and drugs. They fast as do many religions, and their fast lasts nineteen days during the daylight hours from March 2 through 20. Marriage is both a social and a spiritual relationship, and it is not solely about two people. It must and does include the families of the couple. After a couple has freely chosen one another, permission to marry must come from the living parents of both partners, and if that permission is not forthcoming, the marriage cannot take place. It is expected that couples will practice chastity before marriage and will be committed solely to one another after marriage. Divorce is permitted, but it is expected that a couple contemplating divorce will practice patience by waiting a year, during which they will seek counseling and attempt to resolve their differences.

One of the most important concepts in the Bahá'í Faith is that of consultation. There may be a clash of opinions, but all speak their own truths. The goal is genuine group consensus, and this should be true especially in marriage. A decision of fifteen people with eight for an item and seven opposed to it is never a good decision because from the beginning, half the group is against the action. Thus, although it takes longer to reach genuine consensus, this is always the Bahá'í goal, for then everyone is headed in the same direction. Among Latter-day Saints, this is the way the Quorum of the Twelve come to decisions. There is debate, but until there is consensus, no decision is made. This concept of consultation leads to the Bahá'í abstention from involvement in politics, which by its very nature is divisive. Bahá'ís cannot run for office, post political signs in their front yards, or use bumper stickers supporting a candidate. They are encouraged to vote, and they may serve their communities through nonpolitical appointments, but, in harmony with Latter-day Saint doctrine, they believe that where there is contention, the Spirit cannot be present. Thus, they do not enter into confrontational settings of any sort.

If non-Bahá'í persons find the Bahá'í principles and practices attractive and want to contribute to the cause, they cannot, for that is the privilege of the Bahá'ís. Bahá'ís are expected at a minimum to tithe 19 percent of monies they have accumulated after expenses and debts are met.

In the end, life for Bahá'ís is a time of spiritual preparation for the soul's progression toward God in the afterlife. Heaven and hell in the Bahá'í Faith are not places but stages of progression. The soul that is progressing toward God is experiencing a heavenly state, and that soul which is not progressing is distant from God and experiencing a kind of hell. As noted earlier, there is no last judgment or end of time in Bahá'í thought, but rather an ongoing process of endless progression, which sounds very much like the Latter-day Saint concept of eternal progression. However, according to Latter-day Saints, there are definitely a last judgment and final place to which the resurrected bodies and spirits of all persons finally go.

PRACTICES

The Bahá'í calendar is composed of nineteen months, each of nineteen days and with four or five additional days to round out the solar year. Once a month, there is a Feast Day, similar to a Sabbath day in Christianity and Judaism. It is a day for worship, group business, and social interchange. There is the annual fast already mentioned, as well as nine other holy days during the year, during which work is suspended. There is a festival known as Ridvan from sunset of April 20 to sunset of May 2 which commemorates Baha'u'llah's announcement on the island of Ridvan that he was the one for whom the community was waiting. Beyond this, the Bahá'í Faith has few rituals. The one thing all Bahá'ís do is recite the daily obligatory prayer, which appears in short, medium, and long forms. The medium prayer is to be said three times a day—at morning, noon, and night. The short form gives a sense of Bahá'í piety:

> I bear witness, O my God, that Thou hast created me to know Thee and to worship Thee. I testify, at this moment, to my powerlessness and to Thy might, to my poverty and to Thy wealth. There is none other God but Thee, the Help in Peril, and Self-Subsisting.[5]

The goal. The current Bahá'í administrative structure is a religious shadow of what Baha'u'llah has called the human family to create. We are one as a family, and, therefore, the goal is a one-world government brought about through spiritually changed hearts. The Bahá'í structure consists of the Universal House of Justice; National Spiritual Assemblies, each composed of nine members; and, at the local level, Spiritual Assemblies, once again composed of nine members, which support and guide the Bahá'ís in a local community. Bahá'ís spread the faith without pressure. If there is an area where no Bahá'í is living, a family may move to that region to create a presence. As people hear the message, they may choose to join a growing and impressive faith community.

This structure is the precursor of a world commonwealth. The vision for this world order is that there would be a world executive, a world legislative body, a world court, and a world police force drawn from all nations. When confronted with despots and dictators who brutalize their people, the world community would remove them through consultation, or, if absolutely necessary, through a united military force, thus creating a peaceful world. This world community will not happen overnight, however. There must first come a total social breakdown, which will lead to the Lesser Peace, meaning that there will be a complete cessation of war, since everyone will be

Universal House of Justice, Haifa, Israel. Public domain.

exhausted by its brutalities. But it will create a political unity. Out of the Lesser Peace will arise the Greater Peace, which will be a spiritual unity, from which will emerge a new world order as people's hearts are changed by God. This sounds very much like the progression of events that will lead up to the millennial reign of Christ, according to Latter-day Saints. The Bahá'í world order is brought about primarily through a spiritually changed human family, while the Millennium is brought about through the return of Jesus Christ.

— CONCLUSION

There is much that is attractive within the Bahá'í Faith. There is a concept of continuing revelation through which God addresses the human family, revelation that comes in blocks every thousand years and is then progressively unpacked by the Universal House of Justice until the coming of the next Manifestation. There is profound compassion for the human condition and a desire to better humankind. There are excellent moral standards and a commitment to improving the social order, but without confrontation and contention. Guided by God, people can make their world better, and all persons are welcome at the Bahá'í table, if they share similar goals. After all, we are all of the one religion, just following different Manifestations, all of whom God has sent to us.

— NOTES

1. "Major Religions of the World Ranked by Number of Adherents," Adherents.com, last modified August 9, 2007, http://www.adherents.com/Religions_By_Adherents.html#Baha%27i.
2. Bahá'í International Community, "Persecution," accessed November 11, 2011, http://www.bahai.org/dir/worldwide/persecution.
3. Quoted in William S. Hatcher and J. Douglas Martin, The Bahá'í Faith: The Emerging Global Religion (Wilmette, IL: Bahá'í Publishing Trust, 1998), 34.
4. Quoted in Hatcher and Martin, The Bahá'í Faith, 40.
5. Robert E. Van Voorst, Anthology of World Scriptures, 6th ed. (Mason, OH: Cengage Learning, 2008), 338.

CONCLUSION

In any discussion of the nature of the Godhead, Joseph's First Vision needs to be considered. Del Parson, The First Vision, © 1987 Intellectual Reserve, Inc.

CHAPTER 15

CONTRIBUTIONS OF THE RESTORATION

Manifestations of the Holy Ghost are available to people of any faith, if they are seeking truth. God will always respond to their search, so not only are there old truths in all faiths, but there are continually new reminders of truth being given by God to leaders and members within every religious tradition.

We have traveled a long road through many countries and many faiths. At the beginning of this book, we suggested that God was working through all faiths to bring his children back to him, but we had little factual knowledge to test this hypothesis. Hopefully, having walked in the shoes of many faithful people, Latter-day Saints can see the finger of God moving among all of his children while preparing them for the fullness that he has in store for them. If The Church of Jesus Christ of Latter-day Saints does possess the fullness of the gospel, what contributions can it make to the discussion of the great human issues? The church has solid contributions to offer to the following questions: (1) How do we know God?, (2) What is the nature of the divine?, and (3) What is the nature of the human being? This final section will be organized around these questions, some of which we began to answer in chapter 1.

—How Do We Know God?—

Latter-day Saint Christians stand firmly on the ground of revelation. There is no way to know God unless he reveals himself to human beings. Many other Christians hold a similar stance, as do Muslims, Jews, Hindus, Sikhs, and Baha'is. For all Christians, God makes himself known in Jesus Christ as the incarnate Word. It is debated among them whether he can be known also through reason or in nature. For Latter-day Saints, the natural world is proof of God's existence, but we must wait on his self-revelation in Jesus Christ for any real knowledge about him. Muslims believe God has revealed himself to Muhammad, and his Word is incarnate in a book—the Qur'an. Jews hold that God revealed himself at Sinai to Moses and gave his oral and written law, which continues to guide faithful Jews to this day. Hindus and Sikhs hold that God reveals himself in many ways and places and under many names. Baha'is hold that God reveals himself regularly through Manifestations that appear approximately every thousand years. In none of these traditions is God silent. He continues to speak through his Spirit, through a book, or through holy men and women who address anew the problems of daily life.

The unique Latter-day Saint contribution to this discussion is the belief that God has a living spokesperson—a prophet—on earth today who conveys God's will to the human family. Because God continues to speak through a prophet, a portion of the Latter-day Saint canon is open, meaning that there is room to add to the canon. To my knowledge, no other tradition has a doctrine of open canon or of a living prophet like the one among Latter-day Saints.

—What Is the Nature of the Divine?—

Latter-day Saint knowledge of the nature of God is not based solely or primarily on written texts. First and foremost, it is rooted in the First Vision of Joseph Smith, in which the Father and the Son appeared to him when he was fourteen years old. Both Jesus and the Father possessed bodily forms. Thus, from a Latter-day Saint point of view, the traditional doctrine of the Trinity, in which the members of the Godhead are all of one essence, is open to further discussion. Latter-day Saints also believe that the Holy Ghost, while a being of spirit only, also has human form. In any discussion of the nature of the Godhead, Joseph's First Vision needs to be considered.

—WHAT IS THE NATURE OF THE HUMAN BEING?—

PREMORTAL EXISTENCE

It is probably in the area of the nature of the human being that Latter-day Saints have the most to contribute to the general religious discussion. First, among Christians, Latter-day Saints are the only group that believes that life did not begin at conception. In fact, Latter-day Saints believe that there was never a time when human beings were not, for all life is self-subsistent and uncreated, as is God himself (see D&C 93:29). All life—animal or human—existed in a state called "intelligence," which was then clothed with spirit form by God the Father, thereby creating spirit beings that lived in his presence for a period of time. One tradition which shares this sense of uncreated essence extending into all life is Hinduism with its concept of Brahman, but this view questions the ultimate reality of the individual apart from Brahman. Shinto, with its understanding of the kami as a life-force permeating all things and constantly manifesting itself in humans, animals, lakes, rivers, and so forth comes closer to retaining some individuality, since the kami nature continues after death. Perhaps the closest parallel to the concept of the eternal intelligence is the soul in Jainism, which has no beginning and no end and is uncreated, as is premortal intelligence in Latter-day Saint thought. Of course the idea that humans came from somewhere is not new at all in Hinduism, Jainism, Buddhism, and Sikhism, with their doctrines of reincarnation, but in their systems there are multiple mortal existences which are different from Latter-day Saint thought, with only one earth life.

Among Latter-day Saint thinkers, there is not full agreement on the nature of "intelligence." Some, like Elder Bruce R. McConkie, hold that there was a "stuff" of intelligence from which individual spirits were organized (see Abraham 3:22–23).[1] Others, like Elder B. H. Roberts and Truman G. Madsen, believe that "intelligences" are individual entities, without beginning or end, which were incorporated into spirit bodies by God the Father.[2] This author favors the latter position.

The concepts of eternal intelligences and a premortal existence as spirit children of God give added meaning to earthly existence. Humans are not just created to praise and glorify their God and ultimately dwell with him, but in Latter-day Saint thought, humans are eternal and on their way from previously dwelling in the presence of God, through an earthly life of growth, to a future life like God's in his presence.

There is thus a dynamic concept of eternal progression with no beginning and no end. In addition, the concept of eternal intelligences, coupled with the fact that Latter-day Saints believe that matter and energy are just as eternal as God and intelligences, means that God becomes an organizer of already existing entities rather than a God who creates "out of nothing." Thus, the understanding of eternal intelligences gives a new view of both God and human beings.

THE PROBLEM OF EVIL

Understanding the issue of eternal intelligences this way makes a significant contribution to the issue of the origin of evil in the universe. If God created all things, including human beings "out of nothing," it is hard not to blame God for creating evil. If premortal intelligences, however, are as eternal as God is, then God is not the source of evil. Rather, God clothes intelligences with spirit form and affirms agency. He gives his spirit children a chance to grow and change, but each has good and evil inclinations upon which their agency enables them to act. Their choices lead to good and evil in the earthly realm. Thus, human beings are the source of all evil in the world, and despite the choices they make, God will use all their choices, whether good or bad, to bring his work to a glorious conclusion. The Resurrection of Jesus has shown that nothing will ever stand in God's way.

IN THE IMAGE OF GOD

As a product of the First Vision, we learned that not only was Jesus embodied, but so also was the Father. This adds a dimension to the claim that humans are created "in the image of God." Not only do we share the attributes of Deity, such as relationality, rationality, supremacy, love, compassion, and giving, but we also share a common physical form. Hindus would have little problem believing that God could appear as an embodied being, for in their understanding, God is not limited to any one form but could appear in many ways. While Sikhs hold that God is without form, they assert that God can reveal himself in many ways. Muslims and Jews would have a harder time accepting that God has physical form, for this idea raises images of idolatry for both. What Latter-day Saints need to notice, however, is that the attributes of God—not just the bodily form—are very much a part of his image. The issue of "bodily form" is a gap filled through the First Vision, but form is not the total explanation of the "image of God."

THE FALL

In the chapter on Christianity, we looked at some of the contributions Latter-day Saint thought makes to understanding the Fall and the Atonement. Latter-day Saint Christians see the Fall quite differently than other Christians do. It is not a disaster and a Fall downward with Eve being a culprit. Rather, it is a "fortunate Fall" forward, a product of a spiritually informed choice, on Eve's part particularly, through which humankind can actually continue progression toward becoming ever more like God. The trials of life and even death are all part of a process that hones human beings into glorious beings who can live with God and approach being like him.

UNCONDITIONAL EFFECTS OF THE ATONEMENT

Latter-day Saints also contribute to religious dialogue in their understanding of how the Atonement works. While there is usually debate in Christian circles about whether the effects of the Atonement are conditional or unconditional, Latter-day Saint Christians affirm that the effects are both. The unconditional effects of the Atonement remove the results of the Fall—temporal and spiritual death—which all humans received as a product of their birth into mortality. All humans will be resurrected and returned to the presence of God for judgment by the Son.

CONDITIONAL EFFECTS OF THE ATONEMENT

But then what covers our sins? The answer given by Latter-day Saints is that these are dealt with through conditional aspects of the Atonement because they, like Eastern Orthodox Christians, believe that there is cooperation between God and human beings in bringing about salvation. As we have seen, nothing saves human beings from their sins except the Atonement and Resurrection of Jesus Christ, and God expects us to participate in them if we want to be saved from our sinful ways. Because of the agency that humans retain following the Fall, they can respond to God when he approaches them in Jesus Christ. That response is to have a relationship of faith with Jesus, to change the direction of their lives, to submit to the priesthood ordinance of baptism, and then to open themselves to the Holy Ghost, which is God's seal upon them that they have done as he asked them to do. The Holy Ghost also enables persons to live as God would have them live. With the Holy Ghost, they can keep the commandments that God gives them, particularly to love God and to love their neighbors. If we do these things, we are connected into the Atonement, justice is satisfied, and all that God has in store for us will be ours, as long as we continue in a relationship of faith and obedience with Jesus. The critical Latter-day Saint contribution here would be the essential nature of saving *priesthood* ordinances for human progression toward God, which is added to the traditional faith and repentance of many religions.

LIFE AFTER DEATH

Latter-day Saint Christians have much to add to the discussion of life after death. For some of the religions we have studied, there is a cycle of reincarnations to bring people to a spiritual maturity that will enable them to be released from the wheel (Hinduism, Jainism, Buddhism, and Sikhism); there may be little concern for an afterlife (Confucianism, philosophical Taoism, and Shinto); or there may be a doctrine of being with or separated from God in the end (Zoroastrianism, Judaism, Christianity, Islam, and Baha'i). Given the revealed doctrines of the Restoration, particularly those found in Doctrine and Covenants 76 and 138, Latter-day Saints have a good deal to add to human knowledge of what happens beyond the grave.

POSTMORTAL EVANGELISM

Doctrine and Covenants section 138 reveals that mortality is not the only place where persons may hear the fullness of the gospel. If persons of whatever faith pass through death having never heard the full gospel of Jesus Christ, they are not automatically condemned to separation from God, as so many Christians across the ages have believed. Rather, there is a spirit world consisting of spirit prison and paradise. Those who have heard the gospel of Jesus and have received the saving ordinances under the hands of the priesthood go to paradise. Others go to spirit prison, but this is far from a place without hope, for the inhabitants of paradise become missionaries of the gospel to them. There is postmortal evangelism because God is loving and gracious. As suggested in the first chapter of this book, those who have sought truth, no matter what their faith, will find the Truth in their relationship with Jesus Christ and joyfully receive the saving ordinances that others have done for them by proxy. They will then join the missionary force in paradise.

DEGREES OF GLORY

There will, however, come a time when God brings this world to its end, and there will be a final judgment. Doctrine and Covenants section 76 tells us that following the Resurrection and Final Judgment, the end is not just heaven or hell but rather three degrees of glory. The clear differentiating factor between the celestial kingdom, or the highest degree of glory, and the other kingdoms is that those who inhabit it received the testimony of Christ, were baptized by immersion, and received the gift of the Holy Ghost under the hands of "him who is ordained and sealed unto this power" (D&C 76:51–52). Here is the priesthood line as shown in the diagrams. It is this required channel of authority that sets Latter-day Saints apart from all other religious traditions, be they Christian or otherwise. Latter-day Saints believe it is through this priesthood channel that the fullness of all that God has in store is available to us, and that fullness involves dwelling with the Father, the Son, and the Holy Ghost. Those who will inherit the celestial kingdom come to it only through their willingness to humble themselves before Christ and through priesthood authority. This is indeed the "more of Mormonism." It is what The Church of Jesus Christ of Latter-day Saints has to offer to the world—the authority of God through which he can open the celestial kingdom to all who want it, whether they are living or dead and regardless of what religion they practiced in mortality.

Latter-day Saints also hold that this kingdom is where husbands and wives who have been sealed for time and eternity by priesthood authority will dwell eternally with their families. Most people believe that they will live with their loved ones in the afterlife. However, Latter-day Saints are the only persons who say that this comes about through earthly ordinances performed by the priesthood. The eternal nature of the family and the way this may come about is an area in which Latter-day Saints have contributions to make to the broader religious dialogue.

The next degree of glory is the terrestrial kingdom. The people who go there are good people—again, from all faiths—who have done many fine things in life but even in death have refused to participate fully in the gospel. They have seen no need for the ordinances of the priesthood, even though all have had witness borne to them that God asks this of them. Thus, spiritual death once again takes hold, for they are not permitted to enjoy the presence of the Father, although they have the loving companionship of Jesus and the Holy Ghost.

The final degree of glory is the telestial kingdom. This appears to be a broad collection of people who have never denied the Holy Ghost but who may have done all sorts of negative things. They will not be raised until the end of the Millennium, but even so, once raised, they will have the fellowship of the Holy Ghost with them and inhabit a kingdom that is beyond description. Thus, the doctrines of "post-mortal evangelism" and "three degrees of glory" as understood by Latter-day Saints give an answer, which should be considered, to the age-old question, what happens to those who never hear the gospel?

THE LIVING PROPHET

Central to all Latter-day Saint Christian thought is that prophets still live and that the church is headed by a living prophet. It seems incongruous that Jesus suffered all that he did and the Father gave his Only Begotten Son for people of various religions who cannot get along. Did Christ do all that he did so that the religious world could fall into divisiveness and conflict, even within the same faith tradition? Is there no longer anyone to speak the word of the Lord to the human family? Most would say that the Lord's word comes to them through sacred books like the Hindu Bhagavad Gita, the Sikh Guru

Granth Sahib, the Jewish Tanak, the Christian Bible, the Muslim Qur'an, or the Baha'i Kitab-I-Aqdas. Latter-day Saints would wholeheartedly agree with these affirmations, for they too hear God speaking to them from the texts of sacred books. However, their contention is that God does not limit himself to books. He spoke in ancient times through prophets like Abraham, Moses, Elijah, Isaiah, and Jeremiah. He continued after Jesus' death and Resurrection to speak through prophet-apostles like Peter, James, John, and Paul.

President Thomas S. Monson, whom Latter-day Saints accept as prophet today. © Intellectual Reserve, Inc.

Why should that pattern no longer exist? The answer to that question, as we saw in the first chapter, is that an apostasy occurred which removed those prophet-apostles from the midst of the church through persecution.

However, the heart of the Latter-day Saint message is that prophets and apostles with the ancient authority of the divine priesthood have returned to the earth. The restoration of the lost role of prophet began when God the Father and his Son, Jesus, appeared to the fourteen-year-old Joseph Smith in a grove of trees in 1820. From Joseph, that prophetic mantle was passed to Brigham Young and then to his successors, and it is now upon Thomas S. Monson, who is God's prophet, seer, and revelator for both the latter-day church and for the world. The heavens are not sealed. God speaks, and for those who will look and listen, they will know God's will for them in these last days. We no longer need wander in twilight, wondering where God would have us go or trying merely to feel our way along. If we look to the living prophet, we will know God's will in the midst of the chaos of the modern world. We need, however, to look to him, and Latter-day Saints need to offer that opportunity to the world that they might have life and have it more abundantly.

—CONCLUSION—

Most Latter-day Saint Christians hold that the commonalities between the religions can be explained because all have a common root in the gospel that was given to Adam, then successively to Noah, Abraham, and beyond. Over time, the pure gospel became contaminated with the philosophies of men, giving rise to the divergent religious traditions. There is some truth in this viewpoint. It overlooks, however, statements like those of President Spencer W. Kimball and Elder Orson F. Whitney that God *sent* people like Muhammad and the Buddha, Socrates and Plato, Luther and Wesley, Guru Nanak and Baha'u'llah. The world's religions are not just corruptions of an original message but rather the product of a purposeful plan of God to reach all of his children, meeting them exactly where they need to be met. While some of the truths in other faiths may be the product of the original gospel passed on, many had brand new beginnings in meetings between the founder and his God. Falling into this category would certainly be Nanak, Zoroaster, Abraham, Muhammad, and Baha'u'llah. God seems to have given them new messages designed to raise the people of their day to new spiritual heights.

In addition to this, we have seen that manifestations of the Holy Ghost are available to people of any faith, if they are seeking truth. God will always respond to their search, so not only are there old truths in all faiths, but there are continually new reminders of truth being given by God to leaders and members within every religious tradition. God is far from silent among any of his children. Latter-day Saints believe they hear his voice most clearly because they have a living prophet in their midst, but the Holy Ghost moves wherever he wishes, enlightening people everywhere and summoning them to come ever closer to the God and Father who loves them. God's is a glorious, multicolored, and multifaceted tree of faith upon which we all depend and in which we all participate. No persons of any faith are outside God's love, but they are encompassed by it as they find him and his love within their own faith traditions.

There is a saying in Japan that "there are many ways up Mount Fuji." Mount Fuji is, of course, a volcanic cone, and no matter which side persons climb, they end up at the same place. In a sense, this is not a bad analogy for what we have been experiencing in our pilgrimage through the world's religions. From a Latter-day Saint perspective, each faith tradition, because God works in it, leads to the top of Mount Fuji, but all are not the same nor do all contain the fullness that God offers to his children. Latter-day Saint Christians believe, because of the restoration of the *fullness* of the gospel through Joseph Smith, at the top of Mount Fuji is the "more of Mormonism." There persons find the additional channels of grace that augment any other avenues into the Atonement that God may have supplied in their faiths. Thus, the circle becomes complete. Jesus Christ and all the authoritative ordinances that The Church of Jesus Christ of Latter-day Saints offers on earth will be available to all in the afterlife at the top of Mount Fuji.

—NOTE—————————————————————————

1. Bruce R. McConkie, *Mormon Doctrine*, 2nd ed. (Salt Lake City: Bookcraft, 1979), "Intelligence," "Intelligences."
2. Note by B. H. Roberts, in *Teachings of the Prophet Joseph Smith*, comp. Joseph Fielding Smith (Salt Lake City: Deseret Book, 1976), 354; Truman G. Madsen, *Eternal Man* (Salt Lake City: Deseret Book, 1966), 24 n. 5.

INDEX

almsgiving, 58, 107, 280–81. *See also* tithes
  and offerings
Altar of Heaven, 120, *136*, 137
Altar of the Earth, 137
Altars of Land and Grain, 138
Amar Das (Sikh Guru), 101
Amaterasu, 174–75, 184
Amida (also known as Amitabha), 78–80, 87
amrit, 105
Amritdhari Sikhs, 107–8
Amritsar, India, *90*, *100*, 101–2
Anabaptists, 265
Analects of Confucius, 128
ancestors
  China, ancient religion of, 119
  Confucianism, 132–33, 136–39, 141
  Latter-day Saints, 133
  Shinto, 183
  Taoism, 163–64
  See also family
Ancestors, Temple of, 137–38
Angad (Sikh Guru), 93–94
angels. *See* heavenly beings
Anglican Church, *230*, 264–65
Angra Mainyu, 192–93, 196
animals, 47, 305
anointing (in traditional Christianity), 254
anointing (part of LDS ordinances), 252, 254
Antiochus IV, 224
Apocrypha, 233
Apostasy, 10–11, 311
Apostles. *See* prophets and apostles (LDS)
Apostles' Creed, 235
Arabia, Pre-Islamic, 270–71
Arafat, 283
Arjan Dev (Sikh Guru), 94, 101–2
Aryans, 18–19, 21–23, 36, 190, 192
asceticism
  Buddhism, 65–70, 73, 88
  Hinduism, 32–33
  Jainism, 42–47, 55–57
  Sikhism, 97
Asoka, 70–71
assimilated Jews, 214
Assumption, 262
Atash Behram, *188*
Atonement
  Christianity and, 242–43
  conditional effects from our humility,
    244–50
  conditional effects from our pride,
    249–50
  and law of harvest, 26–27
  perfection and, 28

represented by cross, 262–63
  Smith, Joseph, and accessibility of,
    138–39
  unconditional effects, 243–44, 307
Atonement, Day of, 216–17
Aurengzeb, Emperor, 103–4
authority to interpret scripture, 234–35
Avalokitesvara, 78–79, 83, 87, 162, *163*
Avesta, 190

— B —

"Baba Bakala," 103
Bab (in Bahá'í Faith), 290
Babs (in Shi'ite Islam), 276, 290
Ba Gua, 118
Bahá'í calendar, 298
Bahá'í Faith
  administration (governing of people),
    298–99
  afterlife, 298
  alcohol and drugs, 297
  Bab, 290
  Baha'u'llah, 290–93
  community, 299–300
  consensus in, 297
  demographics of, 289
  divorce, 297
  education, 296
  family, 297
  fasting, 297
  festivals, 298
  goal of, 298–300
  God in, 294–95
  Greater and Lesser Covenants, 294–95
  Greater and Lesser Peace, 299–300
  history, concept of, 295
  inclusiveness of, 289, 295, 300
  Islam and, 290, 295
  Latter-day Saint thought and, 291–92,
    296–98, 300, 304
  Manifestations, 294–95, 300
  marriage, 297
  origins of, 290–94
  persecution of Bahá'ís, 289–90
  politics, 297
  prayer, 298
  progression, idea of, 289, 294–95, 298
  revelation, 294–95, 300, 304
  science and religion, 296
  scripture, 294
  sexual relations, 297
  theology, 294–98
  tithes and offerings, 297–98
  truth, 295–96